"In the context of the crisis of the US-led world order and the 'Rise of the South,' this book offers excellent insights into the governance innovations emerging from the South. Surveying examples from all of the world's regions, Gurcan offers a rich and engaging analysis of the history and trajectory of the governance project emerging from the South and of their 'post-hegemonic' potentials."

–Dr Tom Chodor, Lecturer in Politics and International Relations, Monash University, Australia and author of Neoliberal Hegemony and the Pink Tide in Latin America: Breaking Up With TINA?

"Drawing on an impressive array of cases, Gürcan's book provides a provocative and timely analysis of "post-hegemonic" governance projects – alternatives and potential challengers to US-led global governance – emerging from the Global South amid the waning of American power and the crisis of Northern capitalism."

–Dr Kristen Hopewell, Senior Lecturer in International Political Economy, University of Edinburgh, Author of Breaking the WTO: How Emerging Powers Disrupted the Neoliberal Project

Multipolarization, South–South Cooperation, and the Rise of Post-Hegemonic Governance

The crisis of Northern capitalism and failure of hegemonic global governance have created a facilitative environment for post-hegemonic initiatives promoting South–South cooperation. Major Southern countries – especially the BRICS – have taken the lead in pushing for alternative governance mechanisms that are strongly articulated in the areas of economic, financial, cultural, and defense cooperation.

This book focuses on the historical, political-economic, and geopolitical context in which major Southern countries implement a post-hegemonic agenda. Providing a global and comprehensive perspective through a series of focused case studies from Europe, Latin America, Eurasia, and Africa, the author develops a new approach to the multipolarization of world politics based on "global hegemony".

Highly recommended for scholars, students, and activists involved in global political economy, regionalism studies, and international development, this book will be of interest to anyone seeking to develop their understanding of world politics and South–South cooperation.

Efe Can Gürcan is a Lecturer in International Studies at Simon Fraser University and a Research Associate at the Geopolitical Economy Research Group at the University of Manitoba in Canada. He has published over a dozen articles and book chapters on international development, international cooperation, and social movements, with a geographical focus on Latin America and the Middle East. His recent co-authored books are *Challenging Neoliberalism at Turkey's Gezi Park* (2015) and *Neoliberalism and the Changing Face of Unionism* (2016). His latest articles address the geopolitical and political-ecological factors impinging on the Syrian conflict since 2011.

The International Political Economy of New Regionalisms Series
Series Editor: Timothy M. Shaw

The International Political Economy of New Regionalisms Series presents innovative analyses of a range of novel regional relations and institutions. Going beyond established, formal, interstate economic organizations, this essential series provides informed interdisciplinary and international research and debate about myriad heterogeneous intermediate-level interactions. Reflective of its cosmopolitan and creative orientation, this series is developed by an international editorial team of established and emerging scholars in both the South and North. It reinforces ongoing networks of analysts in both academia and think-tanks as well as international agencies concerned with micro-, meso- and macro-level regionalisms.

The Relevance of Regions in a Globalized World
Bridging the Social Sciences-Humanities Gap
Edited by Galia Press-Barnathan, Ruth Fine and Arie Kacowicz

Expanding Perspectives on Human Rights in Africa
Edited by M. Raymond Izarali, Oliver Masakure and Bonny Ibhawoh

The International Political Economy of the BRICS
Edited by Li Xing

Structural Change in Africa
Misperceptions, New Narratives and Development in the 21st Century
Carlos Lopes and George Kararach

Multipolarization, South-South Cooperation, and the Rise of Post-Hegemonic Governance
Efe Can Gürcan

Inclusive Trade in Africa
The African Continental Free Trade Area in Comparative Perspective
Edited by David Luke and Jamie MacLeod

For more information about this series, please visit:
www.routledge.com/ASHSER-1146

Multipolarization, South–South Cooperation, and the Rise of Post-Hegemonic Governance

Efe Can Gürcan

Routledge
Taylor & Francis Group
LONDON AND NEW YORK

First published 2019 by Routledge

2 Park Square, Milton Park, Abingdon, Oxon OX14 4RN
605 Third Avenue, New York, NY 10017

Routledge is an imprint of the Taylor & Francis Group, an informa business

First issued in paperback 2022

Publisher's Note

The publisher has gone to great lengths to ensure the quality of this reprint but points out that some imperfections in the original copies may be apparent.

British Library Cataloguing-in-Publication Data
A catalogue record for this book is available from the British Library

Library of Congress Cataloging-in-Publication Data
Names: Gürcan, Efe Can, author.
Title: Multipolarization, South-South cooperation, and the rise of post-hegemonic governance / Efe Can Gürcan.
Description: Abingdon, Oxon ; New York, NY : Routledge, 2019. |
Series: The international political economy of new regionalisms series |
Includes bibliographical references and index.
Identifiers: LCCN 2018054215| ISBN 9781138600232 (hbk) |
ISBN 9780429470912 (ebk)
Subjects: LCSH: Developing countries--Economic integration. | Developing countries--Foreign economic relations. | Developing countries--Foreign relations. | Regionalism--Developing countries.
Classification: LCC HC59.7 .G836 2019 | DDC 337.09172/4--dc23
LC record available at https://lccn.loc.gov/2018054215

ISBN: 978-1-138-60023-2 (hbk)
ISBN: 978-1-03-233840-8 (pbk)
DOI: 10.4324/9780429470912

Typeset in Times New Roman
by Taylor & Francis Books

Contents

Figures

Abbreviations

ALBA	Alianza Bolivariana para los Pueblos de Nuestra América, Bolivarian Alliance for the Peoples of Our America
AMSA	Articulación de Movimientos Sociales hacia el ALBA, Coordination of Social Movements towards ALBA
BancoSur	Bank of the South
BNDES	Banco Nacional de Desenvolvimento Econômico e Social, National Bank for Economic and Social Development
Brexit	British Exit from the European Union
BRICS	Brazil, Russia, India, China, and South Africa
CIPS	Cross-Border Interbank Payment System
CSN	Comunidad Sudamericana de Naciones, Community of South American Nations
CSTO	Collective Security Treaty Organization
CUFTA	Canada–United States Free Trade Agreement
EU	European Union
FTAA	Free Trade Area of the Americas
ICT	information and communication technology
IIRSA	Integration of Regional Infrastructure in South America
ILO	International Labour Organization
IMF	International Monetary Fund
Mercosur	Mercado Común del Sur, Southern Common Market
NAFTA	North American Free Trade Agreement
NATO	North Atlantic Treaty Organization
OAS	Organization of American States
OECD	Organisation for Economic Co-operation and Development
PDVSA	Petróleos de Venezuela, S. A.
R&D	research and development
RATS	Regional Anti-Terrorist Structure
SADC	Southern African Development Community
SCO	Shanghai Cooperation Organization
SUCRE	Sistema Unitario de Compensación Regional, Unified System for Regional Compensation

SWIFT	Society for Worldwide Interbank Financial Telecommunication
TCPs	Tratados de Comercio de los Pueblos, People's Trade Agreements
Unasur	Unión de Naciones Suramericanas, Union of South American Nations
UNIALBA	Red de Universidades de los Pueblos del ALBA, Network of Universities of the Peoples of ALBA
US	United States of America

Introduction

World politics is experiencing tectonic changes, which are leading to major economic and political instabilities. Arguably, among the most important changes are the crisis of hegemonic governance and a rapidly growing geopolitical multipolarization. Notable examples of such changes include the crisis of Northern capitalism since 2008 and its prolonged effects, which have manifested in a surge in right-wing extremism and the weakening of global governance initiatives, including the North American Free Trade Agreement (NAFTA), the Trans-Pacific Partnership, and the European Union (EU). Particularly, Donald Trump's intention to withdraw from the Trans-Pacific Partnership and renegotiate NAFTA, which he branded as a "trading disaster" (Frisk 2017), attests to the crisis of hegemonic governance. The EU has also been paralyzed by the 2008 economic crisis and political crises such as the Brexit (British Exit) referendum result in 2016. Parallel to the crisis of hegemonic governance is the intensification of geopolitical rivalries, which are being brought to the surface by increasing tensions between the United States of America (US) and other Eurasian powers such as Russia, China, and Iran. This situation has prompted many to suggest that a new cold war is in the offing, especially considering the recent developments associated with the Sino-American military confrontation in the South China Sea; the US military buildup in Asia and near the Russian border; the proxy warfare in countries such as Syria, Ukraine, and Yemen; overt US attempts to evaluate leadership survivability against nuclear strikes in China and Russia; the North Korean conflict; and mutual allegations of hacking (e.g. Black and Johns 2016; Legvold 2016; MacKinnon 2007).

What can be done to prevent these instabilities from culminating in a state of full-scale war and total chaos? The tumultuous state of world politics is largely attributable to painful symptoms of difficulties in adjusting to an emerging multipolar world, in the context of a Northern capitalism in crisis. For this slow adjustment to bring about a peaceful systemic emergence without massive human suffering will depend on the form and strength of alternative global governance and South–South cooperation initiatives that could restrain the global hegemony of Northern capitalism. As these initiatives create alternative governance structures, it is critical to improve our knowledge of these processes. Such knowledge can inform the foreign policies of countries the world over, so that institutionalized and stable patterns of socioeconomic cooperation can emerge. Greater knowledge of the new structures of international governance will also enable better use of the new possibilities of what one could call diplomatic deterrence and power-balancing mechanisms, which have the potential to prevent military confrontation. With these concerns in mind, the present book aims to contribute to crucial debates on how to address the global economic and strategic instabilities attributed to multipolarization. The overall objective is to assess how international state linkages configure the geopolitical and economic patterns of cooperation, collusion, and conflict in a post-hegemonic direction, with particular attention to the historical, normative, and institutional dynamics of these linkages at the regional level. Accordingly, the central theme of this book revolves around the following questions:

What are the leading political-economic and geopolitical factors that have been eroding the influence of hegemonic global governance since the 2000s?

How is the multipolarization of world politics translated into post-hegemonic forms of governance in the Global South?

What are the peculiar manifestations of this process in different regions of the world?

What are the strengths, weaknesses, and prospects of South–South cooperation and post-hegemonic regionalism in institutionalizing alternative forms of international cooperation and power-balancing mechanisms towards growing multipolarity?

The geopolitical economy of post-hegemonic governance and regionalism in the Global South: Towards a conceptual and methodological framework

Recent research in international relations attests to a growing interest in the destabilization of the US-centered world order and multipolarization of global politics (e.g. Acharya 2014; Alcaro, Peterson, and Greco 2016; Amin 2013; Campbell 2016; Mandelbaum 2016; McCoy 2017; Murray and Brown 2012; Stuenkel 2016a, 2016b; Tozzo 2018; Woodley 2017). However, most monographs and edited studies on the Global South's contribution to multipolarization focus on individual major countries, chiefly Brazil, Russia, India, China, and South Africa (the BRICS). Regional and collective governance initiatives remain unaddressed to a large extent, with the exception of the BRICS, on which the literature is burgeoning (Bond and Garcia 2015; Christensen and Xing 2016; Chun 2013; Clegg 2009; Cooley 2012; Gu, Shankland, and Chenoy 2016; Hopewell 2016; Kiely 2015; Kingah and Quiliconi 2016; Miller 2017; Murray and Brown 2012; Pieterse 2017; Roberts, Armijo, and Katada 2017; Slobodchikoff 2014; Stuenkel 2016b; Tselichtchev 2012). A rarity in this otherwise fascinating and valuable literature is book-length accounts on the contribution of multipolarization to South–South cooperation and regional governance: only a few studies have focused on the development of new regional governance initiatives in Latin America or Eurasia (Aris 2011; Bagley and Defort 2015; Marketos 2009; Muhr 2013; Song 2016). Entirely absent is interregional comparative research on how alternative regional initiatives might promote global cooperation and stability in a post-hegemonic direction. This book seeks to advance both our empirical and theoretical knowledge of this newly emerging area by offering a global perspective that incorporates Europe, Latin America, Eurasia, and Africa. It also contributes to Radhika Desai's (2013) theory of geopolitical economy, the uniqueness of which lies in its ability to provide a systematic approach to multipolarity by examining how the geopolitical and economic dynamics of world politics interact to generate global political change. My contribution to geopolitical economy consists of putting the notion of "post-hegemony" at the center of geopolitical economic analysis. Therefore, the significance of my research lies in its advancement of knowledge on post-hegemonic governance, and its development of the concept of post-hegemony as an explanatory tool in geopolitical economy.

In this book, I understand "multipolarization" as the increasing parity in the global distribution of political, economic, cultural, and military power. This process is clearly visible in the transformation of global governance institutions since the 2000s, with a growing emphasis on South–South cooperation. The term "global governance" is used here to indicate the "sum of the many ways individuals and institutions, public and private, manage their common affairs" in world politics (Weiss 2000, 796). In turn, I conceptualize the "South" not as a pre-given category, but rather as a political outcome that designates the middle- and low-income countries of Africa, Asia, and Latin America. It also includes former "Second World" countries such as Russia and rising world powers such as China. These are the countries that choose – albeit in varying forms, degrees of coherence, and levels of engagement – to challenge the global political and economic designs imposed by advanced capitalist countries (Cozzens et al. 2008, 803; Levander and Mignolo 2011). As such, the Global South can be seen as an "imagined community" (Anderson 2006) in an Andersonian sense, insofar as it is an imagined community of nations socially constructed by the states or peoples that see themselves as part of this community. Evoking a certain degree of contention against the Global North (i.e. the advanced capitalist economies), the "South" denomination is not used to dismiss the economic and strategic divergences among low- and middle-income countries. Emblematic of these divergences are India's oscillation between the US and Eurasia (Pande and Thoburn 2016; Tamkin 2017); the persisting rivalry between India and Pakistan, as reflected in China and Russia's differing foreign policy commitments over the Indo-Pakistani question (Chaudhury 2016); and Russia and Iran's disagreements over Assad's Syria (Young 2017). The explanatory potential of the "South" lies rather in discussing the politicization of these countries as they engage in South–South cooperation and solidarity towards multipolarity, to the detriment of a US-centered political system. Relatedly, "South–South cooperation" is used here to designate "the process[es], institutions and arrangements designed to promote political, economic and technical cooperation" (UNCTAD 2010, 1) within the Global South.

As US global hegemony loses its grip, a distinctive feature of the multipolarization of world politics has been the rise of South–South cooperation and regionalism, with Latin American and Eurasian initiatives sharing a common post-hegemonic agenda of governance. The term "region" is derived from the Latin words *regio* (neighborhood) and *regere* (to govern) (Morwood 2005). Regardless of its etymological origin, the term can carry different meanings in different contexts. In the lexicons of geography and sociology, "region" is often used to indicate "micro-regions"; that is, spaces within states that are larger than local areas. However, in this book, "regions" carry the meaning of "macro-regions", which is the common usage in politics and international relations. Macro-regions represent spaces that are larger than the nation-state and smaller than the world-system. While traditional approaches tend to emphasize the pre-given geographical characteristics of regions, contemporary perspectives lay greater emphasis on the fluidity and historicity of definitions of the region across different cultural perceptions and political imaginations (Söderbaum 2003). Accordingly, regionalism is understood here as a set of governance programs and strategies that seek political, economic, and/or cultural cooperation between the states of a region.

"Post-hegemony" speaks to a world no longer characterized by hegemony – "a situation in which one nation-state [i.e. the US in the aftermath of the Cold War] plays a predominant role in organizing, regulating, and stabilizing the global political economy" (Du Boff 2003, 1). The original formulation of post-hegemony was confined to heterodox political-economic practices that challenged neoliberalism in the Latin American context (Briceño-Ruiz and Morales 2017; Riggirozzi and Tussie 2012). In my research, I extend the concept of post-hegemony from its Latin American roots to Eurasia and place additional focus on regional security. Conceived as such, "post-hegemonic governance" describes a situation in which US global hegemony is challenged by a plurality of emerging projects, including the BRICS, Shanghai Cooperation Organization (SCO), and *Alianza Bolivariana para los Pueblos de Nuestra América* (ALBA: Bolivarian Alliance for the Peoples of Our America) – albeit with uncertain prospects that do not necessarily involve direct and sustained confrontation with the US. Therefore, this research retains post-hegemony's original focus on US-promoted neoliberalism, but supplements this with a closer examination of its security and military implications from a geopolitical-economy perspective.

The "post" prefix in post-hegemony is used to highlight how US-led governance structures are being challenged by a plurality of co-existing, competing, and coalescing models, although this Southern challenge to US hegemony does not necessarily involve direct and sustained confrontation with the US. On one hand, BRICS countries and other Southern contenders are creating alternative institutions to confront hegemonic tools of global governance such as the US dollar, the International Monetary Fund, and the World Bank. On the other hand, these Southern contenders have not fully abandoned their efforts to transform hegemonic global governance structures from within; they have also refrained from formulating a *coherent* critique of neoliberal governance principles such as flexible labor and free trade. The Southern challenge to US global hegemony is far from being definitive; several Southern countries continue to maintain economic and military ties with the Global North at the expense of South–South integration. In parallel, the relative decline of US hegemony does not imply that the US has abandoned its status as the global hegemon (Bond and Garcia 2015; Cheru 2011; Hopewell 2016; Kiely 2015; Xing 2016). Ultimately, the complicated heterodoxy of this situation – a global process that is far from certainty and completion – seems to be better captured by the term "post-hegemony" rather than "counter-hegemony". In sum, post-hegemony as a concept allows for a deeper understanding of the ways in which the resistance and activism of the Global South direct the trajectory of multipolarization in world politics.

Since economic and political aspects are interestingly combined in post-hegemonic governance, Radhika Desai's theory of "geopolitical economy" provides the conceptual and methodological basis of this book (Desai 2010, 2013, 2015a, 2015b, 2016). The usefulness of the geopolitical-economy framework for the analysis of post-hegemony stems from how it offers conceptual tools for developing a systematic analysis of multipolarization, global hegemony, and governance in all their complexity. This framework builds on the critique of cosmopolitan and transnationalist views of capitalist international relations, which insist on the decreasing relevance of the nation-state as a unit of analysis (e.g. Bhagwati 2004; Hardt and Negri 2005; Robinson 2004; Wolf 2004). Rather than being directed by a mystical transnational alliance of global capitalist elites, or the spontaneous functioning of global markets, capitalist international relations are mediated through the active involvement of nation-states (see also Gürcan 2015 for a critique of the transnationalist school that parallels the geopolitical-economy framework). Therefore, in the language of geopolitical economy, "economy" is important, because "nation-states [which remain the key actors in capitalist international relations] are material products of capitalist development and its contradictions just as much as are classes" (Desai 2015a, 24). Meanwhile, in understanding capitalist international relations, economy cannot be disassociated from geopolitics, since global politics and hegemonic struggles are primarily shaped by competition between states. Indeed, states are also central to shaping and implementing economic policies (Desai 2013). In addressing the importance of political economy and geopolitics for understanding capitalist international relations, geopolitical economy is particularly concerned with the economic and strategic aspects of US global hegemony and the multipolarization of global politics.

The main assumption of geopolitical economy is that conflict is inherent to capitalist international relations. This essentially stems from the uneven character of capitalism; that is, the economic and sociopolitical inequalities between states and nations. In turn, the combined character of capitalism makes itself felt through the actions of dominant and contender states (e.g. the US versus its main rivals such as China and Russia). These states have the potential to foster global political change by promoting and expanding their own projects of capitalist development (Desai 2013); for example, the US-led project of neoliberal globalization (the Washington Consensus) versus China's state-led capitalism (often branded as the Beijing Consensus). In this study, I focus on Latin American and Eurasian contenders such as Brazil, Venezuela, China, and Russia, which take the lead in constructing development alternatives that confront US hegemony.

The present book uses the method of incorporated comparison. This method seeks to understand the complexity of global phenomena by addressing cross-case commonalities, mutual influences, and interdependencies in tandem with spatial or temporal variations, historical specificities, and internal tensions for a fuller understanding of a global configuration at hand (McMichael 1990, 2000). The idea is to develop a historically grounded theory, rather than to "establish a causal logic that is generalizable outside of time and space relations" (McMichael 1990, 396). Therefore, case selection (e.g. the EU and NAFTA versus SCO and ALBA; BRICS versus the United States) is made based on the principle of historical connectivity and mutual conditioning (McMichael 1990, 2000). In this research, I explore post-hegemony as a global process with historically connected and mutually conditioned regional variants, shaped by this setting vis-à-vis US global hegemony. I will thus engage in a comparative study of the actions of world powers and regional institutions, and then incorporate these comparable cases into a single account of how their complex interaction has resulted in a post-hegemonic cooperation. The first step in my incorporating comparison will be to identify the common elements and regional peculiarities among the incorporation elements; this will be followed by an analysis of the changing patterns of international cooperation, collusion, and conflict in a post-hegemonic direction.

Finally, the main data-interpretation technique employed in this research is process tracing. This method offers an interpretivist lens which allows for the "narrative explanation of a causal path that leads to a specific outcome" (Vennesson 2008, 235). The interpretivist mode of process tracing facilitates a more flexible narrative structure without compromising empirical robustness. Process tracing relies heavily on logical reasoning and evidence gathering based on historical narratives. These are used to identify important landmarks in the development of a phenomenon of interest (e.g. critical junctures), as well as the involved political actors' means, motives, preferences, perceptions, and opportunities (Bennett 2010; Collier 2011; George and Bennett 2005; Vennesson 2008).

Outline of the book

This introduction has offered a conceptual and methodological background to the geopolitical economy of post-hegemony and the multipolarization of world politics. The following two chapters address the crisis of hegemonic global governance in its neoliberal incarnation.

Chapter 1 explores the crisis of "open regionalism" in Latin America, famously known as the laboratory of neoliberalism. I argue that the rise of post-hegemonic governance in the 2000s cannot be understood outside of the context of the socioeconomic calamities of neoliberalism under open regionalism. Most importantly, Latin America's post-hegemonic regionalism emerged as a popular reaction to these very calamities. A case in point is Mexico's entry into NAFTA and the consequent transformation of this country into a "failed state" that represents the crucible of global trafficking in people, weapons, and narcotics. Indeed, the failure of neoliberal governments is epitomized not only in the Mexican case, but also in the series of devastating economic crises in key Latin American countries in 2001 and 2002. The countries most affected by these crises included Argentina, Brazil, and Uruguay, which are all part of the *Mercado Común del Sur* (Mercosur: Southern Common Market) area. Over time, this political and economic environment contributed to the defeat of the Free Trade Area of the Americas project, with the region-wide ascendancy of left-wing governments and social movements in the early 2000s. A major implication of this leftward shift for Latin American regionalism has been the retreat of open regionalism and the undermining of Mercosur's hegemonic position by alternative regional governance mechanisms, even though Mercosur attempted to adjust by adopting a "post-neoliberal" guise resonant of the ALBA and the *Unión de Naciones Suramericanas* (Unasur: Union of South American Nations). As a cautionary note, it is important to acknowledge that providing a clear-cut definition of Latin American post-neoliberalism is no easy task given the heterodox nature of the post-neoliberal policies formulated by left-wing governments. Although post-neoliberalism does not constitute a coherent whole, one could define it with reference to a number of overarching principles as they apply to regionalism. Post-neoliberalism involves de-emphasizing the agenda of economic integration and free trade; extending regional cooperation to extra-economic areas based on a stronger concern with social justice issues; reliance on a developmentalist discourse and active state intervention fuelled by extractivist practices; giving greater weight to infrastructural construction, energy security, and security cooperation; supplementing neoliberal welfare policies, such as conditional cash transfers and targeted poverty programs, with redistributive practices; and promoting participatory forms of democracy, albeit in varying degrees (Hoffmann 2015).

Chapter 2 expands the discussion of the crisis of hegemonic governance by identifying the negative implications of neoliberal policies for the EU. The crux of my argument is that excessive levels of financialization, debt dependency, and deindustrialization have driven the EU economy into the worst crisis in its history. The EU's credibility has been severely undermined by Germany's reluctance to help Southern European countries out of the crisis, and by its insistence on deepening neoliberal austerity measures, blaming crisis-hit countries for their financial irresponsibility and laziness. Moreover, this economic crisis has coalesced with a wide-scale strategic crisis that escalated with the Ukrainian conflict and the Northern intervention in Syria to topple Bashar al-Assad's Baathist regime. The Syrian crisis has triggered massive migratory flows towards Europe, while the Ukrainian crisis has served as the mainstay for the consolidation of Europe's extreme right. The converging impact of these economic and geopolitical crises on domestic politics cannot be overemphasized. Accompanied by the rise of right-wing extremism, the concurrent growth of Euroscepticism, xenophobia, and racism have thus paralyzed the European Union project from within. For these reasons, though once considered to be the poster child of regionalism, the EU is no longer an unrivalled model of global governance.

The remainder of this book delves into alternative practices of post-hegemonic governance beyond neoliberalism and Northern initiatives. Assuming that the BRICS countries provide the historical and material ground for the emergence of post-hegemonic governance, Chapter 3 sets the contextual stage of post-hegemonic practices by teasing out the formation of the BRICS alliance and its strategic implications for the global political economy. Although the BRICS is far from representing a self-coherent historical bloc against US hegemony, it has significantly altered the global balance of power to constrain US dominance and move global politics towards multipolarity. Worthy of notice in this connection are the BRICS' call for a comprehensive reform of the United Nations and the International Monetary Fund; the foundation of a BRICS development bank that rivals hegemonic institutions such as the World Bank and the International Monetary Fund; the BRICS' questioning of the US dollar's hegemony in global trade; the creation of an autonomous contingency fund and credit rating agency; and the pro-Assad attitude of BRICS countries against Northern interests in Syria. In this direction, Chapter 4 uses the case of Africa to extend the book's discussion of how the BRICS contributes to the rise of post-hegemonic alternatives. This continent constitutes a strategic point of convergence of the world's post-hegemonic powers, which constrain the reach of US global hegemony, particularly when it comes to the control of global resources and markets. I address the geopolitical and economic aspects of each BRICS member's engagement with Africa, and portray the continent as a representative case that illustrates the prospects, limitations, and contradictions of post-hegemonic politics. Particular highlights in this regard are the shift from the Global North's verticalist approach of "conditional development assistance" to the Global South's horizontalist discourse of "development cooperation" based on a no-strings-attached attitude. The BRICS' increasing involvement in the continent allows African countries to expand their foreign-policy options and prospects for development, while also diversifying their dependency on extractivism and the arms trade.

The final two chapters turn this book's focus towards the regionalist dimension of South–South cooperation and post-hegemonic governance. Chapter 5 scrutinizes the development, advances, and limitations of Latin America's social justice-centered and developmentalist regionalism in its struggle against neoliberalism and US hegemony. This chapter highlights the role of the Latin American left in advancing the agenda of multipolarization, South–South cooperation, and post-hegemonic regionalism. Therefore, it starts with an overview of the main approaches to the Latin American left; that is, liberal-democratic perspectives, Marxist approaches, and the post-neoliberalism thesis. The cases of ALBA and Unasur as the representatives of Latin American post-hegemonic regionalism constitute the focus of inquiry for the chapter. The historical development, political-cultural background, organizational structure, and innovative practices of these institutions are thoroughly examined. The section on ALBA sheds light on the key institutions that define the innovatory aspects of ALBA's post-hegemonic structure. These include the social missions conceived as vehicles to advance the cause of participatory and bottom-up developmentalism; the model of *grannacionales* – state-led enterprises developed as alternatives to neoliberalism's multinational corporation model; the ALBA Bank and *Sistema Unitario de Compensación Regional* (SUCRE: Unified System for Regional Compensation) currency that challenge the US hegemony in global trade and finance; the teleSUR experience that has significantly regressed the US media monopoly in Latin America; the inclusion of progressive social movements in post-hegemonic regionalization; military regionalization and asymmetric defense strategies against US interventionism; and educational cooperation. This section is followed by one on the Unasur experience, with special emphasis on its major achievements in defense, economic infrastructure building, and regionalization of health. These discussions also include a critical assessment of the Latin American left and its gradual retreat since 2015. The implications of left-wing governments' failure to address excessive dependency on primary commodity exports and to restrain market forces are acknowledged in their connection to the limitations of post-hegemonic regionalism.

Finally, Chapter 6 turns the spotlight onto the state of post-hegemonic regionalism in Eurasia, the peculiarity of which lies in its security-oriented focus, confronting US interventionism and international terrorism. The case of the SCO constitutes the main focus of this chapter, which also offers a window into other key institutions such as the Eurasian Economic Union and the Collective Security Treaty Organization. Of special concern in this chapter are the historical development and institutional structure of the SCO, as well as the underlying strategic imperatives that bind its member states together. Moreover, this chapter features an analysis of priority areas of post-hegemonic cooperation under the SCO's umbrella, such as energy, education, development, and economic infrastructure. The major limitations and contradictions of post-hegemonic transformations are addressed, including Eurasia's neglect of the question of democratic participation and the strength of bilateralism.

References

Acharya, Amitav. 2014. *The End of American World Order*. London: Polity.

Alcaro, Riccardo, John Peterson, and Ettore Greco, eds. 2016. *The West and the Global Power Shift: Transatlantic Relations and Global Governance*. New York: Palgrave Macmillan.

Amin, Samir. 2013. *Beyond US Hegemony: Assessing the Prospects for a Multipolar World*. London: Zed Books.

Anderson, Benedict. 2006. *Imagined Communities: Reflections on the Origin and Spread of Nationalism*. London: Verso.

Aris, Stephen. 2011. *Eurasian Regionalism – The Shanghai Cooperation*. New York: Palgrave Macmillan.

Bagley, Bruce M. and Magdalena Defort, eds. 2015. *Decline of the U.S. Hegemony?: A Challenge of ALBA and a New Latin American Integration of the 21st Century*. Lanham: Lexington Books.

Bennett, Andrew. 2010. "Process Tracing and Causal Inference." In *Rethinking Social Inquiry*, edited by Henry E. Brady and David Collier, 207–220. Plymouth: Rowman & Littlefield.

Bhagwati, Jagdish. 2004. *In Defense of Globalization*. Oxford: Oxford University Press.

Black, J. L. and Michael Johns, eds. 2016. *The Return of the Cold War: Ukraine, The West and Russia*. New York: Routledge.

Bond, Patrick and Ana Garcia, eds. 2015. *BRICS: An Anti-Capitalist Critique*. London: Pluto Press.

Briceño-Ruiz, José and Isidro Morales, eds. 2017. *Post-Hegemonic Regionalism in the Americas: Toward a Pacific–Atlantic Divide?*. New York: Routledge.

Campbell, Kurt. 2016. *The Pivot: The Future of American Statecraft in Asia*. New York: Twelve.

Chaudhury, Nilova Roy. 2016. "India Increasingly Wary of Rising Russia—Pakistan Ties." *Russia Beyond*, December 21. http://in.rbth.com/world/2016/12/21/india-increasingly-wary-of-rising-russia-pakistan-ties_664348

Cheru, Fantu. 2011. "South–South Cooperation: What Prospects for a New Bandung Consensus?" In *South–South Cooperation: Africa on the Centre Stage*, edited by R. Modi, 42–60. New York: Palgrave Macmillan.

Christensen, Steen Fryba and Li Xing. 2016. "The Emerging Powers and the Emerging World Order: Back to the Future?" In *Emerging Powers, Emerging Markets, Emerging Societies: Global Responses*, edited by S. F. Christensen and L. Xing, 3–29. New York: Palgrave Macmillan.

Chun, Kwang Ho. 2013. *The BRICs Superpower Challenge*. Aldershot: Ashgate.

Clegg, Jenny. 2009. *China's Global Strategy: Towards a Multipolar World*. London: Pluto Press.

Collier, David. 2011. "Understanding Process Tracing." *Political Science and Politics*, 44(4): 823–830.

Cooley, Alexander. 2012. *Great Games, Local Rules: The New Great Power Contest in Central Asia*. Oxford: Oxford University Press.

Cozzens, Susan E., Sonia Gatchair, Kyung-Sup Kim, Gonzalo Ordóñez, and Anupit Supnithadnaporn. 2008. "Knowledge and Development." In *The Handbook of Science and Technology Studies*, edited by E. J. Hackett, O. Amsterdamska, M. Lynch, and J. Wajcman, 787–812. Cambridge: MIT Press.

Desai, Radhika. 2010. "The Absent Geopolitics of Pure Capitalism." *World Review of Political Economy*, 1(3): 463–484.

Desai, Radhika. 2013. *Geopolitical Economy: After US Hegemony, Globalization and Empire*. London: Pluto Press.

Desai, Radhika. 2015a. "Introduction: From the neoclassical diversion to geopolitical economy." *Research in Political Economy*, 30(1): 1–44.

Desai, Radhika. 2015b. "Introduction: The Materiality of Nations in Geopolitical Economy." *World Review of Political Economy*, 6(4): 449–458.

Desai, Radhika. 2016. "Introduction: Putting Geopolitical Economy to Work." *Research in Political Economy*, 30(2): 1–21.

Du Boff, Richard B. 2003. "U.S. Hegemony: Continuing Decline, Enduring Danger." *Monthly Review*, 557: 1–15.

Frisk, Adam. 2017. "Donald Trump Again Attacks Canada's Dairy Industry, Calls NAFTA a 'Trading Disaster'." *Global News*, April 20. http://globalnews.ca/news/3392010/donald-trump-canada-dairy-industry-nafta-disaster/

George, Alexander L. and Andrew Bennett. 2005. *Case Studies and Theory Development in the Social Sciences*. Cambridge: MIT Press.

Gu, Jing, Alex Shankland and Anuradha Chenoy, eds. 2016. *The BRICS in International Development*. New York: Palgrave Macmillan.

Gürcan, Efe Can. 2015. "Capitalist Class Formation and U.S. Imperialism." *Review of Radical Political Economics* 47(3). doi:10.1177/0486613414542789.

Hardt, Michael and Negri, Antonio. 2005. *Multitude: War and Democracy in the Age of Empire*. New York: Penguin Books.

Hoffmann, Andrea Ribeiro. 2015. "Politicization and Legitimacy in MERCOSUR." In *The Legitimacy of Regional Integration in Europe and the Americas*, edited by A. Hurrelmann and S. Schneider, 57–74. New York: Palgrave Macmillan.

Hopewell, Kristen. 2016. *Breaking the WTO: How Emerging Powers Disrupted the Neoliberal Project*. Stanford: Stanford University Press.

Kiely, Ray. 2015. *The BRICs, US 'Decline' and Global Transformations*. New York: Palgrave.

Kingah, Stephen and Cintia Quiliconi, eds. 2016. *Global and Regional Leadership of BRICS Countries*. New York: Springer.

Legvold, Robert. 2016. *Return to Cold War*. London: Polity.

Levander, Caroline and Walter Mignolo. 2011. "Introduction: the Global South and World Dis/Order." *Global South*, 51: 1–11.

MacKinnon, Mark. 2007. *The New Cold War: Revolutions, Rigged Elections, and Pipeline Politics in the Former Soviet Union*. Toronto: Random House Canada.

Mandelbaum, Kurt. 2016. *Mission Failure: America and the World in the Post-Cold War Era*. Oxford: Oxford University Press.

Marketos, Thrassy N. 2009. *China's Energy Geopolitics: The Shanghai Cooperation Organization and Central Asia*. New York: Routledge.

McCoy, Alfred W. 2017. *In the Shadows of the American Century: The Rise and Decline of US Global Power*. Chicago: Haymarket Books.

McMichael, Philip. 1990. "Incorporating Comparison within a World-Historical Perspective: An Alternative Comparative Method." *American Sociological Review*, 55 (3): 385–397.

McMichael, Philip. 2000. "World-Systems Analysis, Globalization, and Incorporated Comparison." *Journal of World-Systems Research*, 6(3): 668–690.

Miller, Tom. 2017. *China's Asian Dream: Empire Building along the New Silk Road.* London: Zed Books.

Morwood, James. 2005. *The Pocket Oxford Latin Dictionary.* Oxford: Oxford University Press.

Muhr, Thomas, ed. 2013. *Counter-Globalization and Socialism in the 21st Century: The Bolivarian Alliance for the Peoples of Our America.* New York: Routledge.

Murray, Donette and David Brown, eds. 2012. *Multipolarity in the 21st Century: A New World Order.* New York: Routledge.

Pande, Aparna and Hannah Thoburn. 2016. "Why the India-Russia Relationship Works." *The Diplomat*, December 16. http://thediplomat.com/2016/12/why-the-india-russia-relationship-works/

Pieterse, Jan Nederveen. 2017. *Multipolar Globalization: Emerging Economies and Development.* New York: Routledge.

Robinson, William I. 2004. *A Theory of Global Capitalism: Production, Class, and State in a Transnational World.* Baltimore: Johns Hopkins University.

Riggirozzi, Pía and Diana Tussie, eds. 2012. *The Rise of Post-hegemonic Regionalism: The Case of Latin America.* New York: Springer.

Roberts, Cynthia, Leslie Armijo, and Saori Katada. 2017. *The BRICS and Collective Financial Statecraft.* Oxford: Oxford University Press.

Slobodchikoff, Michael O. 2014. *Building Hegemonic Order Russia's Way: Order, Stability, and Predictability in the Post-Soviet Space.* London: Lexington Books.

Söderbaum, Frederik. 2003. "Introduction: Theories of New Regionalism." In *Theories of New Regionalism: A Palgrave Macmillan Reader*, edited by F. Söderbaum and T. M. Shaw, 1–21. New York: Palgrave Macmillan.

Song, Weiqing. 2016. *China's Approach to Central Asia: The Shanghai Co-operation Organisation.* New York: Routledge.

Stuenkel, Oliver. 2016a. *Post-Western World: How Emerging Powers Are Remaking Global Order.* Cambridge: Polity Press.

Stuenkel, Oliver. 2016b. *The BRICS and the Future of Global Order.* London: Lexington Books.

Tamkin, Emily. 2017. "Is India Playing the United States Against Russia?" *Foreign Policy*, April 17. http://foreignpolicy.com/2017/04/17/is-india-playing-the-united-states-against-russia/

Tozzo, Brandon. (2018). *American Hegemony after the Great Recession: A Transformation in World Order.* New York: Palgrave Macmillan.

Tselichtchev, Ivan. 2012. *China Versus the West: The Global Power Shift of the 21st Century.* Singapore: Wiley.

UNCTAD. 2010. *South–South Cooperation: Africa and the New Forms of Development Partnership.* Economic Development in Africa Report. Geneva: United Nations Conference on Trade and Development.

Vennesson, Pascal. 2008. "Case Studies and Process Tracing: Theories and Practices." In *Approaches and Methodologies in the Social Sciences: A Pluralist Perspective*, edited by Donatella della Porta and Michael Keating, 223–239. Cambridge: Cambridge University Press.

Weiss, Thomas G. 2000. "Governance, Good Governance and Global Governance: Conceptual and Actual Challenges." *Third World Quarterly* 215: 795–814.

Wolf, Martin. 2004. *Why Globalization Works.* New Haven: Yale University Press.

Woodley, Daniel. 2017. *Globalization and Capitalist Geopolitics: Sovereignty and State Power in a Multipolar World.* New York: Routledge.

Xing, Li. 2016. "From Hegemony and World Order to Interdependent Hegemony and World Re-Order." In *Emerging Powers, Emerging Markets, Emerging Societies: Global Responses*, edited by S. F. Christensen and L. Xing, 30–54. New York: Palgrave Macmillan.

Young, Michael. 2017. "Russia, Iran and Their Conflicting Regional Priorities." *The National*, January 28. http://www.thenational.ae/opinion/comment/russia-iran-and-their-conflicting-regional-priorities

1 Neoliberal globalization and the downfall of open regionalism: The Latin American case

Introduction

The predominant paradigm of global political economy in the 1990s was known as the "Washington Consensus", a term coined in 1989 by John Williamson, a British economist. The Washington Consensus sought to overcome the debt crisis of the 1980s through an orthodox prescription that consisted of a set of ten commandments: fiscal discipline, contraction of public expenditure and its redistribution to selected areas, neoliberal tax reform in favour of corporations, liberalization of exchange rates, competitive currency rates, free trade, opening up of the economy to foreign investment, privatization, financial deregulation, and copyright protection. Global governance institutions such as the International Monetary Fund, the World Bank, and the US Treasury were responsible for imposing these commandments on the Global South (Gardini 2010; Knight, Castro-Rea, and Ghany 2014).

Latin America has been called the first test site of neoliberalism, because experimentations with the Washington Consensus began in this region. Following the fall of the Berlin Wall and the collapse of the Soviet Union, Latin America underwent a so-called democratization and transition to a free market economy. However, despite the fact that Latin America became the "backyard" of US imperialism, even neoliberal politicians in this region worried about the rapid pace of neoliberalization throughout the 1990s. Leading countries such as Brazil and Argentina, which serve as the locomotives of the Latin American economy, were struggling with massive debts, disinvestment, stagnation, and hyperinflation. Under these conditions, it was hoped that "open regionalism" would facilitate the region's transition to liberal democracy and neoliberalism through gradual integration into global free trade (Gardini 2010).

What have been the historical underpinnings of open regionalism in Latin America? In what ways has open regionalism been an instrument of US hegemony? What outcomes has the Latin American experience of open regionalism produced, and how have they triggered the upsurge of post-hegemonic regionalism? This chapter addresses the geopolitical-economic background of open regionalism and the key dynamics that brought about its downfall in Latin America. The focus is placed on the main instruments of

Latin American open regionalism. In what follows, I will therefore look at the case of the Free Trade Area of the Americas and the socioeconomic ravages of the North American Free Trade Agreement (NAFTA). This is followed by an assessment of the *Mercado Común del Sur* (Mercosur: Southern Common Market) initiative, which was led by Brazil and Argentina. Then I explore the ways in which this institution attempted to free itself from the influence of open regionalism and joined the post-hegemonic camp.

The ravages of free trade: NAFTA and the Free Trade Area of the Americas

Signed in 1987, the Canada–United States Free Trade Agreement (CUFTA) was the antecedent of NAFTA; the latter was signed in December 1992 and implemented in January 1994. Prior to CUFTA and NAFTA, it was not commonplace to conceive of North America as a region in itself (Bow 2015). Nonetheless, CUFTA's signing became a major controversy during the 1988 elections in Canada. The question of free trade with Mexico spurred widespread contention among both the left and the right during the US elections of 1992 and 1994. The Mexican opposition at that time also voiced concerns about the potential asymmetries that might be generated by free trade with advanced capitalist countries such as the US and Canada. As such, trade asymmetries occupied the forefront of the NAFTA negotiations. Although Mexico was granted the privilege of gradual liberalization for selected agricultural items and exemption of the energy sector from liberalization, NAFTA failed to resolve the problem of asymmetries, since similar privileges were also offered to the US and Canada. For example, Canada did not abolish state subsidies for its cultural industry, and the US preserved its regime of high agricultural subsidies (Bow 2015; Castro-Rea 2014; Zizumbo-Colunga and Seligson 2015).

One of the most noticeable implications of NAFTA's implementation was the abolition of foreign investment and trade restrictions over the first 15 years of the agreement. Furthermore, NAFTA established intergovernmental consultation mechanisms for resolving trade disagreements. It was agreed that disagreements that could not be resolved over 30 to 40 days would be taken over by a Free Trade Commission (Dent and Wilson 2014). Another novelty of the NAFTA regime was the introduction of certain mechanisms that allowed foreign corporations to sue their host country if this country was believed to be imposing policies harmful to corporate interests. These mechanisms have led the Mexican and Canadian governments to pay out millions of dollars in damages. A well-known case was the dispute between Metalclad and Mexico in 1997. This dispute originally arose from a decision by the municipality of Guadalcázar to stop the activities of a Metalclad waste-disposal facility due to suspicions of environmental damage. Eventually, Metalclad was awarded compensation of US$16.7 million under the NAFTA regime (Castro-Rea 2014). A similar dispute took place between

Canada's Newfoundland and Labrador government and a corporation named AbitibiBowater, following the government's decision to revoke the company's right to water and timber use and confiscate its corporate assets. This action cost the government US$130 million in compensation. By October 2010, Canada and Mexico had been subjected to a total of 11 and 19 NAFTA disputes, respectively. Interestingly enough, although the US was subjected to 19 NAFTA disputes, it suffered no penalty at all, whereas Canada and Mexico had to pay CA$157 million and US$187 million, respectively. Even more striking is the fact that the US failed to comply with several of NAFTA's arbitrary decisions (Castro-Rea 2014).

Also emblematic of asymmetries within NAFTA is Mexico's and Canada's dependence on US investment and trade. In 2010, the US accounted for almost 80% of foreign transactions in the other two countries. In the same year, 74.9% of Canada's exports were directed to the US market. Not surprisingly, over 50% of Canada's imports originate from the USA. In 2011, Mexico generated 34% of its national income from exports, over 78% of which were directed to the US market; almost 50% of Mexico's imports came from the USA. However, the 2011 data suggest that only 19% of US exports were directed to Canada and 13% to Mexico. Canada accounts for only 14.2% of total US imports, while US imports from Mexico do not exceed 11.8%. In a similar vein, US foreign investments outpace their Canadian and Mexican counterparts. In 2011, over half of the foreign investment in Mexico and Canada originated from the US, vastly exceeding Mexican and Canadian investments in the US (Castro-Rea 2014).

Ultimately, growing asymmetries within NAFTA seem to have resulted in the strengthening of US influence over Mexican and Canadian politics. Robert B. Zoellick, the neoconservative who presided over the World Bank between 2007 and 2012, has confessed that the NAFTA regime serves not only as a tool for economic supremacy, but also as a weapon that allows the US to impose its own interests on NAFTA members' individual foreign policies. Furthermore, leaked correspondence of John D. Negroponte, a former US ambassador to Mexico and intelligence executive, contains a confession that NAFTA has increased Mexico's dependency on the US and shapes Mexico's foreign policy in favour of US strategic interests (Castro-Rea 2014).

Mexico, as the poorest member of the North American community, was the hardest hit by NAFTA's growing asymmetries. In the 20th year of NAFTA's implementation, Mexico's performance in annual real GDP growth per capita ranked 18th among 20 Latin American countries. Mexico's per capita GDP growth in the period between 1960 and 1980 was recorded as over 98%, which stands in sharp contrast to a mere 18.6% in the first 20 years of NAFTA's implementation. Real wages in 2012 were only 2.3% above their 1994 levels. Mexico's average annual unemployment rate in the period 1990–1994 was recorded as 3.1%; it rose to 5% in 2014 (Weisbrot, Lefebvre, and Sammut 2014; World Bank 2016).

Mexico's agricultural liberalization under the NAFTA regime led to the displacement of nearly 5 million rural families, who were forced to migrate to the US due to the failure of Mexico's neoliberal economy to create adequate employment opportunities. For similar reasons, Mexico's seasonal agricultural employment experienced a growth of almost 3 million over the 20 years of NAFTA's implementation. Between 1994 and 2000, Mexican migration to the US increased by 79%, while the number of Mexican-born persons living in the US soared to 12.6 million in 2009 from only 4.5 million in 1990 (Weisbrot et al. 2014). Even more serious was the transformation of Mexico into a "failed state", one that remains significant in global trafficking of narcotics, arms, and people. In 2016 alone, nearly 23,000 persons in Mexico were victims of armed conflict, making it the deadliest conflict zone after Syria. This situation is closely associated with increasing US demand and customs privileges imposed by the NAFTA regime (Laurell 2015; Persio 2017).

Eventually, once it had experienced NAFTA's colonizing power at first hand, the US proposed the Free Trade Area of the Americas for the rest of Latin America. However, the origins of the Free Trade Area of the Americas can be traced back to the 1990s, when the George H. W. Bush administration first declared the Americas Initiative and the Bill Clinton administration subsequently pushed for a global free trade agenda. Indeed, negotiations for the Free Trade Area of the Americas officially took off in Florida in 1994, during the First Americas Summit of the Organization of American States (OAS). This summit was center stage for a Declaration of Principles in favour of democratization, free trade, and sustainable development (Knight 2014). Accordingly, the regional free trade agenda went hand-in-hand with the strategic aim of diffusing "liberal democracy". In fact, this US-led democratization discourse finds its origin in the OAS, which is known as the world's oldest regional organization. Its historical origins can be found in the 1826 Panama Conference led by Simón Bolívar and the 1889 International Conference of American States organized in Washington. Having distanced itself from Bolívar's legacy over time, this institution has been used by the US to impose its own leadership on Latin America. Not surprisingly, the OAS is headquartered in Washington. Although the OAS failed to put into practice the US economic agenda, it served as a strategic stronghold to diffuse the discourse on free trade and pro-US democracy. As such, Cuba was suspended from the OAS between 1962 and 2009. However, in parallel with the rise of left-wing governments in the 2000s, US authority in the region took a heavy blow when Latin American countries started to pressure the US to reactivate Cuba's OAS membership in 2009 (Dent and Wilson 2014).

The US institutional hegemony in Latin America was not only undermined by the 2009 OAS incident, however. Another historical landmark was the failure of the Free Trade Area of the Americas project in 2005. This project was regarded as the largest and most comprehensive free trade agreement to date: it was expected to bring together 34 Latin American countries with a combined GDP of over US$13 trillion and an annual export potential of over

US$1 trillion (Knight 2014). In the end, the Free Trade Area of the Americas was not implemented. Its failure was mostly due to concerted efforts by Latin America's left-wing social movements and governments, which successfully mobilized workers' and peasants' movements, environmentalists, critical development NGOs, and left-wing political parties. At the level of governmental opposition, perhaps the strongest resistance came from Luiz Inácio Lula da Silva, then President of Brazil. Lula denounced the Free Trade Area of the Americas as the "annexation of Latin America by the USA" (Knight 2014). Lula's decisive attitude found resonance with Mercosur, which was elevated from the status of a mere tool for advancing open regionalism to an emerging alternative to US hegemony in Latin America.

During the 2005 Summit of the Americas, Mexico sided with the US, whereas Brazil and Venezuela denounced the proposed agreement. Increasing regional polarization following the leftward shift of Bolivia and Ecuador in 2006, as well as the rise to office of right-wing governments in Mexico and Colombia, led the Free Trade Area of the Americas to a stalemate. As a side note, Brazilian business circles also remained vigilant in opposing this project; particularly a large number of electronic parts, pharmaceuticals, petrochemical, and export-led agricultural producers who were worried about Brazil's inability to compete with more developed US industries (Castro-Rea 2014; Knight 2014).

Mercosur's transition from open to post-hegemonic regionalism

Mercosur was founded in 1991 through the initiative of Brazil and Argentina. This institution represents the second-largest attempt at regionalism after the European Union (EU), although the rise of the Latin American left later undermined Mercosur's influence. Mercosur was modeled on the EU, but it failed to accomplish its goal of becoming a customs union and common market (Schneider and Hurrelmann 2015). Contrary to the EU experience, Mercosur's regionalization efforts lacked a strong emphasis on supranationalism (Gardini 2010; Hoffmann 2015). Other limitations of the Mercosur experience concern the failure of member states to conform to trade regulations designed by this institution. Moreover, Mercosur's parliament (Parlasur) and the Economic Convergence Fund were instituted only in the late 2000s; since then they have been operated inadequately (Gardini 2010).

In principle, Mercosur's decision-making mechanism relies on member consensus. It also requires its members to incorporate democracy into their own political and legal systems. However, even though a Mercosur court was instituted in 2004, this court failed to establish a region-wide legal system to be adopted by all of the member states. The functioning of this court instead draws on a general reference to the principles of international law. The highest authority in Mercosur's decision-making therefore lies in presidential diplomacy, which overshadows the authority of other institutional bodies. These bodies include the Common Market Council, made up of the Ministers of Foreign Affairs and the Economy; and the Common Market Group, designated as the executive arm of this council. Mercosur also includes a Socioeconomic Advisory Forum endowed with an advisory power, which provides a space for the participation of nongovernmental interest groups (Dent and Wilson 2014; Hoffmann 2015).

In its early years, Mercosur served to moderate the strategic competition between Brazil and Argentina in the aftermath of the Cold War (Knight et al. 2014). Given Argentina's greater dependence on Latin American markets, Mercosur might be said to have been more strategically important for Argentina than Brazil. Brazil, as Argentina's biggest trading partner, is interested in Mercosur to advance its own hegemony in Latin America and counterbalance the regional power of the US (as its own closest trading partners are the US and the EU). As far as Paraguay and Uruguay are concerned, these countries are heavily dependent on the Mercosur economy, given that 30–40% of their foreign trade takes place within the Mercosur area (Gardini 2010).

Mercosur adopted open regionalism throughout the 1990s, during which neoliberalism was the dominant paradigm. Therefore, the main agenda of Mercosur was democratization and the coordination of member states' neoliberal macroeconomic policies. It is plausible to argue that the US-led NAFTA negotiations in the early 1990s, and NAFTA's implementation, provided a friendly environment for the advancement of Mercosur's open regionalism paradigm. On the other hand, both Brazil and Argentina saw Mercosur as a strategic tool to counterbalance US hegemony in the region. It is known that the US pressured Latin American countries to implement the Free Trade Area of the Americas in 2000, but that Mercosur insisted on postponing it to 2005 (Dent and Wilson 2014; Hoffmann 2015).

Mercosur's open regionalism led to member states' regional trade increasing as a proportion of their total foreign trade, from 13 to 23% in the period 1991–1997 (Hoffmann 2015). However, the bankruptcy of neoliberalism and the rise of the Latin American left in the 2000s interrupted Mercosur's dynamism with a series of political crises. The economic crisis experienced by Argentina and Brazil, and the resurgence of left-wing politics, helped to discredit the model of open regionalism. Furthermore, the regional movement against the Free Trade Area of the Americas and neoliberalism (*Alianza Social Continental*: Continental Social Alliance) was also influential in countering the open regionalism paradigm represented by Mercosur (Hoffmann 2015). Mercosur froze Paraguay's membership when the then leftist President Fernando Lugo was impeached by a parliamentary coup in 2012. Moreover, the approval of Venezuela's membership spurred controversies within Mercosur. Although Paraguay's membership was restored in 2013, the country refused to rejoin Mercosur until the end of Venezuela's chairing term (Hoffmann 2015). In the meantime, the post-neoliberal turn in Latin America helped Mercosur to redefine its priorities and shift its emphasis from free trade to welfare and social development. With this aim, a Mercosur Social Institute was instituted in 2007.

The main objective of this institute was to strengthen the social dimension of Latin American regionalism and coordinate the regional quest for alternative social policies. Despite these developments, Mercosur lost its appeal to newly funded regionalist institutions such as the *Unión de Naciones Suramericanas* (Unasur: Union of South American Nations) and *Alianza Bolivariana para los Pueblos de Nuestra América* (ALBA: Bolivarian Alliance for the Peoples of Our America). Until recently, Unasur was hoping to integrate Mercosur into its own structure (Hoffmann 2015). However, the recent retreat of the left in Brazil and Argentina has been directly reflected in Mercosur's leadership, which froze Venezuela's membership in December 2016 (see Chapter 5 for more details on Latin American regionalism).

Review and discussion

Open regionalism emerged in the 1990s as the locomotive of neoliberal globalization in Latin America. The tragic failure of neoliberalism, in parallel with the rise of Latin American left-wing governments and social movements throughout the 2000s, resulted in the downfall of open regionalism. Eventually, the crisis of neoliberalism and upsurge of left-wing movements gave way to the emergence of post-hegemonic forms of regionalism. In view of these developments, this chapter has depicted the socioeconomic ravages of open regionalism, under which the privileged status of US corporations worsened inherited asymmetries in the North American region.

The subordinate position of Mexico under the NAFTA regime is self-evident. An overview of Mexico's performance during the period 1960–1980, compared with the first 20 years of NAFTA's implementation, reveals that this country was better off in the pre-NAFTA era. The NAFTA era has produced a human tragedy in Mexico, which has turned into a failed state due to the neoliberal restructuring imposed by NAFTA. Today, Mexico's dependence on the US under the NAFTA regime has undermined the country's national sovereignty and autonomy in foreign policy, and the country has turned into a center of gravity for international migration and crime.

The destructive effects of NAFTA were duly noted by Latin America's left-wing governments and social movements, and their concerted opposition to the Free Trade Area of the Americas represented a historical victory over global US hegemony. This victory has also had direct ramifications for Latin American regionalism. Mercosur compromised its position vis-à-vis open regionalism and ended up gravitating towards post-hegemonic regionalism, with its emphasis shifting from free trade to social welfare and development. As Chapter 5 reveals, however, even such a tremendous compromise could not prevent Mercosur from being relegated to the sidelines with the advance of post-hegemonic regionalism under the banner of ALBA and Unasur. Yet, before engaging with the kind of regional mechanisms that have significantly debilitated open regionalism and Mercosur, it is important to address the case of the EU, which represents another historical moment in the development of neoliberalism and open regionalism. Mercosur was a failed attempt at open regionalism by countries of the South. The EU, on the other hand, is a Northern initiative and occupies an even more strategic position in the history of hegemonic governance.

References

Bow, Brian. 2015. "Legitimacy, Politicization and Regional Integration in North America." In *The Legitimacy of Regional Integration in Europe and the Americas*, edited by A. Hurrelmann and S. Schneider, 33–56. New York: Palgrave Macmillan.

Castro-Rea, Julián. 2014. "Free Trade: A Tool for US Hegemony in the Americas." In *Re-Mapping the Americas: Trends in Region-Making*, edited by W. A. Knight, J. Castro-Rea, and H. Ghany, 69–82. Farnham: Ashgate.

Dent, David W. and Larman C. Wilson. 2014. *Historical Dictionary of Inter-American Organizations.* Lanham: Scarecrow Press.

Gardini, Gian Luca. 2010. *The Origins of Mercosur: Democracy and Regionalization in South America*. New York: Palgrave MacMillan.

Hoffmann, Andrea Ribeiro. 2015. "Politicization and Legitimacy in MERCOSUR." In *The Legitimacy of Regional Integration in Europe and the Americas*, edited by A. Hurrelmann and S. Schneider, 57–74. New York: Palgrave Macmillan.

Knight, W. Andy. 2014. "The FTAA and its Ultimate Demise." In *Re-Mapping the Americas: Trends in Region-Making*, edited by W. A. Knight, J. Castro-Rea, and H. Ghany, 55–68. Farnham: Ashgate.

Knight, W. Andy, Julián Castro-Rea, and Hamid Ghany. 2014. "Re-Mapping the Americas." In *Re-Mapping the Americas: Trends in Region-Making*, edited by W. A. Knight, J. Castro-Rea, and H. Ghany, 3–38. Farnham: Ashgate.

Laurell, Asa Cristina. 2015. "Three Decades of Neoliberalism in Mexico: The Destruction of Society." *International Journal of Health Services*, 452: 246–264.

Persio, Sofia Lotto. 2017. "Drug War Turned Mexico Into World's Deadliest Conflict Zone After Syria." *Newsweek*, May 10. http://www.newsweek.com/mexicos-drugs-war-created-worlds-deadliest-conflict-zone-after-syria-survey-606558

Schneider, Steffen and Achim Hurrelmann. 2015. "Understanding the Legitimacy of Regional Integration: A Comparative and Mixed-Method Perspective." In *The Legitimacy of Regional Integration in Europe and the Americas*, edited by A. Hurrelmann and S. Schneider, 1–18. New York: Palgrave Macmillan.

Weisbrot, Mark, Stephan Lefebvre, and Joseph Sammut. 2014. *Did NAFTA Help Mexico? An Assessment After 20 Years.* Washington, DC: Center for Economic and Policy Research. http://cepr.net/documents/nafta-20-years-2014-02.pdf

World Bank. 2016. DataBank. http://databank.worldbank.org

Zizumbo-Colunga, Daniel and Mitchell A. Seligson. 2015. "Economic Evaluations and Support for Free Trade in Latin America and the Caribbean." In *The Legitimacy of Regional Integration in Europe and the Americas*, edited by A. Hurrelmann and S. Schneider, 117–134. New York: Palgrave Macmillan.

2 The strategic and economic crisis of open regionalism in Europe

Introduction

European regionalism gained its greatest momentum in the aftermath of the collapse of the Soviet Union, which provided a regional power vacuum to be filled by European powers. Through the 1990s, the European Union (EU) experiment turned into a success story and came to be designated as a role model for regional governance. With 28 member states in its present form, the EU has grown into the world's most successful regionalist institution, with its own parliament, judicial system, and Council of Foreign Relations. However, as this chapter reveals, the strategic and economic crisis of European "open regionalism" has stripped the EU tale of its global appeal under neoliberal policies. As a result, the EU no longer serves as a universal role model for regionalist initiatives in the South.

What are the geopolitical and economic factors that have plunged Europe's long-acclaimed open regionalism into a deep crisis? In this chapter I argue that, faced with converging economic and strategic crises, the EU has lost much of its charm as a role model. The exhaustion of neoliberalism following the crisis of Northern capitalism in 2008 constitutes a major economic factor contributing to the predicament of Europe's open regionalism. At present, Europe is falling apart over excessive financialization and orthodox austerity policies (Stockhammer 2016). Consequently, the slowing down and even disappearance of economic growth in peripheral countries – accompanied by record levels of unemployment – have triggered the resurgence of far-right Euroscepticism and racism. The rise of the European far right has found its expression in France's National Front, Italy's Five Stars, Greece's Golden Dawn, and Hungary's Jobbik (Friedman 2016). In the meantime, while Germany has been less affected by this crisis than poorer countries in Europe, its reluctance to help out the European area and its insistence on maintaining the same neoliberal policies that drove these countries into crisis have shaken member states' belief in the Euro and the EU itself. Another area that has bred mistrust is Germany's pursuance of a neo-mercantilist strategy of development despite the impositions of neoliberal regionalism on poorer countries.

The strategic pillar of this crisis is the geopolitical conflict involving Ukraine and Syria; the key actor in both of these conflicts is Russia.

European integration itself was originally a Cold War project to restrain potential German military expansionism and to contain Soviet Russia. Nowadays, Europe's energy dependence on Russia constitutes a decisive factor that shapes Russo–European relationships (Friedman 2016; Kundnani 2015). However, Northern efforts to contain contemporary Russia by toppling the pro-Russian Ukrainian government in 2014, and attempting to disintegrate President Bashar al-Assad's Syria as a key Russian ally in the region, did nothing but exacerbate racism and xenophobia in favor of the far-right Euroscepticism that had already been fuelled by the economic crisis. Most importantly, the Syrian crisis has resulted in the world's largest humanitarian crisis since the Second World War (Gürcan 2017; Otero and Gürcan 2016), and subsequently the flow of so-called "illegal" refugees into Europe has intensified far-right activism. In parallel, Northern support for far-right nationalist forces in Ukraine has provided an even more facilitative environment for the further strengthening of European fascism.

The first section of this chapter is devoted to the history of Europe's strategic configuration as far as German–European and Russo–European relationships are concerned. The second part addresses Europe's economic crisis in its relationship to neoliberalism. These sections are not placed in order of importance: the chapter opens with strategic factors because Europe's strategic configuration since the Second World War chronologically preceded the neoliberal era.

Germany, Russia, and the European Union's strategic crisis

Europe's political history since the 1950s indicates that the European integration process originally stemmed from strategic concerns about smoothing Germany's future rise and containing Soviet Russia's expansion in Europe. The European Coal and Steel Community – the EU's antecedent – was essentially an attempt to prevent strategic tensions between Germany and France. It was believed that creating a common market for coal and steel would ensure a long-lasting European peace (Kundnani 2015). Similarly, the fall of the Berlin Wall and Germany's unification generated widespread concerns about the military resurgence of a powerful Germany that could dominate the entire European continent. The solution was to create a new momentum for regional integration. François Mitterrand, then French President, believed that a common European currency could prevent Germany's Treasury from dominating Europe (Kundnani 2015).

The so-called "Russian threat" has been another important catalyst for European integration. Convinced that communism was the greatest international threat at the time, the US sought to accelerate European integration in order to contain Soviet power. However, France was reluctant to cooperate with Germany, and while many other European countries embraced US Marshall Plan Aid, they were not eager to initiate a regional integration process (Friedman 2016). In the late 1940s, Britain tended to be optimistic about the survival of its own empire, which would allow it to preserve free trade with its colonies and re-establish the global hegemony of the pound sterling. In the end, however, the fear of Soviet communism and US financial incentives prevailed in favour of regional integration (Friedman 2016).

The catalyzing influence of Russophobia has persisted in contemporary European politics. Europe reacted to the rise of Vladimir Putin's Russia with the EU enlargement process, which since 2004 has involved various Central European countries including Bulgaria, Czech Republic, Estonia, Hungary, Latvia, Lithuania, Poland, Romania, Slovakia, and Slovenia (Kuus 2007). Of course, contemporary Russia's containment by European powers had already been initiated by the bombing of former Yugoslavia in 1999 by the North Atlantic Treaty Organization (NATO), despite the initial promise by then US President Bill Clinton that Northern intervention in Yugoslavia would remain a humanitarian operation. In 1995, NATO had decided not to expand further into Eastern Europe; this promise too was broken with the aim of preventing Russia from building zones of influence in Europe (O'Loughlin and Kolossov 2002). Moreover, throughout the 2000s, the United States and the EU devoted special efforts to supporting the anti-Russian so-called "coloured revolutions" by funding pro-Northern NGOs in the Balkans and Eastern Europe.

The expansion of NATO and European aggression gained new momentum following Russia's intervention in Georgia in 2008 (Friedman 2016). In the same manner, Europe's strategic crisis with Russia took on another dimension following Northern intervention in Syria, where Russia has a strategic naval facility that provides "Russia's only access to the Mediterranean, crucial for both commercial and military purposes" (Gordon 2017). Until 2005, the North had been troubled by the continued Syrian occupation of Lebanon in spite of sanctions. Syria is also known to have facilitated the passage of Sunni terrorists across the Iraqi border with the aim of weakening the US occupation there (Phillips 2015). Moreover, the destabilization of Syria would be desirable for European powers, who were interested in relieving their energy dependency on Russia by opening up alternative routes from energy-rich Arab countries. Last, but not least, Syria's natural resources and strategic position on energy routes – accompanied by the discovery of abundant natural gas reserves in the eastern Mediterranean in 2010 (Engdahl 2013) – attracted regional players such as Turkey and Qatar, which have a vested interest in destabilizing Syria in order to implement their own pipeline projects and counter Iran's regional Shiite influence (Gürcan 2017).

Tragically, Northern intervention against Syria has resulted in a converging strategic and humanitarian crisis, which has had the effect of consolidating European racism and far-right movements in reaction to the influx of migrants. All of this has added to Northern support for Ukrainian ultranationalists against Russia, which has resulted in the merging of an "internationalist" environment between neo-Nazi and other ultra-nationalist groups across Europe (e.g. Draitser 2014; Hughes 2014; Lee 2015; Milne 2014; Pietka 2016; Whelan 2014). Similarly to the Syrian case, Ukraine's strategic importance for Russia concerns both economic and military interests.

Economically speaking, over 45% of the EU's natural gas consumption depends on Russian resources, and most of the energy flow is distributed from Ukraine; hence the importance of controlling this country for both the EU and Russia. It is estimated that 80% of Russian natural gas exports pass through Ukrainian soil, which is why the Russo–Ukrainian rapprochement in 2013 was a worrying development for the EU. As far as Russia's military interests are concerned, Russia is already contained across Baltic and Balkan countries, and it fears further containment in Ukraine (Eriş 2016; Friedman 2016).

The impact of the refugee and economic crisis on European regionalism is well evidenced in poll results by reputable organizations such as the European Commission and Pew Research Center. Regarding the rise of Euroscepticism as part of the economic and strategic crisis of European regionalism, Eurobarometer survey results indicate that, in December 2006, 17% of European public opinion was totally negative and 34% was neutral towards the EU. In December 2013, in the heat of the economic crisis, these percentages soared to 28% and 39%, respectively. This left a mere 31% with a positive opinion of the EU (OECD 2016, 15). Similarly, in a special Eurobarometer survey conducted between 24 September and 3 October 2016, the most important challenges faced by the EU were designated as unemployment, inequality, migration, and terrorism. As many as 45% of respondents identified unemployment as the EU's greatest challenge, whereas 36% pointed to the challenge of social inequalities and migration. According to 31% of respondents, terrorism represented Europe's greatest challenge (European Commission 2016, 4). As far as the rise of European racism and xenophobia is concerned, a 2016 Pew Research Center survey suggested that at least half of the respondents from ten selected European countries believed that the influx of refugees was closely related to the threat of terrorism and economic crisis (Wike, Stokes, and Simmons 2016). Syrian and Iraqi refugees were seen as major threats. Moreover, "in no European Union country surveyed did more than four-in-ten say that having an increasing number of people from many different races, ethnic groups and nationalities makes their country a better place to live" (Poushter 2016).

As a final note, the EU's anti-Russian move towards enlargement has had unintended consequences in terms of widening the gap between rich and poor countries in Europe. The European core represented by richer countries (e.g. Austria, Belgium, Denmark, Finland, France, Germany, Luxembourg, the Netherlands, and Sweden) have consolidated their status within the EU at the expense of homogenizing a peripheral grouping of poorer countries, including South European states (Cyprus, Greece, Malta, Portugal, and Spain), Central European states (Czech Republic, Hungary, Poland, Slovakia, and Slovenia), and Eastern European states (Bulgaria, Croatia, Estonia, Latvia, Lithuania, and Romania) (Magone, Laffan, and Schweiger 2016). Europe's polarization between core and periphery is felt most strongly in the EU's budgetary debates: core countries tend to oppose proposals mostly for budgetary increases. Indeed, following the 2008 economic crisis, the core–periphery polarization has transcended mere budgetary debates. This first Europe-wide economic crisis has radically altered the perceptions of peripheral countries about the EU's status as a charitable organization (Magone et al. 2016). Prior to the economic crisis, certain peripheral countries viewed the EU as a philanthropic institution: many of them had decided to join with the desire of achieving economic and political development. The Italian term *vincolo esterno* (external constraint) made its way deep into the European political lexicon because peripheral countries used to see the EU as an external constraint that guaranteed democratization and accountability. However, political elites in core European countries chose to overlook the ravages of the neoliberal policies that they had imposed, and victimized peripheral countries by alluding to their so-called lavishness, corruption, and laziness. This victimization was also convenient in terms of satisfying Western European electorates, which had been shifting to the right of the political spectrum (Magone 2016; Magone et al. 2016). In the next section, I provide a more detailed picture of the negative implications of peripheralization as they relate to the neoliberal restructuring of European regionalism.

Open regionalism and the ravages of neoliberalism: Making sense of the European Union's economic crisis

Since 2008, Northern capitalism has undergone a deep economic crisis with grave sociopolitical consequences. One of the immediate manifestations of this crisis was the decline and disappearance of economic growth, accompanied by rising unemployment levels in Europe. According to World Bank data, Germany, Italy, and Ireland took the lead in economic contraction, with respective rates of 5.62, 5.48, and 4.57% in 2009. In 2011, Greece's contraction of over 9% shook the entire European economy (Figure 2.1). Furthermore, unemployment levels reached record highs in 2013, soaring to over 26% in Greece and Spain (Figure 2.2). In the same year, youth unemployment rates were over 57% in Spain, 39% in Italy, and 37% in Portugal, not to mention Greece's performance of 58% (Figure 2.3) (World Bank 2016).

In the pre-neoliberal era, Europe's consumption was sustained through relatively high unionization rates; employment-generating public investments; an industry-centered model of economic development; and, subsequently, higher wages. However, the EU reversed this situation by promoting de-unionization, privatization, deindustrialization, and flexibilization of labor, due to which consumption had to be sustained through excessive financialization and indebtedness. Therefore, it is safe to argue that the current economic crisis in the Eurozone is mostly a by-product of neoliberalism imposed by the EU.

Neoliberalism made its entry into Europe following Margaret Thatcher's rise to office in Britain in 1979 and François Mitterrand's decision to do away with France's state-led development model in 1983 (Palley 2013). The region-wide diffusion of neoliberalism resulted from the signing in 1992 of the Maastricht Agreement, and imposed an agenda of anti-inflationary measures,

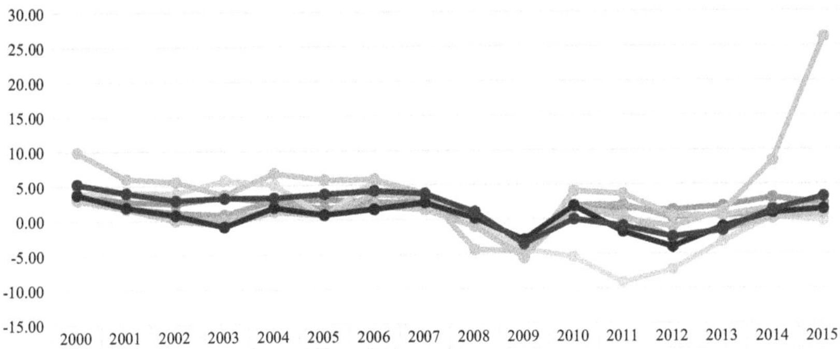

	2000	2001	2002	2003	2004	2005	2006	2007	2008	2009	2010	2011	2012	2013	2014	2015
Britain	3.74	2.73	2.40	3.47	2.53	2.97	2.50	2.56	-0.63	-4.33	1.92	1.51	1.31	1.91	3.07	2.22
France	3.88	1.95	1.12	0.82	2.79	1.61	2.37	2.36	0.20	-2.94	1.97	2.08	0.18	0.58	0.64	1.27
Germany	2.96	1.70	0.00	-0.71	1.17	0.71	3.70	3.26	1.08	-5.62	4.08	3.66	0.49	0.49	1.60	1.72
Greece	3.92	4.13	3.92	5.79	5.06	0.60	5.65	3.27	-0.34	-4.30	-5.48	-9.13	-7.30	-3.24	0.35	-0.22
Ireland	9.91	6.05	5.58	3.67	6.72	5.77	5.87	3.80	-4.37	-4.57	2.03	-0.04	-1.10	1.10	8.46	26.28
Italy	3.71	1.77	0.25	0.15	1.58	0.95	2.01	1.47	-1.05	-5.48	1.69	0.58	-2.82	-1.73	0.09	0.73
Portugal	3.79	1.94	0.77	-0.93	1.81	0.77	1.55	2.49	0.20	-2.98	1.90	-1.83	-4.03	-1.13	0.91	1.45
Spain	5.29	4.00	2.88	3.19	3.17	3.72	4.17	3.77	1.12	-3.57	0.01	-1.00	-2.62	-1.67	1.36	3.21

Britain France Germany Greece Ireland Italy Portugal Spain

Figure 2.1 Annual GDP growth in selected European countries (%)
Source: World Bank 2017, January 13

a common currency, and labor flexibilization on Europe. Another turning point in Europe's history of neoliberalization was the 2009 Lisbon Treaty, which further promoted labor flexibilization and labor cost reduction. Ultimately, excessive financialization and deindustrialization in peripheral European countries amplified these countries' reliance on an import- and debt-driven model of economic development. Not only did financialization and indebtedness contribute to income inequality, but the adoption of a common European currency and fiscal disciplinary measures also left European nation states helpless against a region-wide economic crisis (Busch et al. 2013; Lang 2013; Lapavitsas et al. 2012; Stockhammer 2013).

Europe's financialization can be assessed by looking at the financial intermediation rates of the five most crisis-hit peripheral countries (Greece, Ireland, Italy, Portugal, and Spain) compared with core states (Britain, France, and Germany) in the EU. According to the Organisation for Economic Co-operation and Development (OECD), financial intermediation is "a productive activity in which an institutional unit incurs liabilities on its own account for the purpose of acquiring financial assets by engaging in financial transactions on the market" (OECD 2003). Therefore, financial intermediation reflects the weight of financial transactions within the economy. Figure 2.4

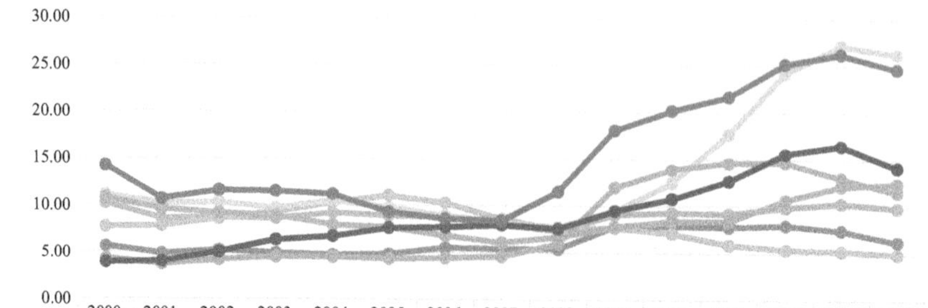

	2000	2001	2002	2003	2004	2005	2006	2007	2008	2009	2010	2011	2012	2013	2014
Britain	5.60	4.80	5.20	4.90	4.70	4.80	5.50	5.40	5.40	7.80	7.90	7.80	8.00	7.50	6.30
France	10.20	8.60	8.70	8.60	9.20	8.90	8.80	8.00	7.40	9.10	9.30	9.20	9.90	10.40	9.90
Germany	7.70	7.80	8.60	9.30	10.30	11.10	10.30	8.60	7.50	7.70	7.10	5.90	5.40	5.30	5.00
Greece	11.10	10.20	10.30	9.70	10.50	9.80	8.90	8.30	7.70	9.50	12.50	17.70	24.20	27.20	26.30
Ireland	4.30	3.70	4.20	4.50	4.50	4.30	4.40	4.60	6.00	12.00	13.90	14.60	14.70	13.10	11.60
Italy	10.80	9.60	9.20	8.90	7.90	7.70	6.80	6.10	6.70	7.80	8.40	8.40	10.70	12.20	12.50
Portugal	3.90	4.00	5.00	6.30	6.70	7.60	7.70	8.00	7.60	9.50	10.80	12.70	15.60	16.50	14.20
Spain	14.20	10.70	11.60	11.50	11.20	9.30	8.60	8.40	11.50	18.10	20.20	21.70	25.20	26.30	24.70

Britain France Germany Greece Ireland Italy Portugal Spain

Figure 2.2 Unemployment rates in selected European countries (%, total labor force)
Source: World Bank 2017, January 13

presents financial intermediation rates for the period 2000–2015. Worthy of special mention is that all the countries in the sample (excluding Greece and Italy) reached a peak in 2008, the year the economic crisis erupted (OECD 2017).

The financial intermediation rate is an indicator that reflects reliance on bank loans rather than on equities and bonds (Deeg 2010, 311–312). Therefore, a sharper indicator of Europe's financialization can be found in the ratio of gross portfolio debt and equity liabilities to GDP (Figure 2.5) (World Bank 2017). Attention should be paid to the fact that all the countries in the sample underwent noticeable increases in their ratio between 2000 and 2007. Particularly noticeable is Greece's ratio, which soared by over 64 percentage points. Similarly, Spain's and Portugal's ratios rose by almost 60 percentage points. France's and Germany's ratios – whose increase was measured at over 40 percentage points – cannot be easily ignored either.

Intertwined with the process of Europe's financialization is indebtedness, which can be assessed based on the debt of households and non-profit institutions serving households as a percentage of net disposable income (Figure 2.6). Greece's ratio was only 30.36% in 2000, but it climbed to 118.48% in 2015. The same ratio increased from 84.22 to 121.78% in Spain and from 110.76 to 208.19% in Ireland (OECD 2017).

Excessive financialization and indebtedness were sustained at the cost of deindustrialization. In the period 2000–2015, the industrial sector's contribution

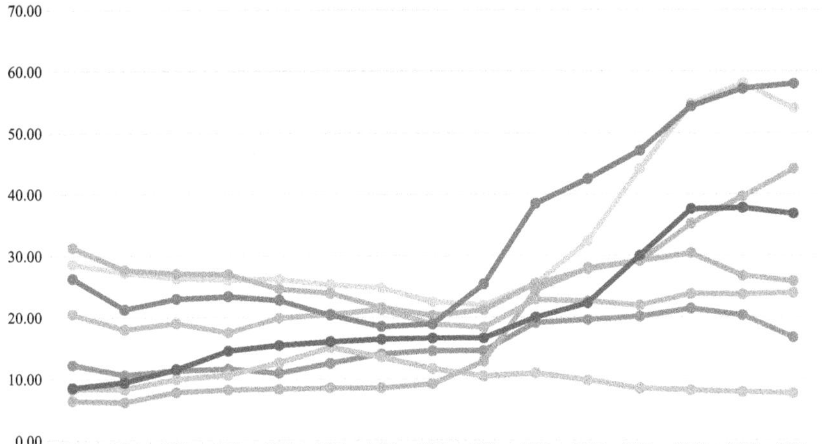

	2000	2001	2002	2003	2004	2005	2006	2007	2008	2009	2010	2011	2012	2013	2014
Britain	12.20	10.60	11.30	11.60	10.90	12.50	14.00	14.50	14.50	19.10	19.60	20.10	21.40	20.30	16.70
France	20.50	18.00	19.00	17.50	19.90	20.50	21.30	18.90	18.40	22.90	22.60	21.90	23.80	23.70	23.90
Germany	8.30	8.30	9.90	10.60	12.60	15.10	13.50	11.60	10.40	10.90	9.70	8.40	8.10	7.80	7.60
Greece	28.60	27.20	26.30	26.10	26.20	25.30	24.80	22.50	22.00	25.50	32.40	44.10	54.70	58.00	53.90
Ireland	6.40	6.20	7.80	8.20	8.30	8.50	8.50	9.10	12.80	24.40	28.00	29.10	30.40	26.70	25.80
Italy	31.30	27.70	27.10	27.00	24.60	23.90	21.60	20.30	21.20	25.50	27.80	29.10	35.20	39.70	44.10
Portugal	8.50	9.40	11.50	14.50	15.40	16.00	16.40	16.60	16.60	20.00	22.30	30.00	37.60	37.80	36.80
Spain	26.30	21.30	23.00	23.40	22.80	20.40	18.50	18.90	25.40	38.50	42.50	47.10	54.30	57.10	57.90

Britain France Germany Greece Ireland Italy Portugal Spain

Figure 2.3 Youth unemployment rates in selected European countries (%, total labor force ages 15–24)
Source: World Bank 2017, January 13

to GDP in Greece fell from 20.99 to 15.69%, while Spain's industry contracted from around 30.74 to 22.56% (Figure 2.7). It is noticeable that in Germany and Ireland – known as Europe's exporting economies – there were declines in industrial employment, which fell from around 33.6 and 28.8% to 28.3 and 18.4% between 2000 and 2014. Industrial employment also declined from 36.1 to 24.9% in Portugal and from 31 to 19.5% in Spain (Figure 2.8) (World Bank 2017).

As a final note on the economic aspects of the crisis of European regionalism, Germany ranks as the world's fourth-largest economy and third-largest exporter (Crawford 2015). Regarded as the EU's locomotive, Germany was also one of the European economies least affected by the 2008 crisis, but so far it has shown little interest in helping out poorer crisis-hit countries. On the contrary, it has exploded the myth of European solidarity by putting the blame on poorer countries for their supposed lavishness, laziness, and corruption, as well as imposing further austerity policies to deal with the crisis situation (Stockhammer 2016). Unlike the model of neoliberal regionalism

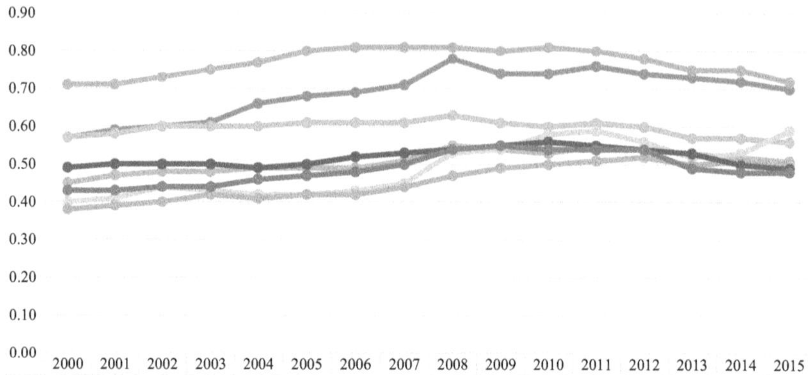

	2000	2001	2002	2003	2004	2005	2006	2007	2008	2009	2010	2011	2012	2013	2014	2015
Britain	0.57	0.59	0.60	0.61	0.66	0.68	0.69	0.71	0.78	0.74	0.74	0.76	0.74	0.73	0.72	0.70
France	0.45	0.47	0.48	0.48	0.49	0.49	0.49	0.51	0.55	0.54	0.53	0.55	0.54	0.53	0.52	0.51
Germany	0.57	0.58	0.60	0.60	0.60	0.61	0.61	0.61	0.63	0.61	0.60	0.61	0.60	0.57	0.57	0.56
Greece	0.40	0.41	0.44	0.43	0.42	0.42	0.43	0.45	0.53	0.54	0.58	0.59	0.56	0.52	0.53	0.59
Ireland	0.71	0.71	0.73	0.75	0.77	0.80	0.81	0.81	0.81	0.80	0.81	0.80	0.78	0.75	0.75	0.72
Italy	0.38	0.39	0.40	0.42	0.41	0.42	0.42	0.44	0.47	0.49	0.50	0.51	0.52	0.50	0.51	0.50
Portugal	0.49	0.50	0.50	0.50	0.49	0.50	0.52	0.53	0.54	0.55	0.56	0.55	0.54	0.53	0.50	0.49
Spain	0.43	0.43	0.44	0.44	0.46	0.47	0.48	0.50	0.54	0.55	0.54	0.54	0.54	0.49	0.48	0.48

Britain France Germany Greece Ireland Italy Portugal Spain

Figure 2.4 Financial intermediation ratio in selected European countries
Source: OECD 2017, January 13

imposed on peripheral European countries, Germany itself has adopted a neo-mercantilist strategy of development (Bellofiore, Garibaldo, and Halevi 2011; Lucarelli 2011). In former Chancellor Gerhard Schröder's period in office (1998–2005), it is known that a major preoccupation of Germany's Foreign Office and its consulates was the facilitation of the national export sector (Kundnani 2015). At present, the German state is seeking to sustain a net export surplus while constraining imports and reinvesting the surplus into productive activities, which is why export revenues have a greater weight than household consumption in the German economy (Crawford 2015; Overbeek 2012). Although Germany has succeeded in reducing its unemployment levels to below 4%, making it one of the best performers among advanced capitalist economies, the squeeze on wages and savings is reflected in a 16% decline of relative unit labor costs in the period 1999–2007, and a decline in the share of GDP going to households from 65% in the early 1990s to 60% in 2016 (Economist 2017a).

The share of exports in Germany's GDP is estimated to be somewhere between 35 and 40%, whereas even in the US – ranked as the world's second-largest exporter – the contribution of exports to GDP remains below 10%. The ratio in China – the world leader in exports – is about 30% (Friedman 2016). Even *Foreign Policy* magazine – known as a mouthpiece for US hegemonism – has not restrained itself from referring to Germany's "arrogant" moral

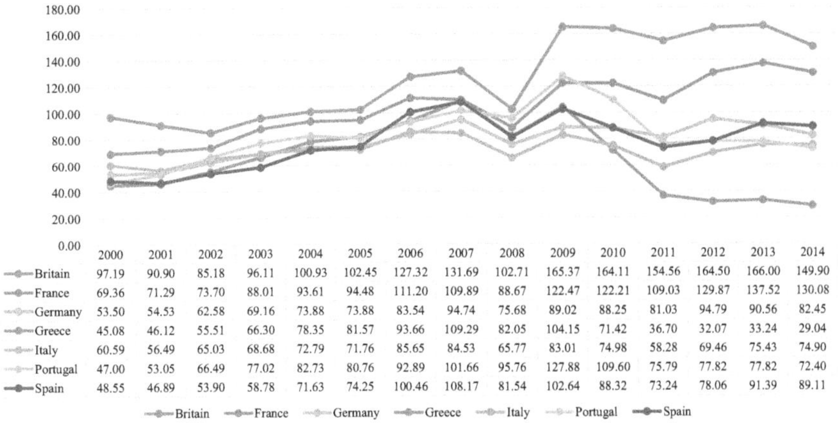

	2000	2001	2002	2003	2004	2005	2006	2007	2008	2009	2010	2011	2012	2013	2014
Britain	97.19	90.90	85.18	96.11	100.93	102.45	127.32	131.69	102.71	165.37	164.11	154.56	164.50	166.00	149.90
France	69.36	71.29	73.70	88.01	93.61	94.48	111.20	109.89	88.67	122.47	122.21	109.03	129.87	137.52	130.08
Germany	53.50	54.53	62.58	69.16	73.88	73.88	83.54	94.74	75.68	89.02	88.25	81.03	94.79	90.56	82.45
Greece	45.08	46.12	55.51	66.30	78.35	81.57	93.66	109.29	82.05	104.15	71.42	36.70	32.07	33.24	29.04
Italy	60.59	56.49	65.03	68.68	72.79	71.76	85.65	84.53	65.77	83.01	74.98	58.28	69.46	75.43	74.90
Portugal	47.00	53.05	66.49	77.02	82.73	80.76	92.89	101.66	95.76	127.88	109.60	75.79	77.82	77.82	72.40
Spain	48.55	46.89	53.90	58.78	71.63	74.25	100.46	108.17	81.54	102.64	88.32	73.24	78.06	91.39	89.11

Figure 2.5 Gross portfolio debt and equity liabilities in selected European countries (% to GDP)
Source: World Bank 2017, January 13

imperialism towards Europe, and to its imposition of neoliberal policies on others despite its own protectionist and export-oriented strategies that deliberately constrain wages and national expenditure (Hockenos 2017). This view is also shared by *The Economist*, a pro-free trade organ, which complains that Germany "saves too much and spends too little" (Economist 2017b, para. 1) while simultaneously championing free trade and globalization.

Europe's export data also point to the fact that neo-mercantilist Germany's economic dependence on Europe is substantially less than Europe's dependence on Germany. Less than half of Germany's exports are directed to the EU area (Friedman 2016). Germany is shifting its focus from European to external markets, which in the long term might turn its foreign policy priorities and commitments away from European countries. For example, Germany is believed to be the largest exporter to the Middle East (Crawford 2015). Meanwhile, China, Russia, and the rest of Eurasia constitute appetizing markets to be conquered in the near future. In 1991, the present EU area received 51.3% of German exports, but in 2010 this rate had fallen to 41%, while on the other hand the share of Germany's Asian exports had gone up to 16% (Szabo 2015).

Review and discussion

Europe's hegemonic neoliberal integration model was once presented as the poster child of neoliberal governance. One of the main factors that rendered

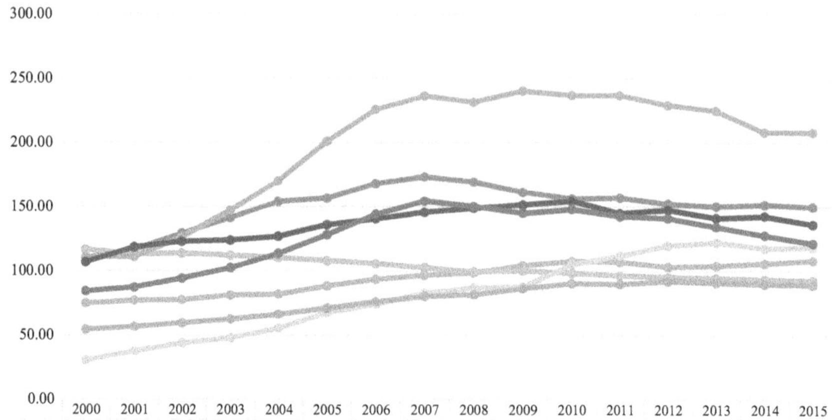

	2000	2001	2002	2003	2004	2005	2006	2007	2008	2009	2010	2011	2012	2013	2014	2015
Britain	109.72	116.29	129.11	141.16	154.25	156.90	168.20	173.32	169.35	161.39	156.21	156.92	152.23	150.28	151.70	150.03
France	74.76	77.03	77.46	81.13	81.93	88.41	93.58	96.65	98.69	104.25	107.53	107.07	103.31	104.16	105.99	108.30
Germany	116.52	112.98	113.58	111.97	110.39	108.06	105.72	102.65	99.40	100.29	98.25	96.49	95.20	94.48	93.65	92.88
Greece	30.36	37.38	43.77	47.80	55.50	67.60	74.12	82.69	86.87	87.64	105.15	111.91	119.85	122.23	117.69	118.48
Ireland	110.76	110.76	126.24	147.22	170.03	201.00	225.86	236.23	231.39	240.25	236.76	236.59	229.14	224.80	208.19	208.19
Italy	54.49	56.54	59.37	62.55	66.23	71.25	76.10	80.16	81.59	86.51	90.39	89.92	92.02	90.72	89.92	89.24
Portugal	106.80	118.26	122.73	123.62	126.78	135.94	140.63	145.74	148.90	151.38	154.36	144.94	147.63	141.32	142.78	136.38
Spain	84.22	87.10	94.13	102.27	113.65	128.22	144.30	154.37	150.23	145.15	148.09	142.40	141.01	134.36	127.90	121.78

Britain France Germany Greece Ireland Italy Portugal Spain

Figure 2.6 Ratio of debt of households and non-profit institutions serving households to disposable net income in selected European countries
Source: OECD 2017, January 13

the EU a charming model was the myth that European integration hinged on the high ideals of democracy, humanitarianism, global peace, and philanthropy. However, it is evident that European integration has in truth been essentially a strategic instrument to counterbalance German power and contain Russia. As far as current geopolitics is concerned, the humanitarian crisis generated by the North's ambition to topple al-Assad's regime in Syria and to provide support for Ukrainian fascists – besides NATO's 2011 military intervention in Libya, which drove that country into deep chaos – nullifies Europe's idealism. Furthermore, the ravages of the neoliberal policies imposed by Europe's regionalism make themselves felt in Europe's bifurcation into a core of rich countries and a periphery of poor countries, as well as the amplification of the 2008 economic crisis under the influence of excessive financialization, indebtedness, deindustrialization, and unemployment. Germany's reluctance to help crisis-hit European countries, and the German position of blaming those countries' supposed lavishness and laziness, demonstrate that the EU is far from being a charitable institution and that it rather represents a club of powerful strategic interests. It is also evident that Germany has retained its

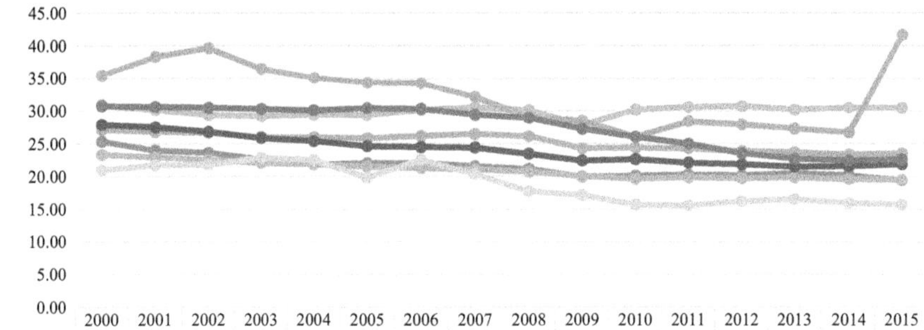

	2000	2001	2002	2003	2004	2005	2006	2007	2008	2009	2010	2011	2012	2013	2014	2015
Britain	25.34	23.96	23.60	22.62	21.79	22.03	22.05	21.54	21.14	19.94	20.11	20.31	20.15	20.50	20.15	19.42
France	23.34	22.91	22.56	22.07	21.85	21.51	21.25	21.06	20.68	20.04	19.60	19.83	19.69	19.84	19.57	19.50
Germany	30.91	30.11	29.36	29.25	29.42	29.40	30.12	30.53	30.06	27.81	30.16	30.57	30.71	30.18	30.53	30.49
Greece	20.99	21.72	21.79	22.87	22.55	19.84	22.56	20.40	17.72	17.13	15.66	15.57	16.21	16.53	15.94	15.69
Ireland	35.43	38.33	39.66	36.48	35.05	34.35	34.26	32.13	28.99	28.48	26.07	28.41	27.93	27.32	26.69	41.65
Italy	27.15	26.80	26.64	25.97	25.97	25.83	26.15	26.49	26.13	24.27	24.37	24.21	23.87	23.70	23.38	23.53
Portugal	27.90	27.51	26.84	25.86	25.40	24.64	24.49	24.39	23.43	22.40	22.62	22.08	21.83	21.47	21.55	21.88
Spain	30.74	30.64	30.49	30.32	30.08	30.43	30.30	29.41	28.96	27.23	26.01	24.97	23.52	22.68	22.41	22.56

Britain France Germany Greece Ireland Italy Portugal Spain

Figure 2.7 Percentage ratio of industry to GDP in selected European countries
Source: World Bank 2017, January 13

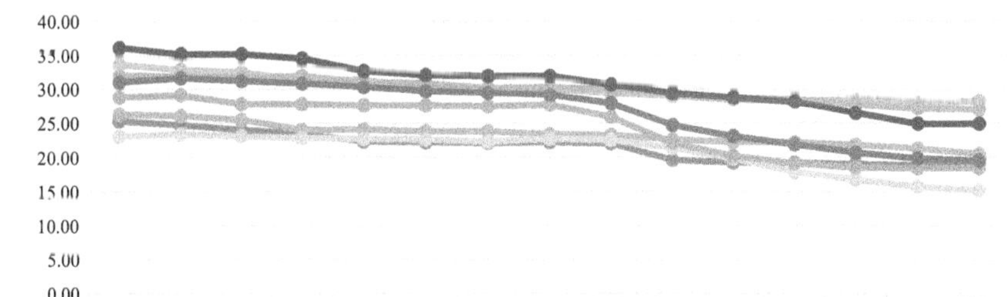

	2000	2001	2002	2003	2004	2005	2006	2007	2008	2009	2010	2011	2012	2013	2014
Britain	25.30	24.70	24.00	23.40	22.30	22.20	22.10	22.20	22.00	19.60	19.20	19.20	19.00	18.80	18.90
France	26.30	26.10	25.50	24.00	24.10	23.80	23.80	23.40	23.20	22.60	22.20	22.20	21.80	21.30	20.50
Germany	33.60	32.90	32.50	31.50	31.40	30.00	29.80	30.00	29.50	29.00	28.50	28.40	28.40	28.00	28.30
Greece	23.00	23.40	23.10	22.80	22.70	22.60	22.30	22.70	22.50	21.40	19.80	17.80	16.70	15.70	15.10
Ireland	28.80	29.10	27.80	27.80	27.60	27.60	27.50	27.70	25.90	22.10	20.20	19.10	18.50	18.40	18.40
Italy	32.00	31.90	31.80	32.00	31.10	30.90	30.20	30.30	30.00	29.40	28.80	28.50	27.80	27.20	27.10
Portugal	36.10	35.20	35.20	34.50	32.70	32.10	32.00	32.00	30.70	29.40	28.80	28.20	26.50	24.90	24.90
Spain	31.00	31.60	31.20	30.80	30.30	29.70	29.50	29.20	27.90	24.70	23.10	21.90	20.70	19.80	19.50

Britain France Germany Greece Ireland Italy Portugal Spain

Figure 2.8 Percentage share of industrial employment in total employment in selected European countries
Source: World Bank 2017, January 13

position as Europe's most powerful economy thanks to its neo-mercantilist strategy of development, while imposing the model of neoliberal regionalism on poorer European states. In the final analysis, the rise of Euroscepticism, racism, and far-right political parties is nothing but a strong indicator of the ways in which Europe's regionalism is suffering from converging economic and strategic crises.

References

Bellofiore, Riccardo, Francesco Garibaldo, and Joseph Halevi. 2011. "The Global Crisis and the Crisis of European Neomercantilism." *Socialist Register*, 471: 120–146.

Busch, Klaus, Christoph Hermann, Karl Hinrichs, and Thorsten Schulten. 2013. *Euro Crisis, Austerity Policy and the European Social Model: How Crisis Policies in Southern Europe Threaten the EU's Social Dimension*. Berlin: Friedrich-Ebert-Stiftung. https://library.fes.de/pdf-files/id/ipa/09656.pdf

Crawford, Beverly. 2015. "German Power and 'Embedded Hegemony' in Europe." In *The Routledge Handbook of German Politics and Culture*, edited by S. Colvin, 329–348. New York: Routledge.

Deeg, Richard. 2010. "Institutional Change in Financial Systems." In *Oxford Handbook of Comparative Institutional Analysis*, edited by G. Morgan, J. L. Campbell, C. Crouch, O. K. Pedersen, and R. Whitley, 309–334. Oxford: Oxford University Press.

Draitser, Eric. 2014. "Ukraine and the Rebirth of Fascism in Europe." http://stopimperialism.org/ukraine-rebirth-fascism-europe/

Economist. 2017a. "The Good and Bad in Germany's Economic Model are Strongly Linked." *The Economist*, July 8. https://www.economist.com/briefing/2017/07/08/the-good-and-bad-in-germanys-economic-model-are-strongly-linked

Economist. 2017b. "Why Germany's Current-Account Surplus is Bad for the World Economy." *The Economist*, July 8. https://www.economist.com/leaders/2017/07/08/why-germanys-current-account-surplus-is-bad-for-the-world-economy

Engdahl, F. William. 2013. "The New Mediterranean Oil and Gas Bonanza. Part II: Rising Energy Tensions in the Aegean—Greece, Turkey, Cyprus, Syria. Global Research." *Global Research*, March 3. http://www.globalresearch.ca/the-new-mediterranean-oil-and-gas-bonanza/29609

Eriş, Özgür Ünal. 2016. "Kriz Sonrası Avrupa Birliği Enerji Politikası" ["The EU's Energy Policies after the Crisis"]. In *Ekonomik Kriz ve Avrupa Birliği* [*Economic Crisis and the European Union*], edited by P. G. Bal and R. İ. Connelly, 157–180. İstanbul: Derin Yayınları.

European Commission. 2016. Special Eurobarometer 451: Future of Europe. http://ec.europa.eu/COMMFrontOffice/publicopinion/index.cfm/Survey/getSurveyDetail/instruments/SPECIAL/surveyKy/2131

Friedman, George. 2016. *Flashpoints: The Emerging Crisis in Europe*. New York: Anchor Books.

Gordon, Sean. 2017. "Russian resolve: Why Syria Matters to Putin." *The Globe and Mail*, April 8. http://www.theglobeandmail.com/news/world/russian-resolve-why-syria-matters-to-putin/article34643406/

Gürcan, Efe Can. 2017. "Political geography of Turkey's intervention in Syria: underlying causes and consequences (2011–2016)." *Journal of Aggression, Conflict and Peace Research*. https://doi.org/10.1108/JACPR-10-2017-0329

Hockenos, Paul. 2017. "Germany Has an Arrogance Problem." *Foreign Policy*, April 27. http://foreignpolicy.com/2017/04/27/germany-is-getting-too-arrogant-merkel/

Hughes, Michael. 2014. "The Neo-Nazi Question in Ukraine." *Huff Post*, March 11. http://www.huffingtonpost.com/michael-hughes/the-neo-nazi-question-in_b_4938747.html

Kundnani, Hans. 2015. *The Paradox of German Power*. Oxford: Oxford University Press.

Kuus, Merje. 2007. *Geopolitics Reframed: Security and Identity in Europe's Eastern Enlargement*. New York: Palgrave Macmillan.

Lang, Dany. 2013. "Financialisation, Income Distribution and the Crisis." *Cambridge Journal of Economics*, 393: 867–870.

Lapavitsas, Costas, A. Kaltenbrunner, G. Labrinidis, D. Lindo, J. Meadway, J. Michell, J. P. Painceira, E. Pires, J. Powell, A. Stenfors, N. Teles, and L. Vatikitis. 2012. *Crisis in the Eurozone*. London: Verso Books.

Lee, Peter. 2015. "Fascist Formations in Ukraine." *Counter Punch*, March 13. http://www.counterpunch.org/2015/03/13/fascist-formations-in-ukraine/

Lucarelli, Bill. 2011. "German Neomercantilism and the European Sovereign Debt Crisis." *Journal of Post Keynesian Economics*, 342: 205–224.

Magone, José M. 2016. "From 'Superficial' to 'Forced' Europeanization in Southern Europe: The Lack of Ownership of National Reforms." In *Core–Periphery Relations in the European Union: Power and Conflict in a Dualist Political Economy*, edited by J. M. Magone, B. Laffan, and C. Schweiger, 87–98.

Magone, José M., Brigid Laffan, and Christian Schweiger. 2016. "The European Union as a Dualist Political Economy: Understanding Core-Periphery Relations." In *Core–Periphery Relations in the European Union: Power and Conflict in a Dualist Political Economy*, edited by J. M. Magone, B. Laffan, and C. Schweiger, 1–16. New York: Routledge.

Milne, Seumas. 2014. "In Ukraine, Fascists, Oligarchs and Western Expansion are at the Heart of the Crisis." *The Guardian*, January 29. http://www.theguardian.com/commentisfree/2014/jan/29/ukraine-fascists-oligarchs-eu-nato-expansion

O'Loughlin, J. and V. Kolossov. 2002. "Still Not Worth the Bones of a Single Pomeranian Grenadier: The Geopolitics of the Kosovo War 1999." *Political Geography* 215: 573–599.

OECD. 2003. Financial intermediation. *Glossary of Statistical Terms*. Paris: Organisation for Economic Co-operation and Development. https://stats.oecd.org/glossary/detail.asp?ID=972

OECD. 2016. *OECD Economic Surveys: European Union*. Paris: Organisation for Economic Co-operation and Development. http://www.oecd.org/eco/surveys/european-union-2016-overview.pdf

OECD. 2017. OECD.Stat. Paris: Organisation for Economic Co-operation and Development. https://stats.oecd.org

Otero, Gerardo and Efe Can Gürcan. 2016. "The Arab Spring and the Syrian refugee crisis." *The Monitor*, January: 16–17.

Overbeek, Henk. 2012. "Sovereign Debt Crisis in Euroland: Root Causes and Implications for European Integration." *Italian Journal of International Affairs* 471: 30–48.

Palley, Thomas I. 2013. "Europe's Crisis without End: The Consequences of Neoliberalism." *Contributions to Political Economy*, 321: 29–50.

Phillips, Christopher. 2015. "Sectarianism and Conflict in Syria." *Third World Quarterly*, 362: 357–376.

Pietka, Bohdan. 2016. "EU's Promotion of Fascism in Eastern Europe." *South Front*, April 1. https://southfront.org/eus-promotion-of-fascism-in-eastern-europe/

Poushter, Jacob. 2016. "European Opinions of the Refugee Crisis in 5 Charts." *Pew Research Center: Fact Tank*, September 16. http://www.pewresearch.org/fact-tank/2016/09/16/european-opinions-of-the-refugee-crisis-in-5-charts/

Stockhammer, Engelbert. 2013. "Rising Inequality as a Cause of the Present Crisis." *Cambridge Journal of Economics*, 393: 935–958.

Stockhammer, Engelbert. 2016. "Neoliberal Growth Models, Monetary Union and the Euro Crisis: A Post-Keynesian Perspective." *New Political Economy*, 214: 365–379.

Szabo, Stephen F. 2015. *Germany, Russia, and the Rise of Geo-Economics*. London: Bloomsbury.

Whelan, Brian. 2014. "Ukraine: Far-Right Extremists at Core of 'Democracy' Protest." *Channel 4 News*, January 24. http://www.channel4.com/news/kiev-svoboda-far-right-protests-right-sector-riot-police

Wike, Richard, Bruce Stokes, and Katie Simmons. 2016. "Europeans Fear Wave of Refugees Will Mean More Terrorism, Fewer Jobs." *Pew Research Center: Global Attitudes & Trends*, July 11. http://www.pewglobal.org/2016/07/11/europeans-fear-wave-of-refugees-will-mean-more-terrorism-fewer-jobs/

World Bank. 2017. DataBank. http://databank.worldbank.org

3 South–South cooperation and the BRICS: Towards a post-hegemonic global governance?

Introduction

The crisis of US hegemonic governance and neoliberalism tells only one part of the story about the multipolarization of world politics and the rise of post-hegemonic governance. The wider context in which these phenomena have occurred can be explored only if due attention is paid to how South–South cooperation has been gaining steam since the 2000s. Therefore, this chapter focuses on the geopolitical economy of the BRICS, which is representative of South–South cooperation. Briefly, the BRICS has fostered the rise of post-hegemonic forms of global governance by providing the necessary material and strategic environment for their growth. To say the least, the Shanghai Cooperation Organization (SCO) experience cannot be considered without understanding the geopolitical challenge of Russia and China in their connection to South–South cooperation. The same also applies to Latin America's post-hegemonic regionalism in the case of Brazil and the *Unión de Naciones Suramericanas* (Unasur: Union of South American Nations).

How does the BRICS contribute to the multipolarization of world politics? What are the strategic implications of the BRICS for South–South cooperation and the erosion of US global hegemony? To what extent has the BRICS' cooperation been developing, and in what direction is it evolving? What are some of the key limitations and challenges of the BRICS' cooperation? In this chapter, I suggest examining global hegemony and multipolarization in six different aspects (economic capacity, military power, territorial domination, population strength, institutional capacity, and cultural influence). Multi-polarization is most visible when it comes to Southern contenders' increasing share of foreign investment and development credit as well as their globally leading status in industrial production, infrastructural development, and high-tech exports. These factors are complemented by the crisis of capitalism and erosion of US institutional power, which facilitate the advance of the BRICS and post-hegemonic regionalism in Latin America and Eurasia.

However, caution is warranted in the interpretation of this process as leading to an inevitable and definitive outcome of "multipolarity". The global influence of US culture is unshaken. Moreover, the US still possesses numerous overseas military bases, and its military expenditure in 2015 (as a percentage of GDP) is over 1.7 times as high as China's. In 2015, the US economy was still larger than its Chinese counterpart by about $7 trillion (World Bank 2017), which becomes even more significant when one considers the fragility of Asian economic growth. In addition, high levels of technological development and economic dynamism in the US are likely to delay the erosion of its global hegemony. Aside from the Asian region, Russia is one of the largest potential rivals of the US, although it is still undergoing severe economic difficulties despite its vast natural resources leveraged against Europe and its strong legacy of military infrastructure inherited from the Soviet Union. Regarding South–South cooperation and the BRICS' challenge to US hegemony, the BRICS is currently far from representing a coherent historical bloc against US hegemony. However, it has significantly altered the global balance of power, moving global politics towards multipolarity and constraining US dominance. This environment is but an expression of the post-hegemonic – rather than counter-hegemonic – transformation of world politics.

Therefore, my main argument is that world politics is undergoing a multipolarization process whose prospects remain uncertain due to the post-hegemonic character of the Southern challenge of US hegemony. Besides the delayed erosion of US hegemony and the strategic weaknesses of Southern contenders, I also attribute post-hegemony to the fact that BRICS countries are pursuing a dual strategy of transforming the hegemonic order from within, while simultaneously attempting to create new international mechanisms to bypass US-led hegemonic institutions. Worthy of notice in this connection are the BRICS' call for comprehensive reform of the United Nations and International Monetary Fund, the foundation of a BRICS development bank that rivals hegemonic institutions such as the World Bank and the International Monetary Fund, the BRICS' questioning of the US dollar's hegemony in global trade, the creation of an autonomous contingency fund and credit rating agency, and the pro-Assad attitude of BRICS countries against Northern interests in Syria.

In the first section, I offer a geopolitical-economic assessment of the multipolarization of global politics in six key areas. US hegemony is assessed in comparison to its main contenders in the Global South. The second and final section places this comparative picture in the historical and political context within which individual BRIC countries (i.e. the main contenders against US hegemony) have emerged as global powers to contribute to the multipolarization of global politics since the 2000s.

Six pillars of global hegemony: A geopolitical-economic assessment of the US and BRICS countries

As far as multipolarity is concerned, it is customary to define global poles with reference to a minimum of six determinants of polar power: economic capacity and dynamism; military power; territorial domination and control of natural resources; population strength; institutional capacity to shape global politics; and global cultural influence (adapted from Murray 2012). These six determinants can also be read as the basic indicators of global hegemony from a geopolitical-economy perspective. The monopolization of these determinants by a sole country (i.e. a hegemon) would correspond to a unipolarizing world order, whereas a situation in which this power monopoly is broken by other countries excelling in several of these areas of power would indicate a multipolarizing order. For example, the 1990s were associated with a unipolar tendency in world politics, whereas the 2000s are identified with the multipolarization of global politics in which global US hegemony is increasingly being challenged by Southern contenders in each of the aforementioned six areas.

I will now look at these six areas to assess the strength of US global hegemony and the multipolarization of global politics. What are some of the key indicators for assessing economic capacity and dynamism? In the first sub-section, I underline China's leading role as the main contender of US hegemony when it comes to the control of global currency, foreign investment, and development credit. BRICS' GDP indicators, contribution to global trade, industrial competitiveness, and foreign direct investment are assessed in comparison with the US economy. This is complemented by an analysis of these countries' performance in research and development, information and communication technology (ICT), and infrastructural development.

The second sub-section examines BRICS' and US military strength based on the Global Firepower Index, military expenditure, and the global arms trade. In the third sub-section, I explore these countries' territorial size as well as their access to energy and energy routes. In turn, the fourth sub-section delves into population strength, which is assessed with reference to the skill levels of populations, along with population size as it relates to military manpower and productive capacity. Following this, I inquire about each nation's institutional capacity to influence global politics in terms of their degree of involvement in global governance mechanisms. The final sub-section addresses each nation's global cultural influence with reference to the Soft Power 30 Index, particularly its education and culture components.

Economic capacity and dynamism

In terms of economic strength, the greatest challenge to US global hegemony comes from China. China undermines US hegemony with its possession of over $2 trillion in currency reserves and US treasury bonds. Furthermore, China is competing with the US in foreign investment in the Global South. For example, Chinese credit to Latin America exceeds the sum of the credit offered by the World Bank and Inter-American Development Bank (MacDonald and Lemco 2011; Stuenkel 2015, 2016). The dominant financial status of the US was already shaken to the core by the introduction of the Euro in 1999 and the quest of Eurasian economies to replace the US dollar with gold or an alternative currency. Since then, the excessive financialization of the US economy and the 2008 economic crisis have undermined the US' status as the world's largest and most dynamic production center. Increasing rates of inequality and unemployment have not only injured the global credibility of the US economy, but have also paralyzed its domestic politics by intensifying racism and xenophobia. Simultaneously, the politicization of US society has shown a historic pace of development, following the nationwide spread of the Occupy Wall Street Movement, black uprisings, and antifascist movements.

The erosion of global US economic power has been accompanied by the ascent of Asia to become the world's center of production. Asia is now the world's largest producer of TVs, computers, and cars, and the second-largest producer of appliances and cell phones. Information technology and the software industry are another strategic area in which Asia thrives (Campbell 2016). A detail worthy of mention, however, is that China's GDP is still much smaller than that of the US, although China has the largest GDP among the BRICS countries (Figure 3.1). GDP per capita offers a more detailed outlook on national economic strength. In this area, too, the US leaves all of the BRICS countries behind. India's GDP per capita, especially, is at a disappointingly low level compared with other BRICS countries, while Russia, China, and Brazil are neck and neck. Respectively, the per capita GDP of

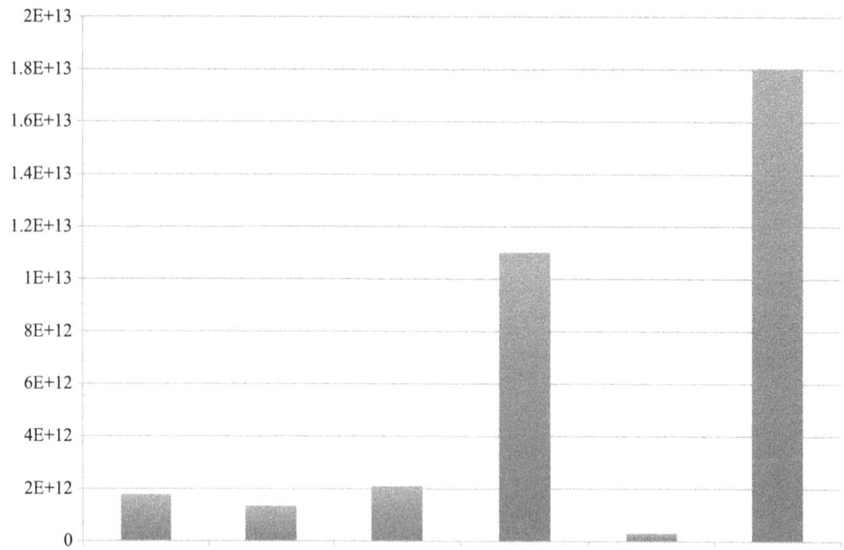

Figure 3.1 GDP size in the BRICS and the United States (2015)
Source: World Bank 2017, January 15

each of these three countries has increased by over 413%, 737%, and 128% between 2000 and 2015 (Figure 3.2).

The US contribution to global trade and production has regressed from 50% in 1945 to 25% in 2005. Similarly, the share of the US dollar in global currency stocks has declined from 66.9% in 2005 to 61% in 2011 (Kiely 2015). The advanced capitalist economies' share of global GDP declined from 80% to 44% between 1960 and 2015, while developing countries' share soared from 20% to 56%. At present, China, India, and Brazil represent 25% of the global economy, while the current share of G7 countries (the US, Britain, France, Germany, Italy, Japan, and Canada) is only 33%. In fact, China has become the world's largest exporter and second-largest economy, and India is known as a global leader in information technology and services. As for Brazil, it is a leading agricultural exporter that is close to outranking the US and the European Union (Christensen and Xing 2016; Hopewell 2016; Kiely 2015).

In a similar fashion, South–South trade has undergone visible increases throughout the 2000s. These exchanges rose from 9.9% of global trade in the period 2000–2001 to 14.5% in 2006–2007 and 16.9% in 2009. The striking fact, however, is that South–South trade cannot even achieve a rate of 50% despite the widely acclaimed rise of the Global South since the 2000s. Moreover, Asian countries make up a large proportion of South–South trade: the share of East Asia is estimated to be as high as 75%, and 40% consists of China alone (Kiely 2015). In 2009, China's exports to India, Russia, and Brazil were recorded as $29 billion, $17 billion, and $14 billion, respectively. Meanwhile, India's exports to China, Russia, and Brazil were $12 billion, $1 billion, and $3 billion (Kiely 2015, 86).

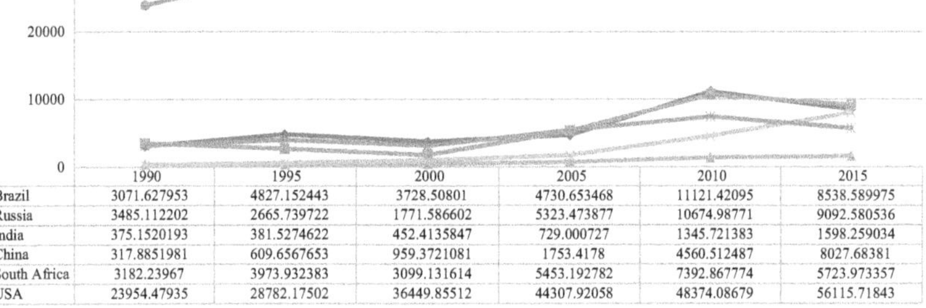

	1990	1995	2000	2005	2010	2015
Brazil	3071.627953	4827.152443	3728.50801	4730.653468	11121.42095	8538.589975
Russia	3485.112202	2665.739722	1771.586602	5323.473877	10674.98771	9092.580536
India	375.1520193	381.5274622	452.4135847	729.000727	1345.721383	1598.259034
China	317.8851981	609.6567653	959.3721081	1753.4178	4560.512487	8027.68381
South Africa	3182.23967	3973.932383	3099.131614	5453.192782	7392.867774	5723.973357
USA	23954.47935	28782.17502	36449.85512	44307.92058	48374.08679	56115.71843

Figure 3.2 GDP per capita in the BRICS and the United States (1990–2015)
Source: World Bank 2017, January 15

While Brazil, Russia, India, and China currently account for 20% of global production (Christensen and Xing 2016; Hopewell 2016; Kiely 2015), it is striking how China and Russia outperform the US when it comes to the size of industry as a percentage of GDP. In 2014, China and Russia's rates were over 43% and 32%, respectively, while the US rate was just 20.69% (Figure 3.3). However, the US seems to have preserved its leadership in research and development (R&D), which made up over 2.7% of its GDP in 2010. As the BRICS' leading R&D investor, China's performance soared from 0.9% to over 1.7% in the period 2000–2010 (Figure 3.4). This is also reflected in its performance in high-technology exports, which were recorded at $554 billion in 2015, compared with US exports of $154 billion (Figure 3.5). Regarding technological competitiveness, it may be noted that the share of ICT goods exports in US goods exports contracted significantly from 20.08% in 2000 to 9.43% in 2015. Although China's share of ICT goods exports was below that of the US in 2000, China has performed outstandingly since then, outrunning the US economy with a share of almost 26.63% in 2015 (Figure 3.6).

BRICS' performance in foreign investment is especially important for understanding the rise of the Global South since the 2000s. In particular, China's performance in foreign direct investment is worthy of special mention. Chinese direct foreign investment rose from $27 billion in 2000 to $230 billion in 2009. Likewise, BRICS' share in global foreign direct investment increased from 1% in 2000 to 10% in 2012 (Kiely 2015). In 2015, China and Russia

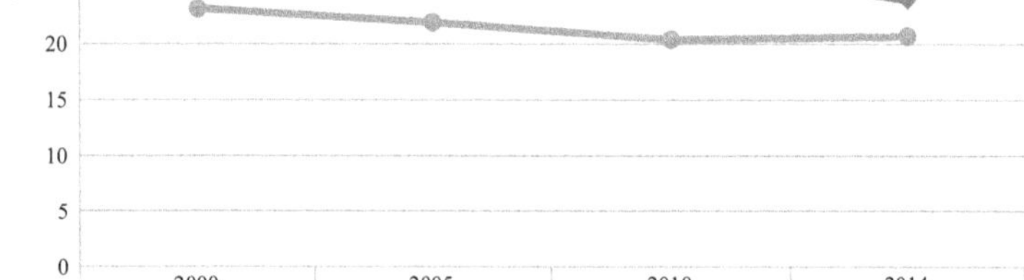

	2000	2005	2010	2014
Brazil	26.74905898	28.4720078	27.37519003	23.96854407
Russian Federation	37.94560823	38.07769631	34.69616575	32.10214024
India	25.99985845	28.13364443	32.42545553	30.00833046
China	45.53725016	47.02376535	46.39606344	43.10295136
South Africa	31.89443081	30.27763655	30.15968832	29.73195175
United States	23.15624289	21.93348557	20.39070263	20.6852981

Figure 3.3 Percentage ratio of industry to GDP in the BRICS and the United States
Source: World Bank 2017, January 15

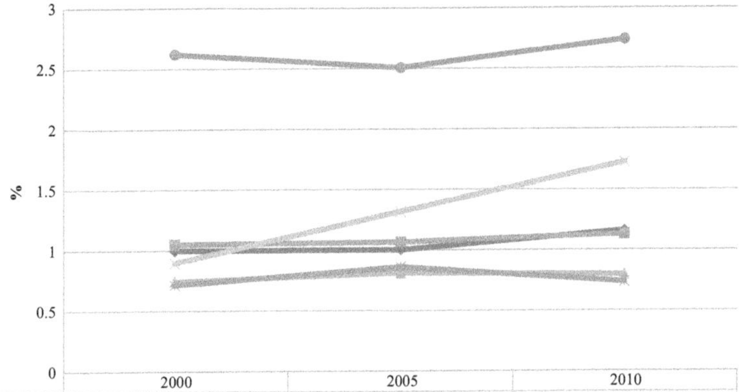

	2000	2005	2010
Brazil	0.998860002	1.001929998	1.159629941
Russian Federation	1.049839973	1.067970037	1.130200028
India	0.743950009	0.810440004	0.797179997
China	0.897669971	1.317929983	1.727200031
South Africa	0.71578002	0.863150001	0.737039983
United States	2.620500088	2.506000042	2.740459919

Figure 3.4 R&D expenditure in the BRICS and the United States (% of GDP)
Source: World Bank 2017, January 15

were neck and neck, closing the gap with the US in terms of the increase in the contribution of foreign direct investment to GDP (Figure 3.7).

No significant economic development is possible without sound infrastructure. While US infrastructure is growing old and suffers from inadequate maintenance, Asia has become a world power in infrastructure building. To give an example, China has the world's tallest building, longest bridge, and longest natural gas pipeline, as well as its largest airport, high-speed rail system, wind plant, dam, port, shopping mall, amusement park, and subway system (Campbell 2016). The US still lacks an advanced high-speed rail system, unlike leading Asian countries such as China, Japan, South Korea, and Taiwan. Moreover, Asian infrastructural advancement is shown by the fact that this region is the world's largest renewable energy producer: China produces more than twice as much renewable energy as the US. China has now become the world's largest producer of wind, water, and solar power (Campbell 2016).

The percentage share of gross capital formation in GDP can be used as an indicator for assessing infrastructural development. This indicator includes "land improvements; plant, machinery, and equipment purchases; and the construction of roads, railways, and the like, including schools, offices, hospitals, private residential dwellings, and commercial and industrial buildings" (World Bank 2017). It is noticeable how China, India, and Russia outperformed the US in gross capital formation in 2015, with rates as high as

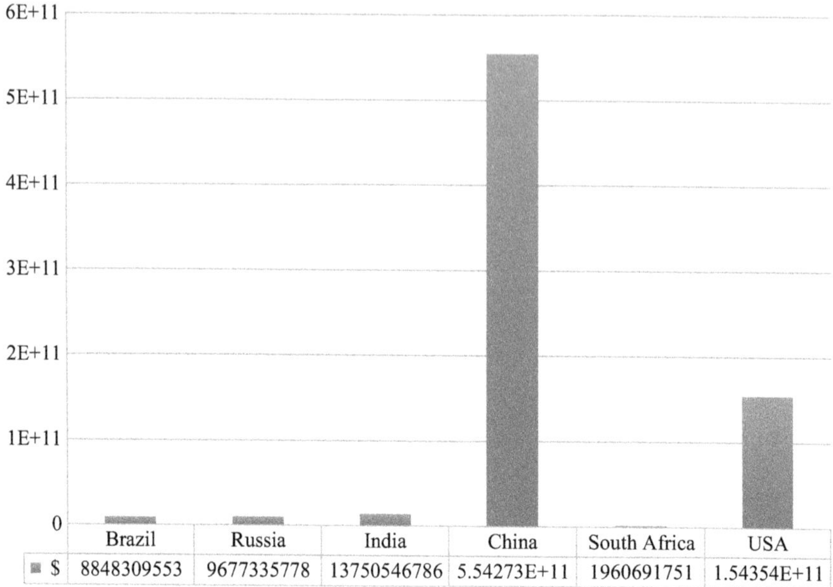

Figure 3.5 Value of high-technology exports in the BRICS and the United States (2015, in current US$)
Source: World Bank 2017, January 15

45.4%, 32.75%, and 22.37%, respectively. The US rate of gross capital formation has declined from 23.57% in 2000 to 20.35% in 2015 (Figure 3.8).

Furthermore, the *Financial Times* global list of the 500 largest companies reveals both the achievements and shortcomings of the BRICS countries when it comes to economic capacity and dynamism. In 2000, only eight companies from the South were represented on the list; this figure rose to 79 in 2010. However, a large number of these companies specialize in banking, energy, mining, and communication, illustrating the South's relative weakness in high-technology sectors such as space science, chemistry, electronics, pharmaceuticals, and information technology (Kiely 2015).

To sum up, most of the BRICS countries seem to have achieved a substantial increase in their GDP per capita, but all of them – even China – are still far from catching up with the US. However, this does not lessen the importance of the BRICS' rise in infrastructural development and global production, in which they have outperformed the US economy. It appears that the BRICS has finally caught up with the US in global trade, and that the gap between the foreign direct investment contribution of the BRICS and the US is closing fast. No less important is the BRICS' superiority over the US in the indicators of technological dynamism and competitiveness; that is, in high-technology exports, especially ICT goods exports.

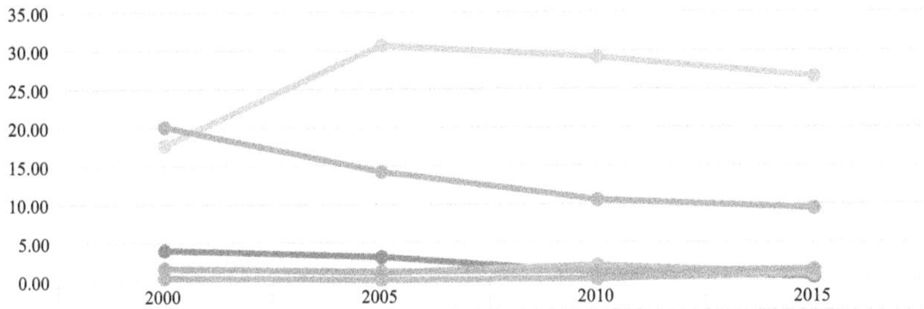

	2000	2005	2010	2015
Brazil	4.05	3.12	1.01	0.45
Russia	0.40	0.18	0.22	0.81
India	1.69	1.11	2.00	0.89
China	17.71	30.72	29.12	26.63
South Africa	1.59	1.25	1.20	1.44
USA	20.08	14.26	10.56	9.43

Brazil Russia India China South Africa USA

Figure 3.6 ICT goods and exports (% of total goods exports, 2000–2015)
Source: World Bank 2017, January 15

Military power

The Global Firepower Index measures military strength by taking into account over 50 factors, including manpower, land systems, air and naval power, financial and logistical capabilities, natural resource access, and geographical factors. According to the Index rankings for 2016, the US is the world's most powerful military power, followed by Russia, China, and India (GFP 2016). The US has used its unequalled military power to contain its potential rivals and slow down their development by controlling natural resources and intensifying ethnic and religious divides in the South, either directly or indirectly. From this angle, the US invasions of Iraq and Afghanistan – which cost the US economy around $4.4 trillion – are believed to reflect US hegemonic ambitions. In the final analysis, however, the US has failed to win an absolute victory in its interventions (Golub 2010) in places such as Iraq, Afghanistan, Syria, Ukraine, and the South China Sea.

Currently, US military expenditure accounts for almost 50% of global military expenditure, and the contribution of NATO to global military expenditure stands as high as 70% (Golub 2010). In terms of military expenditure as a percentage of GDP, the US ranks second to Russia. It comes as no surprise that Russia – which is being targeted by Northern countries in places such as Ukraine and Syria – has significantly increased its military expenditure as a percentage of GDP. Interestingly enough, China is outperformed by India, and Chinese military expenditure decreased slightly as a percentage of GDP between 2005 and 2015 (Figure 3.9). The US is still the world's largest exporter of conventional weapons, accounting for 33% of global arms

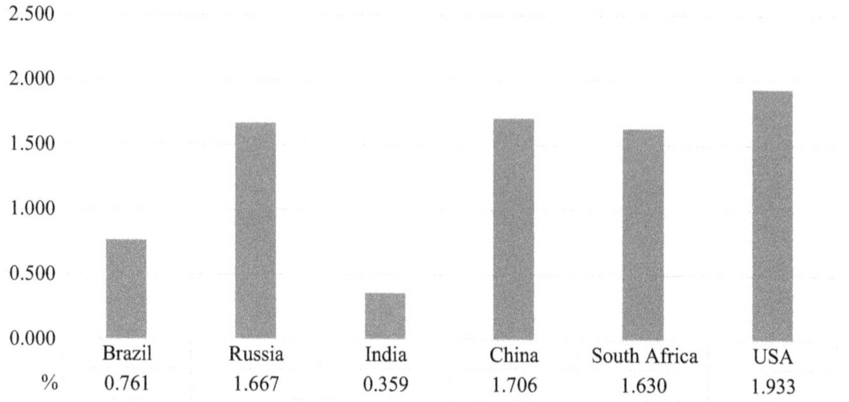

Figure 3.7 Net inflows of foreign direct investments by the BRICS and the United States (% of GDP in 2015)
Source: World Bank 2017, January 15

transfers (UPI 2016). Indeed, none of the BRICS members is on equal footing with the training capacity, air power, and naval capabilities of the US army (Brown 2012).

Rising concerns about the outbreak of a new Cold War between the US and Eurasian powers such as Russia, China, and Iran seem to validate the argument that the deterrent effect of US military power is rapidly waning. As briefly mentioned above, Russia has already outpaced the US in military expenditure as a percentage of GDP, and it ranks as the world's second-largest weapons supplier, accounting for 25% of global arms transfers (UPI 2016). China is the world's third-largest arms exporter with a near 6% share of the global arms trade (UPI 2016). In this area, the Russian interventions in Georgia in 2008, and in Ukraine between 2014 and 2016, are clear demonstrations of how a new Cold War environment can undermine US-centered security concerns. The resilience of the Assad regime and the strengthening of the Russo-Iranian presence in Syria are also among the strongest indicators of US military decline. A further example would be the tensions in 2012 between Iran and the US, known as the crisis of the Strait of Hormuz. The 2015 Baltic Sea crisis between Russia and Northern countries, and the Chinese challenge to US military dominance in the South China Sea, are no less important in the undermining of American military power. The decline of US military deterrence is openly admitted by American officials. According to Deputy Defense Secretary Bob Work, the US sees its "overwhelming operational and technical dominance starting to erode" due to actions of its Eurasian competitors that "aim to deny us access into theaters of operations, and to deny

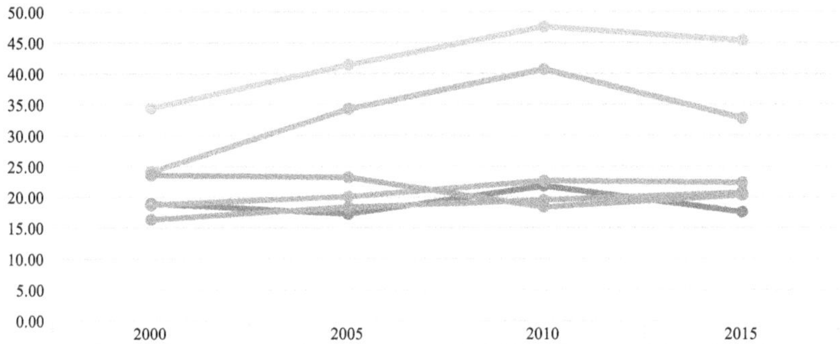

	2000	2005	2010	2015
Brazil	18.90	17.20	21.80	17.61
Russia	18.69	20.08	22.62	22.37
India	24.11	34.28	40.67	32.75
China	34.43	41.39	47.61	45.40
South Africa	16.37	18.31	19.51	20.73
USA	23.57	23.22	18.39	20.35

Figure 3.8 Gross capital formation (% of GDP)
Source: World Bank 2017, January 15

us freedom of maneuver and freedom of action once there" (U.S. Department of Defense 2017).

Territorial domination and control of natural resources

The geographic isolation of the US from the rest of the world serves as a natural shield from global threats, providing it with an invaluable strategic advantage. However, the US is not alone in territorial superiority. It is generally assumed that having a large territory is a potential advantage in terms of greater access to farmland and natural resources. Larger territories might also allow countries to build strategic areas of defense and develop greater resilience to potential nuclear attacks. In this regard, US rivals such as China, Russia, and Brazil also have a territorial upper hand to challenge the unipolarizing ambitions of the US.

Access to energy resources and control of energy routes are important markers for territorial domination. Concerning access to energy resources, the Americans have the world's fifth-largest energy reserves, the largest coal reserves, the fifth-largest natural gas reserves, and eleventh-largest oil reserves. However, leading US contenders are also endowed with substantial access to energy resources. For example, Russia has the world's largest energy reserves, the second-largest natural gas and coal reserves, and the eighth-largest oil reserves. China is also a world power in territorial control and access to energy resources: it is the holder of the world's tenth-largest energy reserves and third-largest coal reserves (Jacobs 2014).

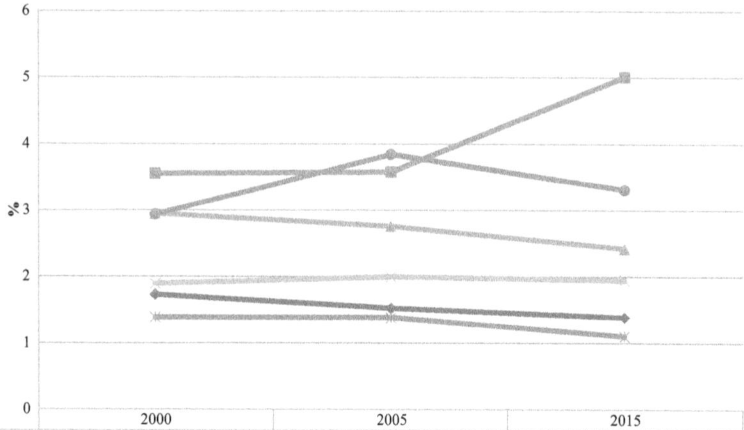

	2000	2005	2015
Brazil	1.730724806	1.524013814	1.386668297
Russia	3.553192072	3.578058264	5.008891223
India	2.948929906	2.754907666	2.421419177
China	1.892938442	2.000424664	1.951019638
South Africa	1.387289781	1.383769392	1.09998226
USA	2.933432016	3.844230435	3.304516449

Figure 3.9 Military expenditure by the BRICS and the United States (% of GDP)
Source: World Bank 2017, January 15

As for the control of energy (and trading) routes as they relate to territorial domination, it is possible to refer to the percentage share of transport services in total service exports as a potentially useful indicator of territorial control and expansionism. Transport services include "all transport services (sea, air, land, internal waterway, pipeline, space and electricity transmission) performed by residents of one economy for those of another and involving the carriage of passengers, the movement of goods (freight), rental of carriers with crew, and related support and auxiliary services [and postal and courier services]" (World Bank 2017). It comes as no surprise that Russia – as the world's largest holder of energy resources – has the highest share of transport services among the BRICS and the US, with a rate of over 30% in 2015. Russia is followed by South Africa (16.4%), Brazil (14.7%), China (13.5%), the US (11.6%), and India (9.2%) (World Bank 2017).

Population strength

A further advantage held by potential US rivals is population strength. Having a large population has the potential advantage of building military strength in terms of manpower and increasing the productive capacity of a nation, especially if the population is young and the state is endowed with a relatively qualified and skilled labor force. The demographic determinant of global hegemony has revealed itself not only in the population size of leading

Eurasian countries, but also in how the share of skilled labor in the Asian workforce is increasing at a fast rate. Asia's transformation into a powerhouse of information technology, software development, electronics and appliance production, and the automotive industry is thus a strong indicator that the US is not alone when it comes to having a demographic advantage and a skilled labor force (Campbell 2016).

The percentage share of the working-age population (persons aged 15 and older) with advanced education provides a clear picture of the skill of the labor force. The International Labour Organization (ILO) defines advanced education to include short-cycle tertiary education, bachelor's or equivalent level, master's or equivalent level, and doctoral or equivalent level (ILO 2017b). Although data on China and India are missing, it is possible to compare the US with Russia, Brazil, and South Africa. In 2009, the US performance was only 32.9%, compared with 55.26% in Russia, 11.28% in Brazil, and 16.04% in South Africa. In 2015, Russia's figure increased to 58.79%, while the US performance was only 35.59%. Brazil and South Africa's scores in 2014 were 14.26% and 16.99%, respectively (ILO 2017a). Nonetheless, the US continues to enjoy a much more sophisticated base of human resources, particularly a skilled and educated labor force (Brown 2012).

Institutional capacity to shape global politics

The erosion of US institutional power is a widely acknowledged phenomenon. Until recently, the US had guaranteed hegemonic status thanks to its control of key institutions of global governance such as the World Economic Forum, World Bank, International Monetary Fund, World Trade Organization, and North Atlantic Treaty Organization. However, the US' insistence on not joining the International Criminal Court or the Kyoto Protocol – as well as its violation of the United Nations Charter in invading Iraq in 2003 – generated widespread discontentment in the international community (Singh 2012). Donald Trump's rise to office as the 45th US President in 2017 seems to have accelerated the erosion of US institutional power, especially after the Trump administration called for a revision of the North American Free Trade Agreement (NAFTA) and withdrawal from the Trans-Pacific Partnership (MacDonald and Lemco 2011; Stuenkel 2015, 2016). At the same time, China – as the world's second-largest economy – has risen to the status of the International Monetary Fund's third-largest contributor after the US and Japan. Worthy of note in this regard are the US failure to ensure univocality at the United Nations; the UN reform demands voiced by the BRICS; and the rise of post-hegemonic regionalism represented by institutions such as the SCO, the Collective Security Treaty Organization, the Eurasian Economic Union, the *Alianza Bolivariana para los Pueblos de Nuestra América* (ALBA: Bolivarian Alliance for the Peoples of Our America), and Unasur. Latin America's social justice-oriented regionalism – as represented by ALBA and

Unasur – has added a new dimension to South–South cooperation via the creation of stable channels for the participation of social movements, alternative media outlets, anti-corporate development enterprises and autonomous pharmaceutical industries, and development banks (Bagley and Defort 2015; Muhr 2013). In turn, Eurasian post-hegemonic regionalism centers on a security-oriented paradigm deployed for deterring US interventionism in the region. Joint military drills, business forums, and university and research networks are the most important activities of Eurasian regionalism Aris 2011; Song 2016). In a similar vein, the BRICS initiative to build an autonomous development bank, contingency fund, and credit rating agency is also a strong indicator of the relative US hegemonic decline in institutional power (de Coning 2015; Kiely 2015; Quiliconi and Kingah 2016; Stuenkel 2015). Equally important is China's new Silk Road initiative, which is a development plan aimed at boosting the economic cooperation and connectivity of Eurasian countries. Officially announced in 2013, this initiative is often compared with the US Marshall Plan that helped to rebuild Europe after the Second World War. The Silk Road initiative is expected to increase China's global prestige thanks to its appealing long-term policy goals and emphasis on infrastructural development (Curran 2016; Shen 2016; Tiezzi 2014).

Global cultural influence

The US still has an unrivalled position as the powerhouse of the global cultural industry. It is home to the majority of the world's most prestigious universities, media outlets, music stars, and motion-picture productions. The US hosts nearly 43 million immigrants; it therefore remains the preferred destination for those who seek to relocate for a better life (Brown 2012). In other words, cultural influence seems to be the area in which potential contenders to US power are weakest. Soft Power 30 is a composite index that measures countries' soft power resources; its educational sub-index looks at "the level of human capital in a country, contribution to scholarship, and attractiveness to international students", whereas its cultural sub-index is concerned with "the global reach and appeal of a nation's cultural outputs, both pop-culture and high-culture" (Portland 2016). Not surprisingly, in 2016 the US was still at the top of both lists. Although China ranked only 28th in the education list, it was listed as ninth in the culture list. Russia's rankings were 20th in the education list and 14th in the culture list. Brazil was at the very bottom of the education list, but 19th in the culture list. India was not even included in either list (Portland 2016).

The rise of BRICS countries and multipolarization

There is more to the multipolarization of global politics and rise of the South than is shown by the numbers, since the historical and political contexts of these processes cannot be fully conveyed in descriptive statistics. Therefore, this section will re-evaluate the conclusions derived from the above comparative assessment in the light of important historical and political developments since the 2000s. Following a historical discussion of the BRICS as a post-hegemonic initiative, each BRICS member (except for South Africa) will be addressed in terms of its contributions to multipolarization and the historical-political context in which these multipolarizing tendencies have taken shape.

The BRICS challenge

The 1980s were named as the "lost decade" of the Global South, and the following decade was no less disappointing for Southern countries, which continued to suffer from the socioeconomic consequences of neoliberal restructuring. The 2000s, on the other hand, represented a historical turning point for the Global South, because leading Southern countries began to voice their concerns about the failure of a US-centered world order and neoliberal orthodoxy to address their vital economic and security problems (Kiely 2015). The struggle of the Global South to transcend the unipolar world order was waged on two different fronts. On the one hand, leading countries made demands to increase their involvement and decision-making power in US-led global governance. On the other, they decided to institute their own instruments of global governance that could challenge the unipolar tendencies in the world order (de Coning, Mandrup, and Odgaard 2015; Quiliconi and Kingah 2016).

The emergence of the BRICS represents a milestone in the development of this bi frontal struggle. The original BRICS acronym was coined in a 2001 report by Jim O'Neill, a former Goldman Sachs executive. According to O'Neill, the BRICS' rise was not necessarily a threat to Northern countries because it generated new market opportunities that could strengthen global capitalism. O'Neill updated his analysis following the 2008 crisis. He predicted that, in terms of economic power, China would outpace the US by 2027; Brazil would outpace Germany by 2029; Russia would outpace Japan by 2037; and India would outpace Japan by 2027 (Kiely 2015).

O'Neill's idea of a BRICS grouping materialized in the period 2005–2006, when the BRIC countries (South Africa was not included at this time) initiated unofficial negotiations at the UN meetings, which culminated in the first official BRIC Summit in Japan in 2009. As Andrew F. Cooper asserts, BRIC's first official summit – as well as BRIC's institutional personality – was catalysed by the 2008 crisis (Cooper 2016). The main themes of this first summit consisted of the US economic crisis, the global food crisis, social justice, and sustainable development. This summit signalled that the resolution of the 2008 economic crisis was too important to be left in the hands of the G8 countries, and that the Global South had to have a say in how to address this crisis. As such, the BRIC summit also called for Brazil and India's inclusion in the United Nations Security Council, and made special reference to the rule of international law and the importance of multilateralism within the UN (de Coning 2015; Kiely 2015).

The second BRIC summit took place in Brazil in 2010 with an agenda for advancing towards multipolarity and democratizing the world order. In this context, an OECD report dating from that time openly admitted that "the world's economic center of gravity has moved towards the east and south, from OECD members to emerging economies" (quoted in Kiely 2015, 10). In the third summit, hosted by China in 2011, South Africa was included in the grouping, which led the BRIC to change its name to the BRICS, thus coming to represent 43% of the world's population. The 2012 summit in India acknowledged the BRICS' role as a platform of global cooperation and dialogue, and reaffirmed its commitment to the rule of international law, multipolarity, development, and global peace. This fourth summit pointed to the need for reforming and democratizing the international financial system by instituting a new development bank; it also voiced a critique of Northern economic protectionism towards developing countries (de Coning 2015; Cooper 2016; Kiely 2015).

The setting up of a new development bank was again a major theme in the fifth BRICS summit in South Africa, which also witnessed the creation of the BRICS Think Tank Council and Business Council, representing prominent entrepreneurs from various sectors. The BRICS Business Council seeks to enhance economic ties among BRICS countries and between state officials and entrepreneurs. It establishes working groups in various sectors and presents proposals and recommendations in the form of annual reports. In turn, the Think Tank Council provides an international network of prominent think tanks, including the China Center for Contemporary World Studies, Russia's National Committee for BRICS Research, Brazil's Institute for Applied Economic Research, South Africa's Human Sciences Research Council, and India's Observer Research Foundation. The Think Tank Council offers proposals and recommendations in strategic areas such as economic growth and development, peace and security, social justice, sustainable development and quality of life, global governance, and knowledge sharing. Similarly, BRICS' 2014 summit saw the creation of a Trade Union Forum, Women's Forum, Civic BRICS, and the BRICS Bank. While the Trade Union and Women's forums were created to elevate the social and labor rights concerns of the relevant movements, the Civic Forum seeks to establish stable channels of dialogue between civil society organizations and state officials.

The BRICS Bank's function was not detailed until the seventh summit in 2015 (de Coning 2015; Cooper 2016; Kiely 2015). The 2015 summit in Russia also witnessed the creation of a Contingent Reserve Arrangement, a $100 billion contingency fund for liquidity support in response to a future balance-of-payments crisis. It was also a turning point in terms of articulating the BRICS' post-hegemonic thrust because it was organized jointly with the summits of the SCO and the Eurasian Economic Union. On the way towards multipolarity, BRICS emphasized the importance of international cooperation in the area of information technology. Finally, up to the time of writing, the eighth summit took place in India, where the BRICS countries took a decisive step towards democratizing the international financial system by deciding to institute an international credit rating agency (de Coning 2015; Cooper 2016; Kiely 2015).

Its historical development aside, what really brings BRICS together? The answer lies partly in the fact that it serves the interests of its members by providing a forum for exchange of ideas and experiences on international development issues, but also in how it helps these countries to "minimize [their] dependence on the USA and possibly to constrain American unilateralism", "stabilizing [the] international environment and [assisting] other developing countries", increasing their global prestige, and "maximiz[ing political] leverage" in the international arena (Glosny 2010, 102). Therefore, the strategic convergences within the BRICS manifest themselves beyond discursive statements of solidarity and cooperation: they are strongly visible in the practical sphere.

In line with its demand for the democratization of global governance, BRICS has insisted on extending the representation of developing countries within the International Monetary Fund and smoothing the rigid hierarchy between creditors and debtors based on the principle of equal partnership. The failure of these reform attempts has resulted in the foundation of an alternative development bank, the Contingent Reserve Arrangement, and a credit rating agency (Quiliconi, Saguier, and Papagnau 2016).

The BRICS Development Bank was instituted with an initial capital of $50 billion, each member contributing $10 billion, with the aim of facilitating the funding of infrastructural and other development projects (Duggan 2015; Quiliconi and Kingah 2016). In turn, the Contingent Reserve Arrangement is designed to provide liquidity protection in order to aid BRICS countries in any future balance of payments crisis. China provides 41% of the Contingent Reserve Arrangement's resources, followed by Brazil, India, and Russia with contributions of 18% each. South Africa contributes 5% (Quiliconi and Kingah 2016). Meanwhile, the credit rating agency seeks to "break the dominance of the big three developed-nation firms [i.e. S&P Global Ratings, Fitch Ratings, and Moody's Investors Service]" (de Wet 2017). The BRICS' major concern about these credit rating agencies is that they tend to represent the long-term interests of Northern companies. Eventually, this BRICS initiative will be tasked with "providing issuers, investors and regulators a better appreciation of relevant risk factors and making the asset class a more attractive investment opportunity" so as to facilitate inter-BRICS investments and the development of a common bond market (de Wet 2017).

Certainly, the BRICS' rise has restructured the global balance of forces to the detriment of US hegemony. However, one should acknowledge that it is still far from emerging as a coherent power bloc. Put differently, the BRICS' transformation into a coherent power bloc is so far only a tendency, which does not offer a guaranteed outcome. This is the reason why strategic divergences within the BRICS are worth exploring, although cooperative tendencies have tended to prevail over conflict and disagreements among these countries. The same goes for South–South cooperation beyond the BRICS' framework. A case in point is the competition between China, India, and Japan (among others) in the South China Sea. Sino-Indian border disputes – as well as India's concerns about China's presence in the Indian Ocean and its restrictions on Chinese companies investing in its economy – constitute sources of potential impediments for the further development of post-hegemonic governance in the Global South. The Latin American region is relatively less contentious than Asia, but low-intensity hegemonic competition between Brazil, Argentina, Chile, and Venezuela should not be overlooked, particularly when it comes to differences between Unasur and ALBA (Cheru 2011; Cooper 2016).

One of the most prominent strategic divergences occurred during the Doha Round debates at the World Trade Organization, which began in 2001 and came to a stalemate in 2008, during the formation process of the BRICS. These debates brought out internal disagreements among BRICS countries. While Brazil and South Africa supported the liberalization of agriculture due to their status as large agricultural exporters, India and China opposed full liberalization, although they agreed to abolish state subsidies. Regarding the liberalization of industrial trade, China proposed mild liberalization, while Brazil took a more protectionist attitude and India demanded full liberalization (Quiliconi et al. 2016). Similarly, Russia defended the Kyoto Protocol until it changed its attitude in 2012, but other BRICS members did not share this view. Moreover, at the 2009 Copenhagen Climate Conference, Russia sided with the US against other BRICS members, who opposed the idea of emission limitations and a climate tax (Duggan 2015).

The BRICS' political incoherence in terms of its position vis-à-vis US hegemony and Northern interventionism was witnessed during the NATO intervention in Libya. In fact, on 17 March 2011, South Africa supported United Nations Resolution 1973, which paved the way for the intervention. The other BRICS members chose to abstain, giving NATO a free hand. It was not until several months later that BRICS' members began to critique this intervention by accusing NATO of manipulating the UN decision (de Coning 2015). This critical attitude demonstrated that the BRICS does in fact have the potential to form a politically coherent bloc.

Such a strategic convergence was also observed in the BRICS' defense of Iran's right to use nuclear energy for peaceful ends, as well as its insistence that only dialogue can provide a solution to the question of Iranian nuclear energy. This added to the BRICS' resolution to back Russia during the Ukrainian crisis and to support UN membership for Palestine. Equally important is the BRICS' collective support for Syria, which played an important role in preventing a direct military intervention by Northern forces (Duggan 2015; Otero and Gürcan 2016). Even so, the collective BRICS support for Syria has shown minor signs of weakening since the 2017 Shayrat missile strike. China's abstention from the UN Security Council vote on a resolution to condemn the alleged chemical attack in Syria, despite Russia's veto (ABC News 2017) demonstrates that the BRICS has not fully learnt its lesson from the Libyan tragedy.

A fuller understanding of the historical and political-economic context of the BRICS' post-hegemonic rise requires specific attention to each member state's individual contribution to multipolarization and South–South cooperation. Therefore, the remainder of this section is devoted to the case of each BRICS member (excluding South Africa) in the order in which they are listed in the acronym BRICS.

Brazil

To begin with Brazil, the rise to office of the President Luiz Inácio Lula da Silva in 2003 represented a historical turning point as the country stepped into a developmentalist era and adopted a more activist foreign policy. Lula introduced the *Programa de Aceleração do Crescimento* (Growth Acceleration Program) in order to boost economic growth and fight inequality through public investments in strategic areas such as energy, transportation, health, construction, and infrastructure (Kiely 2015). Nowadays, the Brazilian Development Bank is the world's second-largest development bank after its Chinese counterpart (Quiliconi and Kingah 2016). Brazil's development has also been led by the so-called "national champions" such as Odebrecht (a conglomerate best known for its activities in the construction sector), Ambev (a large beverage company), Gerdau (the largest North and Latin American long steel producer), Friboi (the world's largest meat producer), Petrobras, and Vale (the world's largest iron ore and nickel producer) (Quiliconi and Kingah 2016).

The agri-food industry occupies a strategic position in Brazil's development strategy. Brazil is the world's largest meat and poultry exporter, and its soybean complex is also important for the provision of animal feed; it is the world's second-largest soybean producer. Equally important is Brazil's ethanol production, which is ranked second in the world (U.S. Department of Energy 2015; World Atlas 2017). Indeed, as one of the world's agricultural powerhouses, Brazil's exports are strategic for the Chinese economy. Brazilian exports to China increased from \$4.5 billion in 2003 to \$46 billion in 2013 (Christensen 2016).

Brazil's *Bolsa Familia* (Family Allowances) was one of the world's largest and most successful conditional cash transfer programs, whose success has been widely acclaimed by such institutions as the United Nations and the World Bank. Between 2003 and 2010, this program provided funding for over 11.4 million households in poverty. Although the model of conditional cash transfers is also part of the neoliberal welfare framework, the originality of Brazil's social policy regime lies in its success in complementing conditional cash transfers with mild redistributive practices (Laurell 2015). In the period 2003–2010, the minimum wage rose by 67%; this was supported by extending public services. Brazil's Gini index thus declined from 0.57 to 0.52 between

1995 and 2008. Similarly, the proportion of households in poverty decreased from 35.8% in 2003 to 21.4% in 2009 (Kiely 2015).

Since 2003, Brazil has increased its presence in global governance institutions, including the G20, G77, the United Nations and the World Trade Organization. Moreover, it is one of the leading countries arguing for UN reform. Its foreign policy has a kind of "Third Worldist" thrust, which was clearly expressed in Lula's slogan of "autonomy through diversification" and Brazil's attempts to prioritize the Global South in its trade deals (Christensen 2016). In this environment, China displaced the US as Brazil's largest trading partner in 2009 (Moore 2009). Indeed, these foreign policy orientations also serve to drive Brazilian capital to expand its business in the Global South. Compelled by these motivations, Brazil has assumed a leading role in Latin American regionalism; hence its close involvement in the *Mercado Común del Sur* (Mercosur: Southern Common Market) and Unasur. In the 2003–2010 period, Brazil's development credit attained $10 billion, and similarly its exports to South America increased by 504% between 2002 and 2011 (Pinheiro and Gaio 2016).

The collapse of Brazil's left with the impeachment of Dilma Rousseff in 2016 provides a strong illustration of the contradictions of post-hegemony in world politics, however. Despite Brazil's social gains in the Lula years, the left did not reverse the privatizations of previous neoliberal administrations and insisted on the continuation of extractivist development strategies despite increasing conflicts with peasant and indigenous communities. Similarly, state investments and incentives to encourage the development of domestic industry failed to generate the expected success and overcome Brazil's dependency on extractivist sectors. A combination of factors, including the fluctuations of global commodity prices and Dilma's alienating attitude towards business elites, has plunged Brazil into the worst recession in its history. Popular angst – which was mainly caused by Dilma's austerity measures in reaction to the economic crisis – eventually resulted, from 2013 onwards, in a long cycle of protests involving right-wing and well-off groups. Precarious sectors of the population also protested, demanding better services and greater social inclusion (Chodor 2015; Quiliconi, Saguier, and Papagnau 2016; Saad-Filho 2017).

Russia

Russia's resurgence in global politics commenced in the 2000s, after Vladimir Putin had risen to power and put an end to the country's eroding prestige since the collapse of the Soviet Union. Interestingly, despite the North's active involvement in Yugoslavia's breakdown with the aim of containing Russia in Europe, Putin's earlier years had been marked by his naïve optimism that "U. S. forces could eradicate the growing Taliban threat that Russian officials viewed as potentially networking with Chechen and Central Asian militant groups" (Cooley 2014, 53). Moreover, Russian public opinion had expressed strong support for closer Russia–US cooperation in world affairs. This environment was, however, reversed by the Northern aggression that was strongly manifested in the US withdrawal from the Anti-Ballistic Missile Treaty in 2002, NATO's decision to expand its membership base in its 2002 summit, and the US invasion of Iraq in 2003. The Northern aggression gained momentum with US regime-change initiatives through the color revolutions across Eurasia, and the European Union enlargement process to further contain Russia (Cooley 2014). Under Putin's leadership, therefore, Russia has gradually been alienated from the North and its presence has been increasingly articulated at the G20 and the World Trade Organization, where it has started to voice its concerns about US unilateralism and the unipolarization of the world order (Korobkov, Kingah, and Jovic 2016). Ultimately, increasing Northern interventionism in strategic countries such as ex-Yugoslavia, Iraq, Afghanistan, Libya, Syria, and Ukraine not only intensified Russia's claim to multipolarity, but also led Russia to a rapprochement with China. Northern interventionism has now become a concern shared by both Russia and China.

Two other key factors that played important roles in the Sino-Russian rapprochement were energy and defense politics (Korobkov, Kingah, and Jovic 2016). Although over a quarter of Russian energy trade is directed to Europe, geopolitical tensions have encouraged Russia to reorient its trade preferences towards Asia in favor of South–South cooperation. Between 2004 and 2015, Russian energy exports to China soared from below $5 billion to $18.9 billion (Henderson and Mitrova 2016). In the period 2010–2014, it was estimated that over 60% of Chinese arms imports came from Russia, although bilateral arms trade with China is fast declining (by almost 78% between 2004 and 2016) thanks to China's efforts to build its own military capability and emerge as a leading global arms supplier (Jiangtao 2017; SIPRI 2017; Wezeman and Wezeman 2015).

Interestingly, the rise of Russia under Putin's rule has gone hand in hand with the expansion of the public sector in the national economy. Since the 2000s, the underlying trend in the Russian economy has been "an increased role of state-owned organizations (including those not directly involved in economic transactions) in the distribution of financial resources and in control over economic agents [as well as] the activation and acquired regulatory functions for newly created vertically integrated organizations in a number of industries, state corporations and other development institutions" (Abramova, Radygina, and Chernova 2017, 21). The share of the public sector in the Russian economy increased from 30% in 2000 to 40% in 2008 (Kiely 2015). By 2016, it was estimated that the state made up almost 50% of the economy (Korobkov, Kingah, and Jovic 2016). The increasing presence of the public sector prevents Northern forces from completely bankrupting the Russian economy. The Russian state is thus involved in strategic companies such as Transneft (the world's largest oil company), Sukhoi (a major aircraft holding company), Rosneft (a major oil company), Sberbank, Unified Energy Systems (a major electricity company), Aeroflot (Russia's largest airline), and Gazprom (a natural gas company that holds the world's largest reserves) (Abramova et al. 2017; Kiely 2015, 56).

Russia's reliance on energy is both a major strength and a weakness of its economy. This finds its expression in the fact that, as of 2011, 20% of Russia's GDP and 60% of its exports came from oil and natural gas (Kiely 2015). On the one hand, its strength in energy helps Russia to thrive in its geopolitical competition with the North. On the other hand, the over-articulation of energy interests inhibits the diversification of Russian industry towards other productive sectors. Nowadays, "Russia's manufacturing sector is … among the most vulnerable sectors of its economy", and "most of the manufacturing subindustries in Russia lag behind global leaders in terms of technology, efficiency in the use of inputs and the quality of manufactured goods" (Kuznetsov, Gimpelson, and Yakovlev 2015, 159). Dependence on the military sector presents another obstacle to Russia's economic diversification in the long run. Russia has inherited a strong military infrastructure, thanks to which it has preserved its status as a top arms exporter. In fact, Russia has become the world's second-largest arms exporter after the US (UPI 2016). Overall, the resilience of the Russian economy, despite heavy dependence on energy markets and Northern pressure, is owed to its relatively qualified labor force and strong companies specializing in construction, metallurgy, informatics, and transportation, all of which were inherited from the Soviet Union. However, a major problem that limits the development of the Russian economy is that much of this inherited economic infrastructure is obsolescent (Korobkov, Kingah, and Jovic 2016). This being said, Russia's growing potential for economic diversification cannot be easily underestimated, and is reflected in strategic sectors such as telecommunications and information technology. Worthy of mention in this regard are Yandex, Kaspersky, Sitronics, MTS, and VimpelCom (Panibratov and Latukha 2014).

India

In the 1990s, India's economic growth was interrupted due to liberalization. While its average annual economic growth was 2.49% in the 1980s, this decreased to 1.57% in the 1990s. However, India's liberalization has followed a relatively slower pace overall (Kiely 2015). India was home to 15% of global anti-dumping actions in the 1995–2006 period; this figure rose to 16.5% in 2011-2012. Similar to Russia's inheritance from the Soviet Union, India's economy derives its strength from the legacy of strong engineering and economic infrastructure in the time of Jawaharlal Nehru, India's first Prime Minister (1947–1964). The relatively qualified labor force inherited from this Nehruvian nationalist and statist era is often associated with the information technology boom in contemporary India (Kiely 2015). At present, India is also regarded as a world leader in pharmaceuticals and the cultural industry (Robbani 2016).

Although India has failed to resolve the question of poverty, castes, and religious conflict, it has emerged as a strategic player in global geopolitics thanks to its large population, high military expenditure, and nuclear arsenal

(Walton 2007). India has taken advantage of its hard power and economic growth to become a leading country in the Global South, which is clearly exhibited in the rise of its aid to the developing world (Pedersen 2016). In the meantime, India's strategic oscillation between the US and Russia (Tamkin 2017), as well as its competition with Pakistan and China in the South China Sea (Mourdoukoutas 2016), are potential sources of instability within the BRICS, although cooperative tendencies seem to be prevailing over conflict so far. India is known to be worried about China's advance in the South China Sea, as well as China's close military and economic relationships with Pakistan and its infrastructural investments in countries such as Myanmar, Bangladesh, and Sri Lanka. However, China constitutes India's largest trade partner, aiding their alliance within the BRICS. Meanwhile, most of India's arms exports still originate from Russia, but this does not prevent it from maintaining its close military relationships with the North (Pedersen 2016). Worthy of particular mention, however, is that India's arms imports from Russia increased by almost 262% in the 2000–2010 period and over 1197% in 2010–2016. In sharp contrast, India's arms imports from the US, United Kingdom, France, Germany and Israel rose by merely 45.45% in 2000–2010 and 151.6% in 2010–2016. Last but not least, the actual volume of imports also reveals Russia's advantage over its Northern rivals in military trade with India. In 2016, India's imports from Russia were over 3322% larger than those from US, UK, France, Germany and Israel (SIPRI 2017; note that the UK data are missing for the year 2000).

China

China's state-led development strategy relies on strong public investments in selected strategic areas, capital controls, and the creation of a qualified labor force (Kiely 2015). The success of this development model originates from China's Maoist period, which has provided it with a relatively strong economic infrastructure, qualified labor force, and welfare practices. Regarding the legacy of Maoism, certain facts refute general misconceptions that the Maoist era was a disaster for China. According to the most conservative estimates, China's average annual economic growth was 5.1% in the period 1963–1978, which included the Great Leap Forward era (1958–1964). As a result of social advances in public health and education, China's average life expectancy rose from 25 in 1931 to 63–66 by 1956. Chinese economic growth continued in the reform era throughout the 1980s, but it really gained momentum in the 1990s when China targeted a total of 120 strategic corporations for support. These corporations operated mostly in areas such as electricity, coal, automobiles, electronic appliances, pharmaceuticals, transportation, aviation, and information technology (Kiely 2015). Consequently, Chinese companies have been steadily increasing their standing in the Fortune Global 500 list, which ranks the world's largest 500 corporations as measured by revenue. By 2017, 120 Chinese companies had made it to the list; for comparison, the US was represented by 126 companies and Japan by 52. Chinese companies featuring in the Fortune Global 500 list operate in strategic sectors including energy, utilities, banking, retail, technology and internet, electronics and appliances, property development, and transportation. State-owned enterprises such as State Grid, Sinopec, China National Petroleum, the Industrial and Commercial Bank of China, China Construction Bank, Agricultural Bank of China, and Bank of China are featured among the top 10 worldwide in the list (Jie 2018).

South–South cooperation has greatly benefited from China's economic success. Most importantly, China has increased its development aid to the Global South. In a white paper published in 2011, China distinguished between Southern and Northern (or Western) aid. China's aid is portrayed as imposing no political conditionality, unlike most Northern aid. The underlying principles of Chinese aid are presented as equality, mutual benefit, and common development (Kiely 2015). While US development aid was recorded at $31 billion in 2010, Chinese aid and low-interest credit in 2009 amounted to $866 million. However, this sum excludes the $25 billion of credit provided by the Chinese Development Bank and Eximbank in 2009 (Kiely 2015). Of particular note is that the China Development Bank "has overtaken the World Bank and the Asian Development Bank as the world's largest financial institution for overseas loans" (Deych 2015, 174). The same also goes for Eximbank, which "has become the world's largest export credit agency" (Deych 2015, 174).

The rise of China as a global financial power is also shown by its leading role in the Asian Infrastructure Investment Bank, which was created in 2016 with the aim of supporting infrastructural development in the Asia-Pacific region. Soon after its creation, the bank had already gained as many as 64 member countries, a number which does not include the United States. It is viewed as a potential rival to US financial power in the region (Hakans and Hynes 2017; Stuenkel 2016). In a similar manner, since 2009 China has devoted special effort to internationalizing the Renminbi and undermining the power of the US dollar as the global currency. Consequently, by 2015 the Renminbi had become the world's third-most-traded currency, and it is soon expected to become fully convertible as Shanghai is fast becoming a global financial center. In this direction, China also created China UnionPay as an alternative to US-owned card payment networks such as Visa and Mastercard. UnionPay eventually became the world's largest bank card group in terms of payment transactions, schemes, and number of cards issued, even surpassing Visa and Mastercard. Likewise, China's Cross-Border Interbank Payment System (CIPS) was established in 2015. CIPS is a payment system that rivals the dominance of Belgium's Society for Worldwide Interbank Financial Telecommunication (SWIFT) (Hakans and Hynes 2017; Stuenkel 2016).

Indeed, South–South trade is closely associated with the rise of China. Its exports to Latin America alone grew sevenfold in the period 2000–2010. In 2009, Chile, Cuba, and Brazil were the largest consumers of Chinese exports in Latin America. These countries were followed by Colombia, Costa Rica, and Peru. Overall, the Latin American region is China's most important primary commodity provider. The Latin American primary commodities in highest demand in China include soybeans, copper, iron ore, and crude oil. It is noteworthy that primary commodity exports occupy a strategic place in the Latin American economy, given that in 2008 these accounted for 87.7% of the region's total exports (Kiely 2015).

China's growing interest in the Global South is not confined to Latin America, however. Africa's exports to China have soared from $1.4 billion in 1995 to $34.4 billion in 2007. The most important items in Africa's exports to China are minerals and mining products (Ghana, Zambia, and Namibia); timber (Cameroon, the Democratic Republic of the Congo, Mozambique, and Tanzania); and oil (Angola, Sudan, Cameroon, and the Democratic Republic of the Congo). As such, the share of oil, minerals, and mining in Africa's exports to China rose from 76% in 2000 to 85% in 2006. In 2003 alone, China accounted for 41% of Sudan's exports and 23% of Angola's exports (Kiely 2015).

There is a wide diversity of opinions about the implications of China's rise. Being pessimistic about the future of US hegemony, John Mearsheimer predicts that the rise of China will result in the intensification of Sino–US tensions parallel with China's increasing determination to keep the US out of Asia (Kiely 2015; Mearsheimer 2006). According to Arthur Waldron, Sino–US tensions could give rise to an Asia-wide war similar to the First World War, which stemmed from Germany's attempts to counter Britain (Kiely 2015; Waldron 1997). Not surprisingly, the US 2002 National Security Strategy pointed to the plans of Eurasian powers, including China, to surpass US military power. Likewise, Robert Kagan believes that China and Russia present a threat to the liberal world order, one that requires vigilance on the part of the US (Kagan 2012; Kiely 2015). Zbigniew Brzezinski cautions that US hegemony is being eroded, adding that the US could reverse this situation by recruiting Russia and Turkey to its ranks against China (Brzezinski 2013; Kiely 2015).

Nonetheless, not every mainstream scholar is pessimistic about China's rise. According to G. John Ikenberry, China does not necessarily present a threat to the liberal world order. On the contrary, the normative strength and coherence of the liberal world order have the potential to orient China's rise to a peaceful path, and in many ways China itself is trying to harmonize with this liberal world order (Ikenberry 2008; Kiely 2015). Joseph Nye further believes that China's success might not be strong enough to outpace the US economy (Kiely 2015; Nye 2011). Approaching the matter from a Marxist perspective, Leo Panitch and Sam Gindin firmly reject the hypothesis that US hegemony is being eroded in the first place. They reduce the Chinese experience to a mere attempt to integrate into a so-called "global capitalism" (Kiely 2015; Panitch and Gindin 2012). In contrast, Joshua Cooper Ramo views China's rise as a counter-hegemonic development: the emergence of a so-called Beijing Consensus against the Washington Consensus. The Beijing Consensus is believed to rely on three principles: acquiring superiority in technological dynamism and innovation; reliance on a sustainable and equitable model of development; and the pursuit of a foreign policy autonomous from Northern hegemony. In Ramo's view, these principles are championed by China and have been increasing their appeal in the Global South (Kiely 2015; Ramo 2004).

Perhaps the most realistic assessment of China's rise within the critical literature comes from Giovanni Arrighi. According to Arrighi, the so-called China miracle is less about the low cost of labor and market economy, and more about socialist infrastructure and planned development (Arrighi 2007). Arrighi has also associated China's rise with US hegemonic decline since the 1970s. Despite the resilience of US hegemony, it is rapidly losing ground due to its long-term failure in countries such as Iraq and Afghanistan, combined with its excessive indebtedness, fiscal deficits, and economic crises. In Arrighi's view, the greatest challenge to US dominance is thus presented by China (Arrighi 2007; Kiely 2015).

Finally, China is widely presented as the sole global power that could rival US hegemony (Campbell 2016; Singh 2012; Walton 2007). Yet China and the Asian region are facing a myriad of challenges that present potential impediments to the future of multipolarity. A case in point is China's growing problem of "ghost cities"; that is, vacant spaces and infrastructure areas that have failed to attract sufficient investment. In the same manner, the continued infrastructural development of China and proper maintenance of newly built infrastructure depend on the stability of economic growth (Campbell 2016). China is also struggling with high levels of socioeconomic inequalities, which in turn cause social upheavals that threaten political and economic stability, as reflected in union activism and rural protests (Gürcan and Mete 2017, 12–13). In particular, China suffers from a chronic migrant labor problem, namely 282 million rural migrant workers (over one-third of the working population) whose basic rights, job and employment security, and access to social services have been restricted (CLB 2017). The degradation of urban living conditions forces many workers to live in "illegal" underground spaces. In Beijing alone, there are an estimated 1 million people living in these conditions (Ross, 2017). With regard to China's growing economic power, its rise in Latin America, Central Asia, and Africa – which severely undermines global US hegemony – is being held back by the sociocultural and environmental insensitivity of certain Chinese corporations (Donette 2012). Sinophobia constitutes a real challenge for China's global expansion in competition with its Northern rivals. No less worrisome is China's intensifying tensions with its neighbors over the control of the South China Sea. This strategic crisis indicates that the rise of Asian economies does not necessarily result in South–South cooperation, given the inability of Asian countries to satisfy their energy needs to sustain their economic growth. Finally, the continuity of the so-called Asian Age of economic development is threatened by environmental disasters caused by rapid economic growth. In 2009, the Asia-Pacific region accounted for half of the world's carbon dioxide production. Between 1980 and 2009, it is estimated that as much as 86% of Asia's population was affected by environmental disasters, and that Asia received up to 42% of worldwide economic losses caused by such disasters (Campbell 2016).

Review and discussion

As discussed in the opening section of this chapter, the erosion of US global hegemony is discernible in several areas. First, US supremacy in the global political economy is undermined by the fact that the center of gravity of global production and exports has been shifting towards the Global South. US financial superiority has been increasingly shaken in the face of a deep-seated economic crisis that has been crippling its economy since 2008. This has found its sharpest expression in how the BRICS countries have increased their share of the foreign investment and development credit going to the Global South. That said, the status of the US as the top performer in GDP per capita, and the fragility of China's development, suggest that US economic superiority is far from having waned completely. Second, the deterrence power of the US military has decreased substantially, although the US still retains its global supremacy in military strength. The loss of military deterrence power by the US is particularly evident in China's persisting resistance in the South China Sea and Russia's assertiveness in Syria and Ukraine. Not only has Russia outperformed US military expenditure as a percentage of GDP, it also, along with China, currently presents a great challenge to US leadership in the global arms trade. Third and fourth, major contenders to US global hegemony draw strength from their territorial advantages and substantial energy access, combined with demographic superiority and an increasing reserve of skilled labor. The fifth and sixth areas in which US global hegemony is being tested are institutional capacity and global cultural influence. Although the global influence of US culture is unrivaled, its decreasing commitment to global governance, the loss of legitimacy of hegemonic global governance institutions, and the creation of alternative institutions in the Global South point to the erosion of US institutional power. In particular, the crisis of hegemonic governance finds its echo in the crisis of NAFTA. In the 1990s, NAFTA was presented as the most advanced model of integration into global capitalism; by 2017, it was being labeled a "trading disaster" by the US President himself. The defeat of the US-led Free Trade Area of the Americas, the subsequent rise of the Latin American left, and the emergence of post-hegemonic regionalism (ALBA and Unasur) constituted further disastrous blows to US institutional power. Likewise, the advance of Eurasian post-hegemonic regionalism (e.g. SCO, the Eurasian Economic Union, the Collective Security Treaty Organization, and China's Silk Road initiative) have significantly eroded US hegemony.

Therefore, the crisis of Northern capitalism since 2008 and the bankruptcy of hegemonic global governance have created a facilitative environment for post-hegemonic initiatives. In particular, the erosion of US global hegemony due to these world-historical developments has cleared the way for a surge of multipolarity in global politics. Consequently, major Southern countries – especially the BRICS grouping – have taken the lead in advancing a new post-hegemonic agenda in the Global South. A distinguishing outcome of this post-hegemonic opening has been the replacement of Northern-led initiatives of international cooperation by South–South cooperation. As discussed in the third section, however, BRICS countries seem to be pursuing a bi-frontal strategy that consists of attempting to conquer hegemonic global governance mechanisms from within, while experimenting with alternative governance tools that have greater autonomy from US hegemony. The BRICS countries' increasing involvement and reform demands within the World Trade Organization, International Monetary Fund, and United Nations are seen as an expression of their attempts to reform the present structure of hegemonic global governance. On the other hand, the challenging of the global hegemony of the US dollar and the proposal to institute an alternative development bank express a claim for autonomous governance.

Despite the geopolitical impact of the BRICS initiative, serious limitations prevent BRICS from becoming a coherent historical bloc against US hegemony; including its continuing dependency on the US economy, the relatively undeveloped and uneven state of South–South trade, and strategic disagreements over issues such as Libya and international trade. Furthermore, an important detail to consider is that the historical and material basis for the BRICS' rise has been the reappropriation of the legacy of state-led experiences of developmentalism. This is the case with China's market socialism, Russia's partially revived Soviet past and its inherited technological and scientific infrastructure, and India's Nehruvian heritage. In the final analysis, it is possible to argue that the BRICS experience sets a development model for other developing countries, particularly when it comes to the carrying out of interventionist industrial policies, the promotion of "national champion" enterprises, the subordination of financial regulation to industrial strategies via stronger regulatory mechanisms, and the promotion of South–South cooperation as autonomous of Northern institutions (McNally 2013; Stephen 2014; Carmody 2013).

References

ABC News. 2017. "After Abstaining on UN Syria vote, China Backs Political Fix." *ABC News.* http://abcnews.go.com/International/wireStory/abstaining-syria-vote-china-backs-political-fix-46770773 [no longer available online].

Abramova, Alexander, Alexander Radygina, and Maria Chernova. 2017. "State-Owned Enterprises in the Russian market: Ownership Structure and their Role in the Economy." *Russian Journal of Economics* 31: 1–23.

Aris, Stephen. 2011. *Eurasian Regionalism – The Shanghai Cooperation.* New York: Palgrave Macmillan.

Arrighi, Giovanni. 2007. *Adam Smith in Beijing.* London: Verso.

Bagley, Bruce M. and Magdalena Defort, eds. 2015. *Decline of the U.S. Hegemony?: A Challenge of ALBA and a New Latin American Integration of the 21st Century.* Lanham: Lexington Books.

Brown, Stuart S. 2012. *The Future of US Global Power: Delusions of Decline.* New York: Palgrave Macmillan.

Brzezinski, Zbigniew. 2013. *Strategic Vision: America and the Crisis of Global Power.* New York: Basic Books.

Campbell, Kurt. 2016. *The Pivot: The Future of American Statecraft in Asia.* New York: Twelve.

Carmody, Padraig. 2013. *The Rise of the BRICS in Africa: The Geopolitics of South-South Relations.* New York: Zed Books.

Cheru, Fantu. 2011. "South–South Cooperation: What Prospects for a New Bandung Consensus?" In *South–South Cooperation: Africa on the Centre Stage*, edited by R. Modi, 42–60. New York: Palgrave Macmillan.

Chodor, Tom. 2015. *Neoliberal Hegemony and the Pink Tide in Latin America.* New York: Palgrave Macmillan.

Christensen, Steen Fryba. 2016. "How Prioritized Is the Strategic Partnership between Brazil and China?" In *Emerging Powers, Emerging Markets, Emerging Societies: Global Responses*, edited by S. F. Christensen and L. Xing, 87–109. New York: Palgrave Macmillan.

Christensen, Steen Fryba, and Li Xing. 2016. "The Emerging Powers and the Emerging World Order: Back to the Future?" In *Emerging Powers, Emerging Markets, Emerging Societies: Global Responses*, edited by S. F. Christensen and L. Xing, 3–29. New York: Palgrave Macmillan.

CLB. 2017. "Migrant Workers and Their Children." *China Labour Bulletin.* http://www.clb.org.hk/content/migrant-workers-and-their-children

de Coning, Cedric. 2015. "BRICS and Coexistence." In *The BRICS and Coexistence: An Alternative Vision of World Order*, edited by C. D. Coning, T. Mandrup, and L. Odgaard, 25–48. New York: Routledge.

de Coning, Cedric, Thomas Mandrup, and Liselotte Odgaard. 2015. "Introduction." In *The BRICS and Coexistence: An Alternative Vision of World Order*, edited by C. D. Coning, T. Mandrup, and L. Odgaard. New York: Routledge.

Cooley, Alexander. 2014. *Great Games, Local Rules: The New Great Power Contest in Central Asia.* Oxford: Oxford University Press.

Cooper, Andrew F. 2016. *The BRICS: A Very Short Introduction.* Oxford: Oxford University Press.

Curran, Enda. 2016. "China's Marshall Plan." *Bloomberg*, August 7. http://www.bloomberg.com/news/articles/2016-08-07/china-s-marshall-plan

Deych, Tatiana. 2015. "BRICS as an Important Actor in Africa." *Insight on Africa*, 72: 169–185.

Donette, Murray. 2012. "The Chinese Dragon." In *Multipolarity in the 21st Century: A New World Order*, edited by D. Murray and D. Brown, 48–79. New York: Routledge.

Duggan, Niall. 2015. "BRICS and the Evolution of a New Agenda Within Global Governance." In *The European Union and the BRICS*, edited by M. Rewizorski, 11–25. Cham: Springer.

GFP. 2016. Countries Ranked by Military Strength. Global Firepower Index. http://www.globalfirepower.com/countries-listing.asp

Glosny, Michael A. 2010. "China and the BRICs: A Real but Limited Partnership in a Unipolar World." *Polity* 421: 100–129.

Golub, Philip S. 2010. *Power, Profit and Prestige: A History of American Imperial Expansion*. New York: Pluto Press.

Gürcan, Efe Can and Berk Mete. 2017. *Neoliberalism and the Changing Face of Unionism: The Combined and Uneven Development of Class Capacities in Turkey*. New York: Palgrave Macmillan.

Hakans, Erik and Phill Hynes. 2017. "China's Challenge to the World Economic Order." *Global Research*, January 17. https://www.globalresearch.ca/chinas-challenge-to-the-world-economic-order/5569145

Henderson, James and Tatiana Mitrova. 2016. *Energy Relations between Russia and China: Playing Chess with the Dragon*. http://www.oxfordenergy.org/wpcms/wp-content/uploads/2016/08/Energy-Relations-between-Russia-and-China-Playing-Chess-with-the-Dragon-WPM-67.pdf

Hopewell, Kristen. 2016. *Breaking the WTO: How Emerging Powers Disrupted the Neoliberal Project*. Stanford: Stanford University Press.

Ikenberry, G. John. 2008. "The Rise of China and the Future of the West." *Foreign Affairs*, 871: 23–37.

ILO. 2017a. Online Database. Geneva: International Labour Organization.http://www.ilo.org/ilostat

ILO. 2017b. Employment by Education. Geneva: International Labour Organization. http://www.ilo.org/ilostat-files/Documents/description_EDU_EN.pdf

Jacobs, Harrison. 2014. "The 17 Countries Sitting On The Most Valuable Energy Reserves." *Business Insider*, February 13. https://www.businessinsider.com.au/countries-with-most-energy-reserves-2014-2

Jiangtao, Shi. 2017. "China Boosts Arms Exports by 74pc, While Cutting Reliance on Outside Providers, Report Finds." *CNBC*, February 20. http://www.cnbc.com/2017/02/20/china-boosts-arms-exports-by-74pc-while-cutting-reliance-on-outside-providers-report-finds.html

Jie, Zhang. 2018. "Global 500: Chinese Companies Race Ahead." *China Daily*, July 20. http://www.chinadaily.com.cn/a/201807/20/WS5b518b77a310796df4df7b77.html

Kagan, Robert. 2012. *The World America Made*. New York: Knopf.

Kiely, Ray. 2015. *The BRICs, US 'Decline' and Global Transformations*. New York: Palgrave.

Korobkov, Andrei, Stephen Kingah, and Jovana Jovic. 2016. "Global Security and Economic Leadership of Russia." In *Global and Regional Leadership of BRICS Countries*, edited by S. Kingah and C. Quiliconi, 93–112. Cham: Springer.

Kuznetsov, Boris, Vladimir Gimpelson, and Andrei Yakovlev. 2015. "Industrialization in the Russian Federation." In *Structural Change and Industrial Development in the BRICS*, edited by W. Naudé, A. Szirmai, and N. Haraguchi, 138–161. Oxford: Oxford University Press.

Laurell, Asa Cristina. 2015. "Three Decades of Neoliberalism in Mexico: The Destruction of Society." *International Journal of Health Services*, 452: 246–264.

MacDonald, Scott B. and Jonathan Lemco. 2011. *Asia's Rise in the 21st Century*. Santa Barbara: Praeger.

McNally, Christopher A. 2013. "The Challenge of Refurbished State Capitalism: Implications for the Global Political Economic Order." *DMS – Der Moderne Staat*, 61: 33–48.

Mearsheimer, John. 2006. "China's Unpeaceful Rise." *Current History*, 1051: 160–162.

Moore, Malcolm. 2009. "China Overtakes the US as Brazil's Largest Trading Partner." *The Telegraph*, May 9. http://www.telegraph.co.uk/finance/economics/5296515/China-overtakes-the-US-as-Brazils-largest-trading-partner.html

Mourdoukoutas, Panos. 2016. "South China Sea Disputes Will Soon Catch Up With Pakistan's Red Hot Stock Market." *Forbes*, January 24. https://www.forbes.com/sites/panosmourdoukoutas/2017/01/24/south-china-sea-disputes-will-soon-catch-up-with-pakistans-red-hot-stock-market/

Muhr, Thomas, ed. 2013. *Counter-Globalization and Socialism in the 21st Century: The Bolivarian Alliance for the Peoples of Our America*. New York: Routledge.

Murray, Donette. 2012. "Introduction." In *Multipolarity in the 21st Century: A New World Order*, edited by D. Murray and D. Brown, 1–16. New York: Routledge.

Nye, Joseph. 2011. "American and Chinese Power after the Financial Crisis." *Washington Quarterly*, 334: 143–153.

Otero, Gerardo and Efe Can Gürcan. 2016. "The Arab Spring and the Syrian refugee crisis." *The Monitor, Canadian Center for Policy Alternatives*, 225: 16.

PanibratovA. and M. Latukha. 2014. "Foreign Expansion of Russian Firms Based on Natural Resources and Technology." In *Successes and Challenges of Emerging Economy Multinationals*, edited by M. A. Marinov and S. T. Marinova. London: Palgrave Macmillan.

Panitch, Leo and Sam Gindin. 2012. *The Making of Global Capitalism: The Political Economy of American Empire*. London and New York: Verso.

Pedersen, Jørgen Dige. 2016. "India as an Emerging Power in the Global Order: On Geopolitics and Geo-Economics." In *Emerging Powers, Emerging Markets, Emerging Societies*, edited by S. F. Christensen and L. Xing, 110–131. New York: Palgrave Macmillan.

Pinheiro, Leticia and Gabrieli Gaio. 2016. "Cooperation for Development, Brazilian Regional Leadership and Global Protagonism." In *Global and Regional Leadership of BRICS Countries*, edited by S. Kingah and C. Quiliconi, 67–91. Cham: Springer.

Portland. 2016. The Soft Power 30. Overall Ranking 2016. London and Washington, DC: Portland Communications. http://softpower30.portland-communications.com

Quiliconi, Cintia and Stephen Kingah. 2016. "Conclusions: Leadership of the BRICS and Implications for the European Union." In *Global and Regional Leadership of BRICS Countries*, edited by S. Kingah and C. Quiliconi, 243–254. Cham: Springer.

Quiliconi, Cintia, Saguier, Zwartjes, and Papagnau, Georgios. 2016. "BRICS: Leadership in the Making." In *Global and Regional Leadership of BRICS Countries*, edited by S. Kingah and C. Quiliconi, 29–48. Cham: Springer.

Ramo, Joshua Cooper. 2004. *The Beijing Consensus*. London: Foreign Policy Centre. https://fpc.org.uk/wp-content/uploads/2006/09/244.pdf

Robbani, Golam. 2016. "India as a Global Power: Capability, Willingness, and Acceptance." In *Global and Regional Leadership of BRICS Countries*, edited by S. Kingah and C. Quiliconi, 135–146. Cham: Springer.

Ross, Eleanor. 2017. "China's Housing Problem: One Million People in Beijing Live in Underground Basements and Bomb Shelters." *Newsweek*, 20 June. https://www.newsweek.com/china-housing-beijing-basement-dwelling-hundreds-underground-627504

Saad-Filho, Alfredo. 2017. "The Implosion of Brazilian Democracy – And Why It Matters." *Critical Sociology*, 43(7/8). doi:10.1177/0896920517731751.

Shen, Simon. 2016. "How China's 'Belt and Road' Compares to the Marshall Plan." *The Diplomat*, February 6. http://thediplomat.com/2016/02/how-chinas-belt-and-road-compares-to-the-marshall-plan/
Singh, Robert. 2012. "The United States: The Eagle Untamed." In *Multipolarity in the 21st Century: A New World Order*, edited by D. Murray and D. Brown, 17–47. New York: Routledge.
SIPRI. 2017. Importer/Exporter TIV Tables. Solna: Stockholm International Peace Research Institute. http://armstrade.sipri.org/armstrade/page/values.php
Song, Weiqing. 2016. *China's Approach to Central Asia: The Shanghai Co-operation Organisation*. New York: Routledge.
Stephen, Matthew D. 2014. "Rising Powers, Global Capitalism and Liberal Global Governance: A Historical Materialist Account of the BRICs Challenge." *European Journal of International Relations*, 204: 912–938.
Stuenkel, Oliver. 2015. *The BRICS and the Future of Global Order*. London: Lexington Books.
Stuenkel, Oliver. 2016. *Post-Western World: How Emerging Powers Are Remaking Global Order*. Cambridge: Polity Press.
Tamkin, Emily. 2017. "Is India Playing the United States Against Russia?" *Foreign Policy*, April 17. http://foreignpolicy.com/2017/04/17/is-india-playing-the-united-states-against-russia/
Tiezzi, Shannon. 2014. "The New Silk Road: China's Marshall Plan?" *The Diplomat*, November 6. http://thediplomat.com/2014/11/the-new-silk-road-chinas-marshall-plan/
UPI. 2016. World's Top 5 Arms Exporters. http://www.upi.com/News_Photos/Features/Worlds-Top-5-arms-exporters/3105/
U.S. Department of Defense. 2017. "Defense Innovation Maintains Military Overmatch Against Adversaries." https://dod.defense.gov/News/Article/Article/1172099/defense-innovation-maintains-military-overmatch-against-adversaries/
U.S. Department of Energy. 2015. Maps and Data – Global Ethanol Production. Washington, DC: Alternative Fuels Data Center. http://www.afdc.energy.gov/data/10331
Waldron, Arthur. 1997. "How Not to Deal With China." *Commentary*, 1033: 44.
Walton, C. Dale. 2007. *Geopolitics and the Great Powers in the 21st Century: Multipolarity and the Revolution in Strategic Perspective*. New York: Routledge.
de Wet, Adri Senekal. 2017. "Brics Keen on Own Rating Agency." *Business Report*, April 10. http://www.iol.co.za/business-report/economy/brics-keen-on-own-rating-agency-8576544
Wezeman, Pieter D. and Siemon T. Wezeman. 2015. *Trends in International ArmsTransfers, 2014*. Solna: Stockholm International Peace Research Institute. https://www.sipri.org/sites/default/files/files/FS/SIPRIFS1503.pdf
World Atlas. 2017. 10 Countries with Largest Soybean Production. http://www.worldatlas.com/articles/world-leaders-in-soya-soybean-production-by-country.html
World Bank. 2017. DataBank. http://databank.worldbank.org

4 The BRICS and Africa's post-hegemonic transformation

Introduction

The previous chapter discussed the BRICS' post-hegemonic character and its importance for South–South cooperation. Here, the geopolitical-economic analysis of the BRICS' leadership in South–South cooperation will be extended to the case of Africa. My overall argument is that BRICS countries' relations with the African continent occupy a strategic place in South–South cooperation, and that the BRICS' African engagement is a major contributor to the multipolarization of world politics in a post-hegemonic direction. BRICS members provide African countries with ample development opportunities by imposing a softer and more flexible conditionality than the Global North. They have been making deliberate efforts at shifting the mainstream development discourse from the verticalism of the Global North's "development assistance" to the horizontalism of "development cooperation", with close attention to the demands of African countries. Infrastructural and social-development cooperation is favored over structural adjustment policies and conditional loans. As such, the BRICS' increasing involvement in Africa is constraining US hegemony, while simultaneously expanding Africa's foreign policy options and prospects for development. However, in practice, the contradictory character of post-hegemony makes itself felt in the peaceful competition of BRICS countries in the African continent and the adverse effects of their involvement, such as increased dependency on extractivism and the arms trade. Accordingly, this chapter is framed in five sections that address the geopolitical economy of each BRICS member's relationships with Africa. The sections follow the order of the countries in the acronym BRICS.

Brazil's rise in Africa under the Lula administration

Prior to the 2000s, Africa was not a priority in Brazil's foreign policy. Particularly in the Fernando Henrique Cardoso era (1995–2002), Brazil's foreign policy had prioritized cooperation with the industrialized countries. Africa became a priority region in Brazil's quest for natural resources and expanding markets only under the Lula administration (2003–2011), which openly declared the continent a foreign policy priority (Suyama, Waisbich, and Leite 2016). Brazil saw a sixfold increase in its trade with Africa, from nearly US $4.2 billion in 2002 to US$27.6 billion in 2011 (Seifert 2013; Stolte 2015). Brazil's foreign direct investment witnessed exponential growth, clearly exemplified by the rise in its investment in sub-Saharan Africa from $29 billion in 2010 to $37 billion in 2011 (Carmody 2013a).

Corporations have assumed a key role in expanding Brazil's investments in the continent. It is estimated that over 500 Brazilian companies operate in Africa's strategic sectors such as construction and real estate, mining, public utilities, energy production, the apparel industry, and food and agriculture. These companies, which include Companhia Vale do Rio Doce, Odebrecht, Camargo Corrêa, and Petrobras, focus mostly on construction and natural resources extraction (de Freitas 2016; Stolte 2015). Interestingly, these companies' increasing activities seem to have fueled a competitive race among BRICS countries. For example, Lula is known to have designated China as a rival in the African continent, which was validated by how Chinese companies took previously agreed projects away from Brazilian companies, for example the Belinga iron ore mine in Gabon. While China typically prefers to rely on its own labor force in its overseas investments, Brazil has gained a better reputation by hiring more local workers. Yet this peaceful competition does not rule out sustained Sino–Brazilian cooperation in Africa, as exemplified by the free distribution of the Earth Resources Satellite (Carmody 2013a, 2013b).

Brazil has become one of the world's largest aid donors: its total foreign aid commitments increased from $120 million in 2006 to $1.2 billion in 2010 (Carmody 2013b). That said, Brazil's official discourse de-emphasizes the notion of foreign aid, instead placing greater emphasis on development cooperation in promoting horizontal rather than vertical dynamics of South–South cooperation, with limited political conditionality. As such, Brazil's involvement in development cooperation includes "an experimental farm in Senegal, health system reform in Angola and a training programme for professionals in Mozambique" (Carmody 2013b, 94) as well as state-funded programs that support the cotton industry in Benin, Burkina Faso, Mali, and Chad. Brazil also runs programs of technical training, incorporating local agricultural knowledge, in Ghana, Kenya, Mozambique, and Angola. Brazilian officials specializing in education, food security, juvenile justice, and management play an active part in development cooperation. The involvement of state institutions such as the Brazilian Cooperation Agency and the Brazilian Agricultural Research Corporation is equally crucial to Brazil's development projects (Carmody 2013a, 2013b). In this direction, Brazil's technical cooperation budget increased by over 700% from 3,342,588 Brazilian reals in 2002 to 27,003,724 Brazilian reals in 2011 (Seifert 2013; Suyama, Waisbich, and Leite 2016). Similarly, Brazil's technical cooperation budget for Africa was below 2 million Brazilian reals in 2002, but increased to 12 million Brazilian reals in 2011. In the period 2000–2014, Brazil's technical cooperation focused mostly on agriculture, education, and health, which respectively accounted for 33%, 23%, and 15% of the total budget (Seifert 2013; Suyama, Waisbich, and Leite 2016).

Lula's foreign policy activism towards Africa was justified by strong normative commitments to international equilibrium, multilateralism, and South–South cooperation. Against this backdrop, Brazil – as a country that received 4 million African slaves in the colonial era and now has the world's largest African population after Nigeria – also capitalized on its historical and cultural proximity to the African continent (de Freitas 2016). In this environment, presidential visits, summits, and high-level conferences between Brazil and Africa became considerably more frequent. Brazil actively lobbied for South Africa's inclusion in the BRICS, the India–Brazil–South Africa Dialogue Forum, and the Africa–South America Cooperation Forum (de Freitas 2016).

Lula's prioritization of relationships with Africa initially received widespread criticism from Brazil's business associations and opposition parties, which considered his activism to be ideologically driven and economic nonsense (Stolte 2015). Lula thus relied heavily on public funding to support Brazilian exports to African countries. For example, the Bank of Brazil and the Banco Nacional de *Desenvolvimento Econômico e Social* (BNDES: National Bank for Economic and Social Development) issued over $4 billion in export credits to support Lula's activism (de Freitas 2016). But normative commitments, political preferences, and ideological biases cannot fully explain Brazil's greater engagement with Africa. In fact, Brazil's partnership with the continent prioritizes resource-rich countries, which also explains the fact that nearly 90% of Brazilian imports from Africa consist of oil and other natural resources. Large Brazilian companies invest to a great extent in the resource sector: these include Odebrecht, Sonangol, and Companhia Vale do Rio Doce, the world's second-largest resource company (Stolte 2015).

Brazil's concentration on resource extraction is perhaps one of the strongest indicators of the contradictory nature of its involvement in Africa. Brazil's economic cooperation seems to promote domestic economic growth, social inclusion, and the redistribution of resources. Meanwhile, in Africa, resource extraction results in forced displacement, greater inequality, and environmental damage. While Brazil does not restrain itself from forming joint ventures with local governments to the benefit of domestic economic interests in the longer run, its biofuel projects in Africa have attracted controversies around deplorable labor conditions and local workers being paid less than their Brazilian counterparts. Another contradictory aspect of Brazil's African engagement relates to the downplaying of human rights in the name of advancing South–South cooperation, despite Lula's former claim to "non-indifference" to human rights abuses. An important example of this is Brazil's continued cooperation with extremely authoritarian regimes such as Zimbabwe (Carmody 2013a, 2013b).

The strategic importance of Russia's limited involvement in Africa

Russia's engagement with Africa has not been as intense as that of Brazil, even though Russia sees the African continent as a strategic site of expansion for its own natural resources and defense companies. Interestingly enough, Russia's foreign policy and national security documents, including the National Security Strategy to 2020 and the Foreign Policy Concepts formulated in 2008, 2013, and 2016, "almost completely neglect Africa" (Arkhangelskaya and Shubin 2013; Oğultürk 2017). By the end of the first decade of the 21st century, Russia had nearly $4 billion invested in Africa, and its African imports recorded an annual growth rate of 19%. However, Africa accounted for only 1% of its global trade, and Russian direct investment in Africa did not exceed 4% of its stock of overseas investments (Carmody 2013b).

Russia's limited involvement in Africa (Kuznetsov, Naumkin, and Zvyagelskaya 2018) can be best explained with reference to its economic limitations and the fact that it is a natural resource-rich country whose energy security does not entirely depend on Africa. Regarding Russia's limitations, it is not as economically powerful or competitive as China, which is Africa's key partner among the BRICS countries (Carmody 2013b). Russia's current economic stagnation is a major impediment to any future Russian economic expansion in the African continent. Nor does the Russian engagement with Africa reflect the idealistic dynamism of Brazil (Arkhangelskaya and Shubin 2013).

As far as energy security is concerned, Russia is already the world's leading energy exporter, with more than a third of the world's proven gas reserves in its possession. It possesses 35% of the world's mineral reserves (Arkhangelskaya and Shubin 2013; Arkhangelskaya and Shubin 2013b). It is known that Russia "in some years exports more oil than Saudi Arabia" (Carmody 2013b). However, mineral resources such as manganese, chrome, nickel, zinc, lead, and bauxite take on a greater relevance for Russia's relationships with Africa, considering that "Russia imports almost 100% of its manganese requirements, 80% of its chrome and 60% of its bauxite" (Arkhangelskaya and Shubin 2013; Oğultürk 2017). Moreover, Russia has lately turned to Middle Eastern and African oil resources in response to growing oil demand among Asia-Pacific countries, Northern sanctions, and fluctuating oil prices (Trickett 2018). Russia is interested in increasing its oil production by investing in Middle Eastern and African resources with lower production costs in order to be able to satisfy the growing Asia-Pacific market, while still maintaining its supply to European markets. Increased oil production is of strategic importance to Russia's economy, especially for financing military and social spending. It is known that Russia's earnings from oil taxes and revenue constitute nearly half of its federal budget. Northern sanctions also constrain Russia's investment options for increased production and lure it to seek ways of bypassing these sanctions via investment opportunities in the Middle East and Africa. As for the issue of global price fluctuations, greater Russian control over Middle Eastern and African oil resources will increase its ability to secure favorable prices for Russian economy (Arkhangelskaya and Dodd 2016; Trickett 2018). Together, Russia and Africa possess the majority of global water and mineral resources, which is why they have a shared interest in protecting and controlling these resources from a geopolitical standpoint. As such, there are over 30 Russian companies operating in Africa's resource-extraction sector. Russian companies are known to have developed a platinum mine in Zimbabwe; they have plans to create an oil refinery in Uganda, and other mineral and energy resource-extraction plans in countries such as Nigeria, Cote d'Ivoire, Ghana, and Equatorial Guinea (Arkhangelskaya and Dodd 2016; Arkhangelskaya and Shubin 2013).

Agriculture plays a role in Russia's economic relations with Africa. Accordingly, cereals occupy an important position in Russia's exports to Africa. In 2010, cereals accounted for 22.58% of Russia's African exports; followed by mineral fuels, oils, and distillation with a total contribution of nearly 16%. In the same year, fruits and nuts made up 27.74% of Russian imports from Africa (Ndambendia 2015). Relatedly, South Africa is a key trading partner for Russia. Russian imports from South Africa increased from over $70 million in 2000 to over $474 million in 2010 and over $628 million in 2017. Russian exports to South Africa amounted to over $33 million in 2000; they increased to over $45 million in 2010 and over $203 million in 2017. However, South Africa represented only 0.28% of Russia's global imports, and Russia's exports to South Africa amounted to just 0.56% of its global exports (United Nations n.d.).

Besides natural resources and agriculture, most of Russia's economic involvement in Africa concentrates on science, engineering and infrastructure, and arms. It is thus important to emphasize that the limited nature of Russia's engagement with Africa does not downplay its importance for the multi-polarization of world politics in a post-hegemonic direction. Russia is involved in some of Africa's most strategic sectors, to the detriment of US hegemony in the continent. Most importantly, Russia's major companies have developed their presence in the African continent, including the Renova Group (specializing in the exploration and production of manganese ore), Nornickel (specializing in the production and mining of nickel), and the EVRAZ Group (specializing in the production of vanadium and steel). Rosatom, Russia's state-run nuclear energy corporation, has committed to supply nuclear reactors to major African countries such as South Africa, Egypt, Tunisia, Nigeria, and Ghana (Borshchevskaya 2017; Kuznetsov, Naumkin, and Zvyagelskaya 2018). It is therefore possible to argue that Russian support for scientific and infrastructural development might contribute to Africa's development in the longer run, even though Russia's focus on the energy and arms sectors has the potential to amplify Africa's dependence on extractivism and its propensity to military conflicts.

Of strategic importance for Russia's involvement in Africa is the arms sector. As argued by Oğultürk (2017), "using arms sales as a point of doorway, Russia has been active reestablishing political, military and business relationships across Africa. Moscow has used this model of arms first, business concession later in many African countries." Russia is known to link its arms deals to capital-intensive mineral and energy projects in Africa. A case in point is the Ugandan oil investment deal in early 2015, which was linked to an arms deal with Rosoboronexport, a subsidiary of Rostec operating under US sanctions. Similarly, countries such as South Africa, Angola, Nigeria, and Ghana have major deals with Russia in both the energy and arms sectors. As such, it would be right to assume that Russia, as one of the world's leading arms exporters, highly values arms trade in its relations with the African continent (Arkhangelskaya and Dodd 2016. In the 2013–2017 period, Africa received as much as 13% of Russia's global arms exports (Wezeman et al. 2018). Russia is also the leading arms exporter to sub-Saharan Africa (TASS 2017). Furthermore, Russia has shown an interest in further expanding its military cooperation with major African countries, as evidenced in joint Russian–Egyptian military exercises and naval drills in 2015–2016 (Borshchevskaya 2017). Russia has reportedly deployed troops in Egypt, and in 2017 made an agreement with that country to use its airspaces and military bases (Neale 2018). Certainly, Russia intends to take advantage of Egypt's proximity to Libya to intervene in the ongoing Libyan conflict.

Russia has crucial geopolitical and economic interests in Libya, which can be broadly summarized in two major points. First, Russia's increasing engagement contributes directly to the multipolarization of world politics by constraining Northern powers' prestige and military influence. The general opinion about the Libyan crisis is that the Northern intervention for regime change in Libya, and the North's lack of engagement after Gaddafi's death, are the chief factors contributing to the chaotic environment of the post-Gaddafi era. Therefore, Russia sees the Libyan conjuncture as a great opportunity to fill the power vacuum created by the Northern powers (Neale 2018). Russia had also shown interest in constructing naval bases on Libya's eastern coasts in 2008 and 2009. Therefore, Russia's increasing involvement in post-Gaddafi Libya could be indirectly associated with its intention to increase its global military influence by contributing to the multipolarization of world politics. In Russia's quest for global military influence, against the backdrop of its intensifying confrontation with the Northern powers, the Mediterranean basin is of crucial importance. Relatedly, Libya's proximity to Europe is a great source of concern for European powers, who have already been suffering a historic wave of migration from Arab Spring countries. Russia's political, economic, and military involvement would certainly force its hand in influencing Europe's geopolitics (Eljarh 2018; Neale 2018). Second, Gaddafi's death dealt a huge economic blow to Russia, which lost contracts worth billions of dollars in strategic sectors such as energy, construction, infrastructure, and defense. Russia is now interested in regaining its former economic concessions in the face of Northern economic sanctions and stagnation. Russia is therefore seeking both to contribute to Libya's reconstruction efforts and to exploit its vast oil resources (Eljarh 2018; Kuznetsov, Naumkin, and Zvyagelskaya 2018; Neale 2018).

India's rise in Africa

Among the BRICS countries, India is also an important player in the African continent. India's involvement in Africa is perhaps most pronounced in development cooperation, natural resources, food trade, and energy. Indian aid and development cooperation have really gained momentum under the Narendra Modi government (Kumar and Stanzel 2016). Its investments have reached a total of $54 billion since 1997, making it the fifth largest foreign investor in Africa (Ministry of External Affairs 2017).

In its efforts at advancing development cooperation, India has focused on key areas such as agriculture, infrastructure, health, education, science, and information technology. These areas play significant roles in boosting India's prestige in the African continent. In contrast to China's concentration on large infrastructural projects, however, India lays greater emphasis on smaller-scale development projects (Kumar and Stanzel 2016). It is estimated that India has extended 152 lines of credit to 44 different African countries, amounting to as much as $8 billion since 2015. These lines of credit are directed to the development of infrastructure, public transport, clean energy, irrigation, agriculture, and manufacturing capacity. Besides several ongoing or completed development partnership projects in the form of Grant-in-Aid projects or concessional loans, India has committed to additional lines of credit that amount to $10 billion directed to development projects. It is also committed to grant assistance worth $600 million for the period 2015–2020. India's other projects in Africa include capacity-building interventions such as the building of vocational training centers, IT parks, and centers of excellence, as well as the supply of vehicles, ambulances, agricultural equipment, IT equipment, medical devices, medicines, and other items. Furthermore, India has initiated private partnership programs in the health sector and a massive Pan African e-Network Project, which focuses on tele-education and tele-medicine in 48 different African countries. In the area of education, India has committed to provide 50,000 scholarships to African students in 2015–2020 (Ministry of External Affairs 2017).

Natural resources are of primary importance for India's engagement with Africa. India produces over 90% of the world's cut-and-polished diamonds. It imports $10 billion worth of rough diamonds annually, and nearly 80% of these imported diamonds originate from Africa (Carmody 2013b). Even in 2006 – prior to the Modi era, which witnessed the intensification of Indo-African bonds – "India got 12% of its gold imports, 79% of its phosphates, 91% of its nuts and 16% of its copper from the continent" (Carmody 2012, 121).

Food and agriculture also occupy important places in India's dealings with the African continent, evidenced by the fact that "20% of investment by Indian companies in Africa is now in the food, beverages and tobacco sector"

(Carmody 2013b). Not only are population growth and poverty major concerns for India; the neoliberalization of Indian agriculture and concomitant agricultural disinvestment severely threaten India's food security. For example, pulses are a major source of protein in the Indian diet, and estimates suggest that India's demand is likely to rise faster than its production. This situation encourages India to accelerate offshore agro-investments and land grabs, not only for pulses, but also for edible oils and energy security. Africa is an important venue for these agro-investments and land grabs as the cost of agricultural production in Africa is nearly half that in India, thanks to the availability of cheap labor and the possibility of using less fertilizer and pesticide (Carmody 2013b). Indeed, Indian agro-conglomerates see land grabbing as a strategic opportunity for capital accumulation rather than a food security issue. However, land grabs fuel already existing racial tensions, exacerbate inequality through dispossession and limiting local communities' access to natural resources, and lead to long-term environmental problems due to the poor regulation of land use in Africa (Batterbury 2018). In this respect, it is highly relevant to note that 70% of the foreign investment in Ethiopia's agricultural land comes from India (Carmody 2012).

In India's foreign policy, food security goes hand in hand with energy security. In 2013, India was the third-largest country for energy demand. It requires a constant supply of energy in order to maintain its economic growth, but estimations suggest that it will run out of coal reserves in 40 years (Carmody 2013b; IEA 2015). By the end of 2014, India's remaining recoverable barrels of oil amounted to 24 million; but the country needs over 1.4 billion barrels annually due to increasing demand. This has prompted India to intensify its foreign land-grabbing efforts for increased biofuel production derived from different cropping systems (IEA 2015). For similar reasons, countries such as Nigeria, South Africa, Ghana, Angola, and Egypt are among India's top trading partners in the energy sector. In 2015, as much as 73% of India's total African imports originated from these countries, with the greatest contributions coming from mineral fuels, lubricants, and related materials including coal and crude oil. It is estimated that mineral fuels and lubricants constitute 57% of India's total imports from Africa (Taylor, Van der Merwe, and Dodd 2016). Finally, India's corporate presence in Africa is felt in various other sectors. Tata Group, one of India's largest conglomerates, maintains operations in 11 African countries with a total investment of nearly $145 million. It is estimated that 20% of India's pharmaceutical exports go to Africa; this is mainly attributable to the involvement of major pharmaceutical companies such as Cipla and Ranbaxy (Taylor, Van der Merwe, and Dodd 2016).

China as the leading post-hegemonic power in Africa

China has no rivals among the BRICS countries in its capacity to engage the African continent. Unlike Russia, China has seen Africa as a top foreign policy priority, especially in the 2010s. In building trust relationships with

Africa, China became involved in peacekeeping and conflict management by sending troops and providing financial support. Unlike Northern powers, however, the Chinese involvement was driven by the principles of impartiality, unconditionality, and national sovereignty, which rule out foreign interference and use of sanctions as security-building tools (Sicurelli 2013). However, China's principles came under heavy criticism from Northern powers and pro-Northern politicians in Africa for allegedly impeding the democratization of African states by remaining impartial towards authoritarian regimes (Duchâtel, Gowan, and Rapnouil 2016; Kumar and Stanzel 2016; Sicurelli 2013). China's role as a security provider is perhaps most visible in its activities in United Nations peacekeeping missions and in cooperation with the African Union. In 2016 alone, nearly 2200 Chinese peacekeepers served in Africa. China's navy has extended the number of its ports in the African continent and has constructed a permanent military base in Djibouti. Relatedly, China has become a major arms supplier for Africa. In the 2011–2014 period, China provided as much as 24% of the conventional arms supplied to sub-Saharan Africa. All of this goes hand in hand with large quantities of low-cost, good quality small arms and light weapons provided by China to African countries (Eisenman and Shinn 2018).

Africa is the biggest recipient of Chinese aid, which was estimated at nearly $30 billion in the 2000–2013 period alone (Kumar and Stanzel 2016). Similarly, China's Exim Bank has become the largest loan provider to Africa, outranking the World Bank (Carmody 2013b). Between 2000 and 2014, China offered an estimated $86.3 billion in loans, which were mostly directed to infrastructure projects with no strict political conditionality. However, it is worth noting that in practice China's unconditionality means minimum conditionality. Rather than impose a long list of harsh conditions such as privatization, liberalization, and democratization, China expects African countries to remain open to trade and investment. In certain contracts, another condition imposed by China concerns concessions provided to Chinese companies for employing Chinese workers and cooperating with Chinese companies rather than fully relying on local workers and companies. Compliance with Chinese foreign policy priorities such as the One-China policy is also an important condition for securing China's fuller support (Eisenman and Shinn 2018).

In 2014, Africa was home to at least 250,000 Chinese workers, whose presence in Africa was due to China's increasing involvement in the continent. Moreover, it is alleged that the available official figures are an underestimate, and that the number of Chinese nationals working in Africa may be as high as 1 million (Kumar and Stanzel 2016). In this environment, it is estimated that Africa now receives a quarter of Chinese exports to developing countries, whereas China's foreign direct investment saw a 19-fold growth in the 2000–2006 period alone (Carmody 2013b). Currently, South Africa is the recipient of as much as 40% of China's total foreign direct investment stock in Africa. In return, as an act of goodwill, China has committed to restraining its textile exports to South Africa. Having signed a comprehensive strategic partnership agreement with South Africa, China largely imports South African minerals and exports manufactured goods, including machinery and textiles (Carmody 2013b).

It would thus be naive to argue that China has made Africa a top priority in its foreign policy out of pure benevolence. China's major state-owned companies have developed vested interests in Africa's strategic sectors, including the energy sector (e.g. in the oilfields in South Sudan, and investment of over $100 billion in the African mining industry by 2014); infrastructure (e.g. $13.8 billion in railways in East Africa); and manufacturing (e.g. garment manufacturing in Ethiopia and Rwanda) (Kumar and Stanzel 2016). Similarly, Chinese investments are strongly represented in Africa's service sector, especially with the involvement of Huawei and ZTE. WeChat, China's biggest internet-based mobile messaging platform and social network (similar to WhatsApp and Facebook), has already entered the African market (Kumar and Stanzel 2016).

By 2009, China had become Africa's largest trading partner. Approximately 85% of China's African imports consist of raw materials, including oil, minerals (e.g. copper, iron, cobalt, manganese, and tantalum), and hardwood timber, a majority of which is supplied by South Africa, Angola, the Democratic Republic of Congo, South Sudan, and Zambia. China largely exports high-value manufactured products to Africa, particularly textiles, electronics, machinery, and transport equipment (Eisenman and Shinn 2018; Kumar and Stanzel 2016). On one hand, China's increasing exports contribute to the availability of cheaper and affordable goods in the marketplace. On the other hand, Africa's increasing dependency on imports from China has the potential to hold back local industry. In Ghana's case, for example, a major concern is that Chinese textile exports have started to depress local textile production and to force the closure of textile plants. Similarly, Africa also seems to have developed increasing levels of export dependency on China. The 2015 figures indicate that over 40% of the total exports of Eritrea, the Central African Republic, Angola, Sudan, Mauritania, and the Democratic Republic of Congo go to China. The rates for Zambia and Liberia are 28% and 27%, respectively (Langan 2017).

China's foreign direct investment reflects the extent to which it values natural resources in its engagement with Africa. In 2011, 31% of Chinese foreign direct investment to Africa went to oil and mining. This figure is followed by other strategic sectors: 20% banking and finance, 16% construction, and 15% manufacturing, with the remaining percentage represented by services, technology, wholesale and retail, agriculture, and real estate (Eisenman and Shinn 2018). To give an example of China's quest for African natural resources, it has been keen to cultivate close relations with Zambia, which has serious debt problems amounting to as much as 29% of its GDP (Hill 2018; Mariam 2017). China is the world's largest consumer of copper, and Zambia is among the world's top ten copper producers. Most of Zambia's recent debt is owed to Chinese state-owned companies and is used for building roads, airports, and power plants. Even though China's contributions to developing Zambia's infrastructure cannot be overemphasized, China is often accused of neocolonialism by African politicians for taking advantage of Zambia's indebtedness, imposing poor working conditions, and engaging in illegal extractive activities. These problems have even led to diplomatic incidents, as in the case of the arrest of 31 Chinese nationals for involvement in illegal mining in Zambia (Hill 2018; Mariam 2017; South China Morning Post 2017). Regarding poor working conditions imposed by Chinese companies operating in Africa, it has been reported that most companies do not provide overtime payments, rely heavily on short-term contracts with no benefits, and offer better working conditions to migrant Chinese workers than to native Africans (Carmody 2013b). In Zambia's case, for example, certain trade union officials acknowledge China's contributions to their country, but they also point to the need for stricter labor regulations in order to ensure better working conditions, constrain corruption and other illegal activities, and prevent violent clashes between local workers and Chinese companies. Despite these shortcomings, China continues to enjoy much higher popularity in Africa than Europe or North America, as clearly reflected a 70% favorability rate in the 2015 Pew Global Attitudes survey (Carmody 2013b; Dollar 2016).

South Africa as the BRICS' bridge to the African continent

South Africa cannot be easily compared with other BRICS countries on an equal footing. By the International Monetary Fund's calculations, in 2017 South Africa ranked only 33rd among the world's largest economies (IMF n. d.). It has the world's 25th largest population and 24th largest surface area. Even Jim O'Neill, who coined the acronym BRIC for emerging economies, argues that there are bigger economies in the Global South with better performance and greater influence than South Africa; including Indonesia, Turkey, and Saudi Arabia (Carmody 2013b). Moreover, South Africa is among the world's most unequal societies. This inequality is not only a legacy of the apartheid era (1948–1994), but also due to South Africa's liberalization policies in the post-apartheid years (Carmody 2013b). Equally important is that South Africa's regional influence is often overstated, mainly because this country is regarded with utmost suspicion by many African countries for its "sub-imperial role", allowing Africa's exploitation by its white-dominated companies and by Northern countries under the guise of "multilateralism". Similarly, South Africa's calls for good governance, democratization, and the rule of law in the early post-apartheid years are known to have offended Africa's authoritarian regimes (Carmody 2013b; Prys 2012).

South Africa's economic and symbolic position in the African continent, rather than its global influence, is what makes this country a privileged member of the BRICS grouping. By 2012, South Africa had become the world's third-largest sender of foreign direct investment to the least developed countries, behind only India and China (Carmody 2013b). As Africa's second-largest economy, South Africa's investment focuses mostly on infrastructure and telecommunications, mining, oil, petroleum, and gas. Moreover, international donors, business communities, and the world's leading economies see South Africa as the catalyst for African development and a springboard that facilitates foreign access to African markets (Carmody 2013b; Prys 2012). As a reliable partner for foreign countries interested in the African continent, the quality of South Africa's economy is evidenced in its ranking of ninth in the Index of Government Economic Power, which measures economic power with reference to government revenue, foreign exchange reserves, exports of goods and services, and human capital (Basu et al. 2011; Carmody 2013b). The South African state is thus portrayed as having the highest levels of state capacity in Africa.

Furthermore, South Africa is a globally leading producer of chrome, diamonds, gold, and platinum (Scholvin 2014). Endowed with a high level of human capital, it has accumulated a substantial amount of know-how for extraction and production. This allows South African companies to mine coal in Nigeria, Zambia, and Zimbabwe; diamonds in Angola, the Democratic Republic of Congo, Namibia, and West Africa; and gold in East and West Africa (Scholvin 2014). Similarly, illustrating how South African corporations benefit from high levels of human capital, it is estimated that out of Africa's top 20 companies, 17 originate from South Africa: these "suppl[y] minerals and agricultural raw materials to the outside world … and provide the service infrastructure" (Carmody 2013a, 236). "South African-based financial service providers such as Absa Bank and Nedbank, retailers such as Pick 'n' Pay and Shoprite, telecommunication firms such as MTN and Vodacom, and numerous small and medium-sized tourism companies have all gained dominant positions" throughout Africa (Scholvin 2014, 103–104). These companies also take advantage of South Africa's strong energy sector and transport infrastructure, which bind the continent together:

> Half of the region's paved roads and railroads, as well as its seven largest ports, are in South Africa, and the country has a near monopoly on both telephones and host computers in the region. South Africa accounts for 82 per cent of all energy consumption in SADC; Eskom, a South African parastatal, provides approximately 45 per cent of Africa's energy supply and is the seventh-largest power generator in the world.
>
> (Prys 2012, 45)

Therefore, South Africa is in a position to systematically encourage regional expansion and corporate penetration through bilateral ties, infrastructure projects, and the publicly owned Industrial Development Corporation, which invests in regional projects and provides cost-sharing schemes with the private sector (Carmody 2016). While the trade between the BRICS countries and Africa recorded a tenfold growth between 2000 and 2009, from $16 billion to $157 billion, this growth was mainly due to South Africa's contributions (Carmody 2013b). China – South Africa's foremost sponsor for its accession to the BRICS grouping – has become South Africa's largest trade partner. China's closer engagement with South Africa is of strategic importance for the Chinese manufacturing industry, which requires South Africa's middlemanship for the provision of minerals and agricultural raw materials (Carmody 2013b).

Symbolically, South Africa exhibits a strong commitment to business-friendly values such as multilateralism, democracy, and the rule of law. It participates actively in multilateral institutions by expanding its global prestige in the eyes of international donors, business communities, and the world's leading economies. The creation of the South African Development Partnership Agency and the election of a South African politician – Nkosazana Dlamini-Zuma – to lead the African Union in 2012 represented milestones in South Africa's increasing global prestige (Carmody 2013b). Besides chairing international organizations such as the United Nations Conference for Trade and Development, South Africa also became involved in the India–Brazil–South Africa Trilateral Alliance and assumed a leading role in the Non-Aligned Movement and the World Trade Organization. Having promoted humanitarian campaigns such as the prohibition of landmines, and engaged in conflict mediation in international disputes such as that between Libya and the North over the 1988 Lockerbie bombing, South Africa has consolidated its global image as a "bridge between the North and South" (Prys 2012).

South Africa's close engagement with Africa is strongly manifested in its leading role in African regionalism. In fact, the African continent has a rich diversity of regional cooperation mechanisms. But very few of these mechanisms are in good shape, mostly due to the preponderance of weak states devoid of effective bureaucracies and an adequate level of capacity for territorial control (Söderbaum 2003). Africa's enduring colonial legacy renders most of these states extremely dependent on extra-regional trade with Europe, extractive sectors, foreign assistance, and peace-building missions. Consequently, most of the continent's effective regional cooperation mechanisms focus predominantly on internal security issues and open regionalism. This situation significantly constrains Africa's post-hegemonic potential, particularly in comparison with Eurasia and Latin America (Söderbaum 2003).

Africa's leading regional cooperation mechanisms are the Southern African Development Community (SADC) and the African Union. Not surprisingly, given its regional economic influence, South Africa is a leading force in these organizations (Prys 2012). SADC, as a successor of the Southern African Development Coordination Conference, is one of Africa's oldest regional organizations, along with the African Union. Established in 1992 to promote the region's socioeconomic development and security, SADC has 15 members: Angola, Botswana, the Democratic Republic of the Congo, Lesotho, Madagascar, Malawi, Mauritius, Mozambique, Namibia, Seychelles, South Africa, Swaziland, Tanzania, Zambia, and Zimbabwe. Since the mid-1990s, SADC's vision of regional development has increasingly shifted from an import-substitutionalist model to an outward-looking open regionalism centered on free trade and market integration (Muntschick 2018). In 2001,

SADC-led regional cooperation gained momentum through an institutional reform that centralized its administration and strengthened the member states' decision- and policy-making capacity. In 2008, the SADC created a free trade area, which currently includes 13 of its members, leaving out Angola and the Democratic Republic of the Congo. Despite these reforms, however, the SADC has been unable to overcome its problem of institutional weakness and make significant advances in implementing organizational decisions (Muntschick 2018).

In its present form, SADC has a complicated institutional structure; given the relative triviality of its contributions to the post-hegemonic restructuring of world politics, it is beyond the scope of the present chapter to give full details. SADC's most important bodies include the Summit of Heads of State or Government (its highest decision-making body) and the Organ on Politics, Defense and Security, which is responsible for promoting regional security. The Organ – whose performance is often described as "largely ineffectual" (Nathan 2012) – is home to the SADC Brigade and the Regional Peacekeeping Training Center, which were created as part of the organization's peace-building efforts. SADC's Tribunal was designed as its supreme judicial and dispute-settlement body; however, it was dissolved in 2012. The Secretariat manages SADC's administrative functions, but contrary to earlier expectations it has not gone beyond an advisory role. This is due to institutional weakness caused by a combination of several factors, including national rivalries, understaffing, and underfinancing. SADC was expected to create a customs union in 2010 and monetary union in 2016, but has not yet done so (Muntschick 2018).

Finally, the African Union – a continuation of the Organization of African Unity – presently includes 55 African countries. South Africa's role in the African Union is critical given its status as one of the organization's largest financial contributors and a leading actor in its peace and security efforts (Akokpari 2016). The Assembly, consisting of the heads of state or government of member states, is the African Union's highest authority. Its other important organs include the Executive Council, which contains the ministers of foreign affairs; the Permanent Representatives Committee, which includes nominated representatives who assume advisory roles to the Executive Council; the Economic, Social, and Cultural Council, which represents the continent's civil society organizations; and the Commission, which assumes the organization's administrative tasks (Muchie, Lukhele-Olorunju, and Akpor 2013; Touray 2016). The African Union also includes the African Commission on Human and Peoples' Rights, whose mission as a quasi-judicial body is to promote and protect human rights through investigative activities; and the New Partnership for Africa's Development, an economic development program that aims primarily to eradicate poverty, promote sustainable growth, integrate Africa in the global economy, and encourage women's empowerment programs (Muchie, Lukhele-Olorunju, and Akpor 2013; Touray 2016). Certainly, the African Union's sophisticated institutional structure, which takes a comprehensive approach to regionalism, constitutes a significant achievement in African affairs, given that the continent is characterized by fragile states and widespread conflicts.

However, though the African Union's potential for regional cooperation cannot be neglected, this organization is far from realizing its ambitious aim of supra-national integration. The African Union's potential is greatly hampered by a significant lack of funding and a constrained capacity to implement and monitor organizational decisions. The African Union's "ambition–capacity gap" has led to limited success in key areas, including peacekeeping, where the organization has been unable to maintain its operations; human rights protection, where the organization's operations have remained scattered and uncoordinated; and human development, where the organization has failed to achieve concrete successes aside from the creation of a Pan African University and scholarship programs (Touray 2016).

Review and discussion

What have been the implications of the BRICS' involvement in Africa for the multipolarization of world politics in a post-hegemonic direction? What is the geopolitical and economic importance of the BRICS' engagement in Africa? What are the prospects and contradictions of the BRICS' rise in the African continent? The study presented in this chapter has been guided by these questions with the aim of understanding the geopolitical-economic dynamics of Africa's post-hegemonic transformation. Geopolitical and economic dynamics are the most pronounced aspects of the BRICS' cooperation in Africa, the driving force of which has derived mainly from the quest for natural resources, the energy sector, and arms trade.

In the case of Brazil, whose cooperation with Africa gained significant pace in the Lula years, one observes the accentuation of development cooperation as opposed to development aid. Brazil brings to the fore social development programs and infrastructural projects without explicit political conditionality; driven by the principles of domestic economic growth, social inclusion, and the redistribution of resources. Brazil's closer engagement with Africa seems to have intensified competition between Brazilian and Chinese firms, and Brazil's hiring of local labor – as opposed to China's insistence on hiring imported labor – has received greater notice in this environment. However, such friendly competition does not rule out Sino–Brazilian development cooperation in the African continent.

As for Russia, as a resource-rich country its involvement in Africa is especially important in terms of the Russian intention to ensure control of the global energy market and sustain its global strength in arms trade. In the meantime, Russia's intervention in the Libyan conflict reflects its intention to constrain US military expansionism in the region and enhance its global military influence. Russia's development cooperation with Africa does not rely on strict political conditionality: its conditionality is mostly tied to arms trade and energy deals, in a less prescriptive and more implicit manner than that of its Northern counterparts.

Like the other BRICS countries, India's engagement with Africa is driven primarily by a quest for natural resources and energy security. However, India has also emerged as a leading actor in development cooperation with Africa. Its approach to development cooperation differs from China's in that India prioritizes smaller-scale projects and capacity-building interventions as opposed to China's emphasis on large-scale infrastructural projects.

Unarguably, China is the leading post-hegemonic power on the African continent. As with the other BRICS countries, China's conditionality does not pursue an explicit and prescriptive approach; instead it is closely tied to minor foreign policy commitments and economic concessions. Likewise, China's participation in Africa's peacekeeping missions, growing share in the African arms trade, and naval expansion contribute at first hand to geopolitical multipolarization. No less important in this regard is China's status as Africa's largest trading partner and main provider of loans and foreign direct investment. Although China's increasing involvement in Africa raises concerns about its alleged "neocolonial" intentions, China remains more popular than Europe or North America.

Finally, South Africa is Africa's leading economy and regional political actor, but its engagement with other African countries does not necessarily involve a post-hegemonic character. South Africa is widely perceived as a "sub-imperial" actor, and its regional initiatives do not go beyond the open regionalist paradigm of the 1990s. Even though its global influence and economic power are not on an equal footing with the other BRICS countries, South Africa is part of the BRICS thanks to Africa's strategic importance and its own status as the continent's middleman.

References

Akokpari, John. 2016. "South Africa and the African Union's Peace and Security Architecture: Old Responsibilities and New Challenges." *Brazilian Journal of African Studies* 1(2): 28–47.

Arkhangelskaya, Alexandra and Nicola Dodd. 2016. "Guns and Poseurs: Russia Returns to Africa." In *Emerging Powers in Africa. International Political Economy Series*, edited by Justin van der Merwe, Ian Taylor, and Alexandra Arkhangelskaya. New York: Palgrave Macmillan.

Arkhangelskaya, Alexandra and Vladimir Shubin. 2013. *Russia's Africa Policy*. SAIIA Occasional Paper 157. Johannesburg: South African Institute of International Affairs.

Basu, Kaushik, Supriyo De, Rangeet Ghosh, and Shweta. 2011. *The Evolving Dynamics of Global Economic Power in the Post-Crisis World: Revelations from a new Index of Government Economic Power*. Working Paper for Ministry of Finance, Government of India. http://kaushikbasu.org/Index%20of%20Government%20Economic%20Power.pdf

Batterbury, Simon and Frankline Ndi. 2018. "Land-grabbing in Africa." In *The Routledge Handbook of African Development*, edited by J. A. Binns, K. Lynch, and E. Nel, 573–582. London: Routledge.

Borshchevskaya, Anna. 2017. "From Moscow to Marrakech: Russia Is Turning Its Eyes to Africa." *The Hill*, September 21. http://thehill.com/opinion/international/351684-from-moscow-to-marrakech-russia-is-turning-to-africa

Carmody, Pádraig. 2012. "A Global Enclosure: The Geo-Logics of Indian Agro-Investments in Africa." In *Handbook of Land and Water Grabs in Africa: Foreign Direct Investment and Water Security*, edited by John Anthony Allen. London: Routledge.

Carmody, Pádraig. 2013a. "Globalising Solidarity or Legitimating Accumulation? Brazilian Strategies and Interests in Africa." *Irish Studies in International Affairs* 24: 81–99.

Carmody, Pádraig. 2013b. *The Rise of the BRICS in Africa: The Geopolitics of South–South Relations*. London: Zed Books.

Carmody, Pádraig. 2016. *The New Scramble for Africa*. Cambridge: Polity Press.

Dollar, David. 2016. *China's Engagement with Africa: From Natural Resources to Human Resources*. Washington, DC: Brookings Institution. https://www.brookings.edu/wp-content/uploads/2016/07/Chinas-Engagement-with-Africa-David-Dollar-July-2016.pdf

Duchâtel, Mathieu, Richard Gowan, and Manuel Lafont Rapnouil. 2016. *Into Africa: China's Global Security Shift*. London: European Council on Foreign Relations. https://www.ecfr.eu/page/-/Into_Africa_China's_global_security_shift_PDF_1135.pdf

Eisenman, Joshua and David H. Shinn. 2018. "China and Africa." In *The Palgrave Handbook of African Colonial and Postcolonial History*, edited by Martin Shanguhyia and Toyin Falola, 839–854. New York: Palgrave Macmillan.

Eljarh, Mohamed. 2018. "Russia's Ambitions in Libya." *Valdai Discussion Club*, February 20. http://valdaiclub.com/a/highlights/russia-s-ambitions-in-libya

de Freitas, Marcus Vinicius. 2016. *Brazil and Africa: Historic Relations and Future Opportunities*. Washington, DC: German Marshall Fund of the United States. http://www.gmfus.org/file/7424/download

Hill, Matthew. 2018. "Zambia to Seek Restructuring of Debt to China After IMF Warning." *Bloomberg*, February 13. https://www.bloomberg.com/news/articles/2018-02-13/zambia-to-seek-restructuring-of-debt-to-china-after-imf-warning

IEA. 2015. *India Energy Outlook: World Energy Outlook Special Report*. Paris: International Energy Agency. https://www.iea.org/publications/freepublications/publication/IndiaEnergyOutlook_WEO2015.pdf

IMF. n.d. IMF Data. Washington, DC: International Monetary Fund. Accessed August 13, 2018. https://www.imf.org/en/Data

Kumar, Sunaina and Angela Stanzel. 2016. "India and China: A scramble for Africa?" *European Council on Foreign Relations: Commentary*, July 29. https://www.ecfr.eu/article/commentary_india_and_china_a_scramble_for_africa_7086

Kuznetsov, Vasily, Vitaly Naumkin, and Irina Zvyagelskaya. 2018. *Russia in the Middle East: The Harmony of Polyphony*. Moscow: Valdai Discussion Club. http://valdaiclub.com/files/18375/

Langan, Mark. 2017. *Neo-Colonialism and the Poverty of 'Development' in Africa*. New York: Palgrave Macmillan.

Mariam, Alemayehu G. 2017. "Chinese Neocolonialism in Africa." *Pambazuka News*, September 7. https://www.pambazuka.org/global-south/chinese-neocolonialism-africa

Ministry of External Affairs. 2017. "Question No. 153: Indian Aid to African Countries." *MEA Media Center*, July 26. New Delhi: Government of India. http://www.

mea.gov.in/lok-sabha.htm?dtl/28705/QUESTION+NO153+INDIAN+AID+TO+AFRICAN+COUNTRIES

Muchie, Mammo, Phindil Lukhele-Olorunju, and Oghenerobor Akpor, eds. 2013. *The African Union Ten Years After. Solving African Problems with Pan-Africanism and the African Renaissance.* Pretoria: Africa Institute of South Africa.

Muntschick, Johannes. 2018. *The Southern African Development Community (SADC) and the European Union (EU)*. New York: Palgrave Macmillan.

Nathan, Laurie. 2012. *Community of Insecurity: SADC's Struggle for Peace and Security in Southern Africa.* Farnham: Ashgate.

Ndambendia, Houdou. 2015. *Africa Trade and Investment with BRIC Nations in a Changing Economic Landscape: The Role of China.* MPRA Paper No. 71675. https://mpra.ub.uni-muenchen.de/71675

Neale, Erin. 2018. "Russia: Is Syria's Fate Libya's Future?" *Atlantic Council*, February 14. http://www.atlanticcouncil.org/blogs/menasource/russia-is-syria-s-fate-libya-s-future-2

Oğultürk, Mehmet Cem. 2017. "Russia's Renewed Interests in the Horn of Africa as a Traditional and Rising Power." *Rising Powers Quarterly* 2(1): 121–143. http://risingpowersproject.com/quarterly/russias-renewed-interests-in-the-horn-of-africa-as-a-traditional-and-rising-power/

Prys, Miriam. 2012. *Redefining Regional Power in International Relations: Indian and South African perspectives.* London: Routledge.

Scholvin, Sören. 2014. *The Geopolitics of Regional Power: Geography, Economics and Politics.* London: Routledge.

Seifert, Jurek. 2013. "New Asymmetries or Old Patterns? South–South Cooperation between Brazil and Angola." Presented at the European Conference for African Studies (ECAS)Africa in a Multipolar World, Lisbon, June 27–29.

Sicurelli, Daniela. 2013. "The Security Culture of the African Union Adapting and Reacting to External Models." In *Mapping Agency Comparing Regionalisms in Africa*, edited by Ulrike Lorenz-Carl and Martin Rempe, 17–34. London: Routledge.

Söderbaum, Frederik. 2003. *The New Regionalism in Africa*, edited by J. Andrew Grant. London: Routledge.

South China Morning Post. 2017. "Chinese Nationals Held in Zambia over Illegal Mining." *South China Morning Post*, June 4. https://www.scmp.com/news/china/diplomacy-defence/article/2096858/chinese-nationals-held-zambia-over-illegal-mining

Stolte, Christina. 2015. *Brazil's Africa Strategy: Role Conception and the Drive for International Status.* New York: Palgrave Macmillan.

Suyama, Bianca, Laura Trajber Waisbich, and Lara Costa Leite. 2016. "Brazil as a Development Partner under Lula and Rousseff: Shifts and Continuities." In *The BRICS in International Development*, edited by Jing Gu, Alex Shankland, and Anuradha Chenoy. London: Palgrave Macmillan.

TASS. 2017. "Russia–Africa: A Structural Approach to Cooperation in the New Economic Reality." *TASS: Business & Economy*, May 29. http://tass.com/sp/948360

Taylor, Ian, Justin Van der Merwe, and Nicole Dodd. 2016. "Nehru's Neoliberals: Draining or Aiding Africa?" In *Emerging Powers in Africa: A New Wave in the Relationship?* edited by Justin Van der Merwe, Ian Taylor, and Alexandra Arkhangelskaya, 107–128. New York: Palgrave Macmillan.

Touray, Omar Alieu. 2016. *The African Union: The First Ten Years.* Lanham, MD: Rowman & Littlefield.

Trickett, Nicholas. 2018. "Why Putin's Oil Maneuvers Will Keep Russia in the Middle East." *The Washington Post*, April 5.

United Nations. n.d. UN Comtrade Database. Accessed August 13, 2018. https://comtrade.un.org/data/

Wezeman, Pieter D., Aude Fleurant, Alexandra Kuimova, Nan Tian, and Siemon T. Wezeman. 2018. *Trends in International Arms Transfers, 2017*. Solna: Stockholm International Peace Research Institute. https://www.sipri.org/sites/default/files/2018-03/fssipri_at2017_0.pdf

5 The Latin American left and post-hegemonic regionalism: The regional quest for social justice and development

Introduction

The BRICS coalition is not the only instance in which the intensification of South–South cooperation and multipolarization of global politics have been observed at the expense of US hegemony. The Latin American left's challenge of post-hegemonic regionalism is equally important in this regard. Since the 1980s, the Latin American left had been considered by many to be historically defeated. Yet the 2000s witnessed a tremendous surge for Latin America's left-leaning social and political movements, which attained unparalleled strength and influence (Gürcan 2013; Gürcan and Bakiner 2015). This region-wide turn to the left was initiated by the rise to power of Hugo Chávez after the Venezuelan presidential election of 1998. There followed the accession to office of left-leaning leaders in countries such as Chile, Brazil, Argentina, the Dominican Republic, Uruguay, Bolivia, Honduras, and Nicaragua. By 2010, self-designated leftist figures had ascended to power in countries that accounted for more than 60% of the region's population, gaining the electoral support of over 50% of Latin Americans. Despite a number of major electoral setbacks for the left since 2015, Latin America has grown to be the epicenter for political struggles worldwide, especially those geared to eroding the ideological monopoly of neoliberalism and the regional influence of the United States (Ballvé 2006; Barrett, Chávez, and Rodriguez-Garavito 2008; Burbach, Fox, and Fuentes 2013; Petras and Veltmeyer 2011; Saad-Filho 2005; Singham 2015). Combined with the growing dynamism of various social movements, the Latin American left has thus come to transform the basic terms of political debate on a myriad of key issues; including socioeconomic equality; social security; human rights; indigenous politics; environmentalism; reproductive rights; and the treatment of ethnic, cultural, and gender minorities (Gürcan and Bakiner 2015).

This chapter revolves around the following questions: What is the peculiarity of Latin America's post-hegemonic regionalism within the context of a regionally ascending left? What kind of historical background is this regionalism built on? What are the normative and institutional settings that help the Latin American left to put this post-hegemonic agenda into effect? My underlying argument is that Latin America's post-hegemonic regionalism has been characterized by an agenda of social justice and development that refutes US neoliberal hegemony. As discussed in Chapter 2, Latin America's open regionalism was a predominant framework for regionalism in the 1990s, which found its strongest expression in the *Mercado Común del Sur* (Mercosur: Southern Common Market), the North American Free Trade Agreement (NAFTA), and the Free Trade Area of the Americas. The central concerns of open regionalism were free trade and economic integration. However, the crisis of Latin American regionalism and the rise of social movements and the political left undermined the relevance of open regionalism. A radical paradigm shift occurred from economic integrationism to a social justice-oriented and social developmentalist regionalism against US hegemony. The *Alianza Bolivariana para los Pueblos de Nuestra América* (ALBA: Bolivarian Alliance for the Peoples of Our America) and *Unión de Naciones Suramericanas* (Unasur: Union of South American Nations) led the way in bringing post-hegemonic regionalism from the margins to the mainstream of Latin American politics. ALBA's most successful activities concentrate on areas such as development, cultural integration, social movements, education, food security, and defense. Similarly, Unasur has made its name heard most strongly in the areas of defense, infrastructural development, and health.

In what follows, I thus focus on the case of post-hegemonic regionalism with reference to the Latin American left as well as the ALBA and Unasur experience. The first section presents an overview of key concepts and debates about the Latin American left and sheds light on their implications for post-hegemonic regionalism. The second and third sections explore the ALBA and Unasur experiences; including their historical development, symbolic underpinnings, institutional settings, and innovatory practices.

Three major approaches to the Latin American left: Liberal democracy, Marxism, and post-neoliberalism

The notions of social justice, developmentalism, and the left constitute the underlying concepts of this chapter. Social justice is referred to as an "ideal condition in which all members of a society have the same basic rights, protections, opportunities, obligations, and social benefits" (Barker 2003, 404). In turn, developmentalism speaks to a development strategy in which the state assumes a strategic role in promoting economic and sociocultural development (Mhone 2004). For the practical purposes of this chapter, I use the term "left" to designate an array of political or social movements, including both moderate reformers and revolutionaries, that rhetorically – if not substantially – prioritize the issues of social justice, equality, and democracy (Katz 2005; Zibechi 2003). In fact, social justice, equality, and democracy appears to be a recurring theme that runs through much of the discussions in the existing literature on the definition of the left. For example, in Castañeda's definition, the left is portrayed as "a current of thought, politics, and policy that stresses social improvement over macroeconomic orthodoxy, egalitarian distribution of wealth over its creation, sovereignty over international cooperation and democracy" (Castañeda 2006, 32). A vague reference to democracy also appears in Richard Flacks' definition of the left as "a body of thought … that seeks to expand the capacity of the people themselves to make the decisions that affect the conditions and terms of everyday life" (Flacks 1988, 100). In turn, Hugh Stretton emphasizes the equality component of the left by defining it in terms of political actors' support for reducing inequalities (Stretton 1976, 2). The same goes for Juan Pablo Luna and Cristóbal Rovira Kaltwasser's definition, which frames the left as "a political position, which is characterized by the idea that the main inequalities between the people are artificial and thus seeks to overcome them by active state involvement" (Luna and Kaltwasser 2014, 4). Similarly, Levitsky and Roberts conceptualize the left as "political actors who seek to employ public authority to protect individuals and groups from market insecurities, reduce social and economic inequalities, and strengthen the voice of underprivileged groups" (Levitsky and Roberts 2011b, 5). Tony Hilfer views the left "as a politics aimed at restructuring the socioeconomic order so as to equalize wealth and power" (Hilfer 2014, 2). It is hoped that the wide spectrum offered by this literature might help to capture the widely acknowledged "heterogeneity" of the Latin American left (Ellner 2014; Lievesley and Ludlam 2009; Rodríguez-Garavito, Barrett, and Chávez 2008).

The liberal-democratic critique of the Latin American left

One may discern a minimum of three major approaches to the Latin American left in the extant literature: the liberal-democratic camp, Marxist approaches, and the post-neoliberalism thesis. The liberal-democratic camp builds its arguments on Jorge Castañeda's dichotomization (Castañeda 2006) between the "good" and the "bad" left (Levitsky and Roberts 2011b; Lynch 2007; Moreno-Brid and Paunovic 2010; Vargas-Llosa 2007; Weyland 2010). According to Castañeda, the new Latin American left is divided into what he calls the "pragmatic, sensible, realistic, honest, responsible, and humanized" left (e.g. Brazil, Chile, Uruguay); and the "nationalist, populist and statist", or simply dishonest and irresponsible left (e.g. Venezuela, Bolivia, Nicaragua, Argentina) (Castañeda 2006, 2008; Castañeda and Morales 2008). Similar language is used elsewhere to differentiate between the so-called "vegetarian" and "carnivore" left (Vargas-Llosa, 2007, 60); or between social democracy and populism (Lynch 2007, 378). In a similar vein, Kurt Weyland proposes to categorize the Latin American left into the "moderate left" and "contestatory left" (Weyland 2010). Parallel with Castañeda's categorization, Weyland concludes that the moderate left performs better as to economic development, social justice, and democracy. He expresses his dislike of the fact that the contestatory left, represented by Venezuela and Bolivia, ended up undermining liberal democracy because of its emphasis on participatory democracy, which allegedly resonates with majoritarianism rather than genuinely deepening democracy (Weyland 2010). According to Weyland and his colleagues, one of the major good points of the moderate left, represented by Brazil and Chile, is its respect for liberal democracy and "existing political institutions"; it dedicates its efforts to finding common ground with the opposition instead of "rewriting the political rules" (Madrid, Hunter, and Weyland 2010, 141–142). Using Castañedaian language, these scholars also brand the radical left as "inefficient, imprudent, and irresponsible" (Weyland 2011, 73–74).

The Castañeda/Weyland framework finds resonance in the work of Steven Levitsky and Kenneth M. Roberts. According to these authors, the new Latin American left is differentiated in terms of levels of institutionalization of political parties and social movements as well as the nature of the political authority in place (Levitsky and Roberts 2011b, 12). As far as levels of institutionalization are concerned, Levitsky and Roberts distinguish between established organizations that have longstanding effects (Chile, Brazil, etc.) and recently created organizations that simply serve as electoral vehicles for leaders or movements who challenge the pre-existing institutional structure (Venezuela, Bolivia, etc.). As for political authority, they identify movements dominated by individual figures and movements that disperse power (Levitsky and Roberts 2011b, 12–13). Despite their critique of Castañeda, however, Levitsky and Roberts cannot keep themselves from resorting to dichotomization between moderation ("good left") and radicalism ("bad left").

Another important attempt at categorization comes from Jon Beasley-Murray, Maxwell A. Cameron, and Eric Hershberg (Beasley-Murray, Cameron, and Hershberg 2010). While acknowledging the diversity of the Latin American left, these writers argue that differentiation within the left can be better assessed once the focus of attention is shifted to the question "why is liberalism insufficient in Latin America?" (Beasley-Murray, Cameron, and Hershberg 2010, 13). Accordingly, they praise the democratic potential of indigenous movements as long as they remain within the confines of the "basic liberal rights and freedoms" (Beasley-Murray, Cameron, and Hershberg 2010, 13, 16) rather than revolutionizing conventional liberal-democratic institutions. The same argument is reasserted elsewhere: the need for "peacefully and (more or less) legally transforming the system" (Cameron and Sharpe 2010, 77) without resorting to revolutionary violence or transforming property relations via class struggle. Ultimately, this perspective unintendedly reproduces Castañeda's "bad left" thesis to the extent that those who attempt to violate bourgeois legality can be demonized as the enemies of liberal democracy. In a similar vein, the negative implications for democratization of US interventions, economic blockades, and coup attempts are not systematically engaged by the liberal camp.

Finally, Francisco Panizza suggests categorizing the new Latin American left with reference to forms of political representation (Panizza 2009). His categorization is predicated on a liberal-democratic account which echoes that of Beasley-Murray and his colleagues: he tends to favour liberal over participatory democracy due to the latter's "well-known problems of legitimacy, mobilization bias and representation" (Panizza 2009, 224). In analyzing internal differences within the left, Panizza identifies three forms of representation, namely those associated with parties, social movements, and personalist leaders. For example, Venezuela is seen as being low in party representation, low–medium in social representation due to limited autonomy in movement participation, and high in personalist representation. Brazil is low in personalist representation and high in party representation because Lula's leadership was constrained by institutional checks and balances and higher levels of institutionalization in the Workers' Party. Somehow, Brazil's performance in social representation is rated as medium–low – that is, better than Venezuela's performance – probably due to higher levels of autonomy rather than the intensity of social mobilization (Panizza 2009).

In Bolivia's case, party representation is assessed as low, whereas social and personalist forms of representation are high. Argentina is medium in party, high in personalist representation because of the Kirchners' charismatic leadership, and exhibits relatively high levels of institutionalization within the Peronist left (Panizza 2009, 189–193). Surprisingly, Panizza (2009) presents Argentina's performance in social representation as being better than Brazil's, although much of liberal-democratic and even Marxist accounts in the literature complain about higher levels of co-optation in social movement organizing, and lower levels of dispersion in the sharing of political power, in Argentina (Levitsky and Roberts 2011a, 2011b; Robinson 2008).

The Marxist critique of the Latin American left

The so-called "left turn" in Latin America was postulated on a strong rejection of neoliberalism in discourse. However, the left's strategic setbacks in Venezuela, Bolivia, Brazil, and Argentina since 2015 seem to have rekindled the debates about how leftist Latin America's governments really were, and whether the left presented a genuine challenge to neoliberalism in practice. Pessimistic accounts of Latin America's left turn have been voiced from the Marxist camp. For example, James Petras posits that the rise to eminence of left-wing regimes in Latin America hardly entails a radical rupture from neoliberalism, contrary to the radical discourse of the socialism of the twenty-first century (Petras 2011). This discourse is officially represented by Venezuela's Bolivarian socialism, but it can also be associated with the ideal of communitarian socialism in Evo Morales' Bolivia and the project of "Citizens' Revolution" in Rafael Correa's Ecuador. A common trait of this continental discourse speaks to the critique of Soviet socialism for its anti-democratic political system. It is also characterized by departure from the armed guerrilla struggle towards democratic electoral strategies, anti-imperialism, and diversification of the political agenda towards gender equality and environmental justice (Burbach, Fox, and Fuentes 2013; Gürcan and Bakiner 2015; Lievesley and Ludlam 2009; Rodríguez-Garavito et al. 2008). Another crucial commonality shared by most leftist governments in Latin America is a popular reaction to the "economic crises and corruption scandals linked to structural adjustment reforms multiplied throughout the region" (Rodríguez-Garavito et al. 2008, 9). According to Petras, however, regardless of the political diversity of Latin America's left governments, they tend to be closely involved with multinational corporations and their extractivist projects (Petras 2011). For example, Venezuela, which remains an oil-dependent country, has failed to resolve the question of inequality, introduce sweeping agrarian reform, or reverse class hierarchies by imposing progressive taxation and suppressing bourgeois interests from the ranks of the state bureaucracy (Petras 2011). Petras' portrayal of Venezuela is strongly echoed by others, who observe that the private sector "takes up a larger share of the economy that it did before Chávez came to office" (Beasley-Murray, Cameron, and Hershberg 2010, 9). A similar situation is observed in Ecuador's "Citizens' Revolution", which has imposed restrictions on trade union strikes and allowed for greater foreign ownership in strategic areas, including mining and energy resources, telecommunications, banking, and commercial exports (Petras 2011). Despite tremendous achievements in the area of indigenous rights and autonomy, Bolivia has increasingly relied on the cooperation of foreign-owned extractive industries and large landowners (Petras 2011; Veltmeyer and Petras 2014).

According to Henry Veltmeyer and James Petras, the kernel of Latin American development lies in "new extractivism", that is, the re-primarization of the development model by focusing on export-oriented resource extraction through mining, fossil fuel collection and biofuels, land grabbing, and soy monoculture. New extractivism has taken advantage of rising global primary commodity prices since the early 2000s to the benefit of state taxation and multinational corporations. However, in the process it has intensified social conflicts (Veltmeyer and Petras 2014). In Latin America, the new extractivist agenda has been advanced under the cover of a progressive rhetoric of social inclusion, resource nationalism, and sustainable management of resources to superficially smooth the effects of class polarization (Veltmeyer and Petras 2014).

In line with Veltmeyer and Petras, Jeffery R. Webber and Barry Carr concur that the programs of most of Latin America's leftist governments amount to a continuation of the neoliberal capitalist project (Webber and Carr 2013). Webber infers that new left policies in Latin America constitute "a tactical response of the ruling classes to adjust to the social contradictions generated by the implementation of neoliberalism in the region while preserving the underlying class-project and the successes it has enjoyed" (Webber 2010, 227). Webber goes on to associate Latin America's left with Antonio Gramsci's notion of "passive revolution", in which "capacities for social mobilization from below are co-opted, contained, or selectively repressed, while the dominant classes' political initiative is restored" (Webber 2017b, para. 16). According to Webber, Bolivia is a case in point regarding the Latin American left's limitations. This country underwent an insurrectionary cycle with the outbreak of the Water and Gas Wars between 2000 and 2005; this was, however, interrupted by a return to conventional parliamentary politics and eventually the reconstitution of neoliberalism. Bolivia's political economy after the insurrectionary period was marked by greater integration into global markets, combined with heavier reliance on exports of hydrocarbons and minerals. Increasing government revenue was not reflected in social spending, which substantially decreased as a proportion of GDP. Accompanied by growing inflation rates, precarious labor conditions persisted alongside high poverty and inequality levels (Webber 2011). William I. Robinson similarly concludes that Latin America's left has represented the power of dominant classes and a mystical force that he calls the "transnational capitalist class", through which "many of the Pink Tide states were able to push forward a new wave of capitalist globalization with greater credibility than their orthodox and politically bankrupt neoliberal predecessors" (Robinson 2017, para. 5).

The post-neoliberalism thesis

Certain observers of the Latin American left, who are not as pessimistic as the Marxist camp, assert that the continental shift to the left led to the opening of a new era, which came to be called post-neoliberalism. These scholars caution, however, that the post-neoliberal era in Latin America does not imply a transcendence of neoliberalism. Rather, they all concur that this era corresponds to an interregnum period rather than the definitive end of neoliberalism (Sader 2009; Yates and Bakker 2014). Perhaps best represented by progressive social movements, post-neoliberalism thus involves an incoherent set of utopian-ideological projects to transform society beyond the neoliberal imaginary. In turn, institutional reforms and other pragmatic measures are traditionally associated with center-left governments (Yates and Bakker 2014, 3). In this sense, post-neoliberalism can be seen as a "discontinuity within continuity" (Macdonald and Ruckert 2009, 6), in which both center-left governments and social movements react to the socio-economic contradictions of neoliberalism via a wide range of policy alternatives. Continuity implies that neoliberal macroeconomic policies such as moderate inflation rates, balanced budgets, trade liberalization, flexible labour, full-fledged commodification, and cash transfers are slightly revised and reappropriated by center-left governments; perhaps with the exception of Bolivarian Venezuela. Discontinuity suggests that state power is used to correct market failures, partially renationalize some of the strategic sectors, expand the scope of redistributive welfare mechanisms, and deepen democratic participation at varying levels (Macdonald and Ruckert 2009, 7–8). For similar reasons, Jean Grugel and Pía Riggirozzi seem to use the term post-neoliberalism interchangeably with neostructuralism; they agree that the post-neoliberal era is but a reaction to excessive marketization, unemployment, and technocratic democracies (Grugel and Riggirozzi 2012, 3). Again, post-neoliberalism is deployed by center-left governments to pragmatically restrain neoliberalism by enhancing the social responsibilities of the state through increased taxation and management of exports, selective protectionism, pacts between labour and business, and inclusionary citizenship rights (Grugel and Riggirozzi 2012, 4–5, 12).

Far from framing post-neoliberalism as a coherent and standardized policy model, the post-neoliberalism thesis of the Latin American left acknowledges the pluriformity that comes from country-specific, institutional, and sectoral conditions (Macdonald and Ruckert 2009, 18; Yates and Bakker 2014, 22). The Argentine case is emblematic of the conceptual flexibility of post-neoliberalism. According to Federico M. Rossi (2015), the inclusion of progressive movements in policy-making and welfare networks cannot be simply reduced to a mere instance of populist co-optation to advance the neoliberal-capitalist agenda, as alleged by other researchers (Castorina 2014; Robinson 2008; Vivares, Echenique, and Ozorio 2009). Rossi (2015) prefers to depict the rise to eminence of progressive movements such as *piqueteros* as a struggle for recognition and reincorporation into society. These movements had previously been ignored by neoliberal governments: the so-called "postneoliberal" (Rossi 2015, 18) environment encourages them to mobilize as legitimate actors with authentic claims to access to employment, water, health, vocational training, and education. Meanwhile, these movements have turned into primary agents of social transformation rather than simply co-opted subjects of the *kirchnerista* apparatus (Rossi 2015, 3–4, 6, 16). As of 2005, a number of *piquetero* movements – such as *Federación de Tierra, Vivienda y Hábitat, Movimiento Evita*, and *Barrios de Pie* – had started to assume secondary roles in the executive and legislative branches, including the ministries of Social Development, Federal Planning, and International Relations. By 2007, several *piquetero* leaders had taken office in federal and provincial governments. These "outcomes were the result not of co-optation of the movement but of an expansion of the number of legitimate actors" (Rossi 2015, 15).

Miguel A. Rivera-Quiñones maintains that the Argentine post-neoliberalism experience is represented by the *kirchnerista* "national-popular" project, whose defining characteristic has been the paradigmatic shift of the locus of the economy from unproductive financial activities towards a productive system (Rivera-Quiñones 2014, 69, 73). Another defining characteristic of the so-called national-popular project consists of a considerable growth in the export sector, especially in transgenic soy exportation. This was heavily encouraged by high global commodity prices, which contributed to an annual trade surplus averaging $12 billion in 2004–2010 (Rivera-Quiñones 2014, 67–68). Rivera-Quiñones emphasizes that revenues generated from the taxation of soy exports constituted the backbone of the Kirchners' social programs. As such, Argentina's national capitalism obtained significant improvements, including a 200% increase in the minimum wage between 2003 and 2010 and a 34% real wage increase by 2009 (Rivera-Quiñones 2014, 71). Rivera-Quiñones stresses that "industrial growth, debt reduction, trade surpluses, international reserves accumulation, the end of the International Monetary Fund's disciplinary power, and growing social expenditure all exemplify a very different process of capital accumulation from the one that was dominant before the 2001 crisis" (Rivera-Quiñones 2014, 83). On the other hand, striking continuities can be observed with neoliberalism; particularly the strategic importance of foreign exchange and tax revenues and the growing economic weight of multinational corporations such as Cargill, Nidera, Dreyfus, Bunge, and ADM (Rivera-Quiñones 2014, 83).

Christopher Wylde maintains that Argentine post-neoliberalism is characterized by a turn to a state-centric neodevelopmentalist model (Wylde 2016). The prefix "neo" in neodevelopmentalism indicates that Argentina has not simply returned to an import-substitution model consolidated with widespread social programs. Instead, it gives greater weight to export-led development and continues the neoliberal logic of safety-net welfare that is selectively geared toward families rather than systematically tackling poverty and inequality (Wylde 2011). Meanwhile, the state consolidates its position as an agent of redistribution and market regulation with greater emphasis on tax collection in order to expand public expenditure. Wylde contends that the deepening of the post-neoliberal model under Cristina Fernández de Kirchner has worsened political and economic unsustainability, as previously anticipated by Richardson (Wylde 2016). The deterioration of global markets, especially after 2011 (IMF 2017), has exposed Argentina's excessive vulnerability to international demand and price fluctuations. Cristina Kirchner's inability to control inflation rates, coupled with the imposition of import restrictions, has further alienated the Argentine middle classes. Tax impositions on the rural sector have antagonized business interests and led to an unlikely coalition against *kirchnerismo*, which has since resulted in political polarization and the collapse of the multi-class alliance originally foreseen by Néstor Kirchner (Wylde 2016).

In sum, without discarding the Marxist critique of Latin America's dependency on extractivism, the post-neoliberalism thesis seems to capture the complexity and heterogeneity of the Latin American left in a more nuanced way, beyond the liberal-democratic dichotomy of the moderate versus radical left. Far from merely facilitating the region's integration into global capitalism, the experience of the Latin American left can thus be seen as a crucial factor that advances the multipolarization of global politics at the expense of US global hegemony. Therefore, the remainder of this chapter shifts the focus from leftism to post-hegemonic regionalism led by Latin America's leftist governments: that is, ALBA and Unasur. These organizations will be examined in terms of the normative framework and institutional settings that have molded their development.

The ALBA experience of post-hegemonic regionalism

ALBA's emergence coincided with the rise of the Latin American left in the early 2000s. The idea of an ALBA-like regional cooperation was officially brought onto the agenda for the first time in the Integrated Cooperation Agreement signed by Cuba and Venezuela in 2000. The idea was then voiced by Hugo Chávez himself during the 2001 Summit of Caribbean Countries. State-level commitments to build a post-hegemonic institution were also supported by the continental movement against the Free Trade Area of the Americas among left-wing social movements and political parties struggling against neoliberalism. Ultimately, the joint involvement of Latin America's political- and social-movement left resulted in ALBA's official foundation in 2004. Nowadays, ALBA has 11 member states: Antigua and Barbuda, Bolivia, Cuba, Dominica, Ecuador, Grenada, Nicaragua, Saint Kitts and Nevis, Saint Lucia, Saint Vincent and the Grenadines, and Venezuela (Muhr 2013b).

The Presidential Council is the highest authority in ALBA's institutional structure. This structure also includes the Political Council of foreign ministers; the Economic Council of ministers of the economy, finance, trade, and development; the Social Council of ministers of social affairs in areas related to education, health, employment, and culture; and the Social Movements Council of anti-neoliberal and anti-imperialist social movements from member and non-member countries (unions and peasants' movements, international solidarity networks, gender movements, indigenous movements, development NGOs, environmentalists, and human rights advocacy groups). These councils are tasked with advising the Presidential Council in their respective areas. They also host the work of special area committees such as the Committee of Women and Equal Opportunities, the Committee for the Defence of Nature, and the Committee for Sovereignty and Defence (Borbón 2015, 78–79; Domínguez 2015, 245).

ALBA's normative framework

ALBA's regionalism draws its powerful symbolism from Latin America's rich history of struggle against colonialism and imperialism. The Spanish acronym for the Bolivarian Alliance for the Peoples of Our America, ALBA, means "dawn". The name refers to Simón Bolívar, the Venezuela-born liberator whose dream of uniting the entire Spanish-speaking Americas inspired generations of Latin American intellectuals and politicians. The choice of 'Our America' [*Nuestra América*] is also quite intentional, referring to the title of the famous essay written by José Martí, the intellectual forefather of Cuban independence, who promoted the cultural solidarity of Latin America in the face of emerging American imperialism in the late nineteenth century. Needless to say, out of the multiplicity of the interpretations associated with the legacies of Bolívar and Martí in Latin America (Dawson 2010), the leaders of these pioneering regional integration efforts select a specific historical lesson – one that advocates anti-imperialist pan-American solidarity. Similarly, *Patria Grande* constitutes an underlying slogan of ALBA regionalism. This is associated with the legacy of Simón Bolívar and Francisco de Miranda, Bolívar's antecedent as a military leader and revolutionary. Miranda participated in the French Revolution and in wars of independence against Spanish colonialism; he is regarded as the forefather of Latin American regionalism, having proposed the foundation of a Latin American federation in 1790 (Gürcan and Bakiner 2015; Gürcan 2010).

ALBA's anti-imperialism finds its sharpest expression in its claim for fair trade, juxtaposed to the free trade conception of multinationals and hegemonic global governance. Economic cooperation treaties signed under the ALBA system are called *Tratados de Comercio de los Pueblos* (TCPs, People's Trade Agreements) rather than conventional Free Trade Agreements. This semiotic shift aims to unsettle the identification of trade with profit maximization. Instead, the promoters of TCPs argue that the goal of trade should be to enhance the fair distribution of prosperity for all members of the participating societies. Likewise, multinational companies created under the ALBA system are called *grannacionales* (an approximate translation would be "great-nationals"), rather than "multinational" corporations. Accordingly, some observers associate ALBA's approach with the principle of "cooperative advantage" as the basis of mutual economic relations, rather than the comparative (and by corollary, competitive) advantage model advocated by standard economic theories (Artaraz 2012; Gürcan 2010; Gürcan and Bakiner 2015; Muhr 2013b).

The emphasis of ALBA's post-hegemonic regionalism on social justice and development is well reflected in its achievements, which can be summarized in a rather long list: the growth of literacy through targeted programs delivered to around 3 million people so far; the promotion of local development through *grannacionales*-supported social missions; the expansion of free public health services and the provision of scholarships for medical students with the active support of the Latin American School of Medicine; the development of autonomous cultural and communications networks free from the yoke of US imperialism and corporate media (e.g. teleSUR, ALBA TV, and ALBA Houses); the creation of a free trade network supported by a development bank and an autonomous currency free from the yoke of the US dollar (the ALBA Bank and *Sistema Unitario de Compensación Regional* (SUCRE: Unified System for Regional Compensation); the founding of a regional university network (ALBA Universities); the development of a post-hegemonic collective defense paradigm embodied in the ALBA School of Defense and Sovereignty; and the championing of food security and sovereignty.

However, despite ALBA's strong anti-imperialist discourse and emphasis on endogenous development, critical scholarship on the Latin American left does not portray a rosy picture of how this discourse has translated into policy making (e.g. Petras 2011; Veltmeyer and Petras 2014; Webber and Carr 2013; Robinson 2017). Faced with the challenge of extractivism, Latin America's post-hegemonic regionalism does not seem to have systematically tackled its contradictory results, which bring Latin American contender states closer to the dominant paradigm of neoliberal globalization through the pillage of natural resources, free trade, and high dependency on global markets. It is known that, although energy-related projects are essential for ALBA, ALBA has disregarded criticism by certain social movements about the potential environmental damage that could be induced by ALBA members' energy-related projects. A case in point is that of the South Gas Pipeline. This project was challenged by environmental organizations concerned about its reported damages to the Amazonian area; their concerns went unheard by ALBA (Serbin 2012, 158–159).

Therefore, extractivism is not merely important in terms of assessing the left's commitment to anti-imperialism and multipolarization. Its importance also comes from the relationship between extractivism and the left's commitment to indigenous rights and environmentalism, insofar as maintaining or enhancing the former leads to environmental degradation and the splintering of indigenous territories (Webber 2017a). Regarding the relationship between extractivism and Latin American post-hegemonic regionalism, most of ALBA's projects are funded through Venezuela's petrodollars (Yeates 2014, 35; Riggirozzi 2012, 29). Venezuelan petrodollars have assumed a key role both in funding ALBA and in keeping the ALBA countries together. The centrality of Venezuelan petrodollars is shown in the fact that as much as 71.5% of Venezuela's transfers, investments, and grants to ALBA members and other countries are estimated to have originated from the resources of *Petróleos de Venezuela, S. A.* (PDVSA) and the sale of discounted oil in various forms (Borbón 2015, 80–81; Riggirozzi 2012).

Empirical evidence on extractivism reveals the severity of this situation. Extractivism can be briefly defined as "the super-exploitation of natural resources and the export of primary goods – hydrocarbons, metals and minerals, agricultural produce and biofuels – on a vast scale" (Webber 2017a, 157). Accordingly, to assess extractivism, one can use World Bank data to calculate the sum of agricultural raw materials, fuel, and ore and metal exports. Looking at the data for Bolivia, its share of extractivist exports in total exports increased from 67.9% in 2005 (the year of Evo Morales' electoral victory) to 77.4% in 2015. The performance of Venezuela, the leader of ALBA regionalism, worsened from 77.6% in 1998 to over 98% in 2015. The case of Brazil – the leader of post-hegemonic regionalism in Latin America – is equally revealing. Although Brazil is known as a global biofuel producer, biofuels exports are not included in these calculations due to data unavailability. However, biofuels are not Brazil's sole extractivist sector: it is also regarded as a world leader in the soybean trade. Therefore, Brazil's exports in raw materials reflect the general extractivist trend on its part. Brazil's rates soared from 17.3% in 2002 to 22.7% in 2015 (World Bank 2016). Certainly, these trends impede economic diversification, render extractivist countries extremely vulnerable to the fluctuation of global prices, and eventually weaken the popular base of leftist governments by fostering economic stagnation in the long run.

Another factor that further complicates Latin America's excessive dependency on extractivism is China's increasing engagement in the region. Unarguably, the Latin American economy has greatly benefited from China's involvement, especially since the 2010s (Bárcena et al. 2015). China has become Latin America's second-largest import source and third-largest export destination. However, China also seems to amplify Latin America's extractivism due to the region's "clear commodity bias in exports to that country [which] hinders attempts by the region's governments to move towards a more diversified, knowledge-intensive and socially and environmentally sustainable productive and export structure" (Bárcena et al. 2015, 48). Latin America's top five exports to China were iron ores, soy, copper, unrefined petroleum, and copper ores, which amounted to as much as 69.7% of this region's total exports to China in the 2010–2014 period (Barragán and Castillo 2017). Moreover, Latin America has become a popular destination for China's foreign direct investment. Chinese investment amounted to $7,342,000,000 to over $7.3 billion in the 1990–2009 period. However, in 2010 alone this rose to $13,712,000,000 over $13.7 billion. Worthy of emphasis here is that most of China's investment in the region concentrates on oil, mining and gas, which leads to severe socio-environmental conflicts (Bárcena et al. 2015). In fact, China's status as both the leading force in the multipolarization of world politics at the expense of US global hegemony and an instigator of extractivism in Latin America reflects the post-hegemonic character of contemporary transformations in world politics.

ALBA's post-hegemonic institutional setting

ALBA has created innovatory mechanisms to advance a post-hegemonic agenda, including *grannacionales*-supported social missions, new financial instruments as alternatives to hegemonic institutions such as the International Monetary Fund and World Bank, alternative media and education networks, and anti-imperialist defense schools. Based on the geopolitical economy framework, it is possible to argue that the creation of these alternative governance institutions presents a multifrontal challenge to US hegemony in the areas of international development, communication, cultural integration, civil society, education, and security. In the area of international development, ALBA's social missions were adapted from Chávista practices of state-supported local development in Venezuela. Venezuelan social missions are basically welfare programs that aim to reduce poverty, increase food security, improve housing, expand public health services, and promote education. By 2010, ALBA Caribe Fund had allocated around $15.4 million across 84 development projects in 11 different countries. ALBA's most acclaimed missions are *¡Yo, Sí Puedo!* ("Yes, I can!") and Milagro. The Milagro Mission, led by Cuban oculists, has reached 1.54 million patients since 2005. *¡Yo, Sí Puedo!*, meanwhile, has developed its own literacy program and adapted it to 14 different cultural contexts in 28 countries. By 2009, over 3.8 million illiterate people had benefited from the program (Hirst and Sabatini 2015; Muhr 2010; Muhr 2013a).

ALBA's development agenda of fair trade has been sustained through a number of post-hegemonic mechanisms such as *grannacionales*, ALBA Bank, and SUCRE. The ALBA vision of development and fair trade draws on the principles of solidarity, complementarity, cooperation, mutual interest, and peoples' sovereignty. Within this framework, ALBA has created several *grannacionales* in strategic areas such as food, the environment, science and technology, energy, industry and mining, health, communication, transportation, and tourism. *Grannacionales* are state-owned corporations that are allowed to cooperate with private corporations. From the point of view of geopolitical economy, these institutions have a potential to curb the power of US-backed multinational corporations because their corporate decisions are made by a board of representatives from member states (Gürcan and Bakiner 2015).

The ALBA Bank was initiated in 2008 as an alternative to the US-led International Monetary Fund and World Bank. It had an initial capital of $1 billion, 85% of which was provided by Venezuela itself. ALBA Bank's main responsibilities are funding social missions; *grannacionales*; and infrastructural, commercial, and productive investments (Borbón 2015; Hirst and Sabatini 2015). ALBA's financial structure is complemented by the SUCRE system, which seeks to push Latin America away from the yoke of the US dollar and relieve the obligation of ALBA states to accumulate US dollars for their import needs. Therefore, this system is designed to eventually weaken Latin America's dependence on the US economy. In 2014 alone, the ALBA zone saw over 5000 SUCRE transactions with a total worth of $2 billion. Estimates suggest that SUCRE transactions account for almost half of current Venezuelan–Ecuadorian trade. SUCRE also coexists with ALBA's own barter system, which is mostly used in the barter of Venezuelan oil with other export items. For example, Dominica provides Venezuela with English books, expertise in natural resources, and tourism services in return for oil. Oil has always been part of ALBA solidarity practices, which find their strongest expression in how the payment period of 50% to 60% of Petrocaribe's oil sales has been extended to 25 years with a two-year grace period and low-interest credit (Azzellini 2016; López and Lo Brutto 2016).

The media power that ALBA has developed serves as a major catalyst in the post-hegemonic integration of the entire region, and is particularly relevant for the manifestation of multipolarization and hegemonic struggles from a geopolitical economy perspective. To understand the significance of ALBA's media initiative, it is vital to note that prior to the 2000s, Latin American media was characterized by high levels of concentration of ownership and content importation. In 1996, according to Salö (2007), only 6% of audio-visual imports in Latin America originated from within the region, while 86% of the imports came from the US. By 1998, the percentage of TV programs coming from the region had reached 30%. TeleSUR was launched in 2005 in reaction to the media hegemony of CNN, NBC, Univision, and Fox News, which together controlled 85% of the news sector in Latin America. At the time, TeleSUR was jointly owned by Venezuela (51%), Argentina (20%), Cuba (19%), and Uruguay (10%) (Guerra 2012; Macpherson 2006). The channel emerged with the slogan of "Our North is the South" along with an advisory board that included Nobel Peace Prize-winner Adolfo Pérez Esquivel, writer Tariq Ali, Free Software Foundation creator Richard Stallman, and actor Danny Glover. In line with its post-hegemonic thrust in the field of cultural integration, teleSUR's programming included programs that aimed at creating a shared imaginary of Latin America by hosting artists from the region, featuring local traditions and customs, and broadcasting films and documentaries (Gürcan 2010; Gürcan and Bakiner 2015).

Grannacionales were also involved in ALBA's attempts at cultural integration. Founded in 2008, ALBA Cultural offered programs that promoted fine arts, literature, and radio and television. Special support was provided for creating a movie sector that could confront US propaganda. Similarly, ALBA Audiovisual supported Venezuela's *Villa del Cine* with the aim of promoting a national cinema. ALBA's cinematic sector was also represented by Venezuela's Amazonia Films, *Red de Distribución y Exhibición Audiovisual* (Network of Audiovisual Distribution and Exhibition) with branches in several countries, and Cuba's Alternative Network of Audiovisual Production. Similarly, ALBA Culture hosted audiovisual training workshops in Bolivia and international movie production workshops in Ecuador. In addition, ALBA's Audiovisual Production Plan facilitated the creation and diffusion of short movies and documentaries. Besides these activities, ALBA has twice organized Olympic games in Cuba and has hosted several festivals, award ceremonies, and exhibitions (Villazana 2013).

Besides *grannacionales*-supported social missions, new financial support instruments, and alternative media networks, ALBA's innovatory mechanisms include the Council of Social Movements. This council supports the work of the Council of Presidents and Council of Ministers in deepening the cooperation process. Aside from ALBA's internal functioning, the Council of Social Movements functions as a counter-hegemonic vehicle tasked with infusing ALBA's agenda of regional cooperation into civil society and influencing ALBA's own agenda in line with the aspirations of left-wing movements. The council is responsible for presenting its proposals and projects to the Council of Presidents and evaluating the work of the latter, as well as assisting the work of the *grannacionales.* In many respects, the Council of Social Movements has emerged as the catalyst for a regional norm-creation effort (horizontalism, inclusion, complementarity, cooperation, solidarity, coexistence, direct and participatory democracy, social justice, and equity) that aims to eradicate the exclusionary legacy of neoliberalism in the continent. The Council of Social Movements affirms that its main task is to contribute to the development of common agendas for the benefit of the people, in addition to the implementation of a new development paradigm relying on the principles of participation and assistance through social movements (Gürcan 2010; Gürcan and Bakiner 2015). In practice, however, this council is undermined by weak institutionalization: "the relationship between social organizations and ALBA's decision-making bodies and implementation of social programs (social missions) remain vague" (Serbin 2012, 162).

Another bottom-up initiative parallel to the Council of Social Movements has been the *Articulación de Movimientos Sociales hacia el ALBA* (AMSA: Coordination of Social Movements towards ALBA). This is said to involve critical social movements from 28 Latin American countries, including the *Movimento dos Trabalhadores Rurais Sem Terra* (Landless Rural Workers' Movement), *Frente Popular Darío Santillán* (Darío Santillán Popular Front), *Organización de Solidaridad con los Pueblos de Asia, África y América Latina* (Organization in Solidarity with the People of Africa, Asia, and Latin America), *Vía Campesina, Coordinador Nacional Agrario de Colombia* (National Agrarian Coordinator), *Movimiento de Liberación Nacional* (National Liberation Movement of Mexico), *Movimiento de Campesinos de Santiago del Estero* (Santiago del Estero Peasant Movement), *Central de los Trabajadores de Argentina* (Workers' Center of Argentina), and *Movimiento Campesino Paraguayo* (Paraguayan Peasant Movement). Most of these movements represented the backbone of the historic struggle against the Free Trade Area of the Americas, which eventually culminated in the emergence of ALBA (AMSA 2012a, 2012b).

AMSA defines itself as a regional initiative made up of critical social movements that are driven by such values as anti-imperialism, anti-neoliberalism, anti-patriarchalism, equality, freedom, and emancipation. AMSA's primary task has been to build broad and permanent networks of solidarity, dialogue, and exchange among Latin America's leftist movements. Relatedly, AMSA has also been interested in producing a collective voice within social forums. AMSA itself formulates its concrete tasks as follows: the struggle against militarization, military bases, the criminalization of social protest and the aggressions of the empire; the battle against multinational companies, privatization and denationalization; confronting the climate crisis and protecting the rights of Mother Earth, the rights of indigenous peoples of Our America and the struggle for living well; and international solidarity among various peoples (AMSA 2012a, 2012b). Therefore, AMSA takes part in regional activism and mobilization on a wide range of issues, including the struggle against the Canadian mining industry, solidarity with the Paraguayan people after the impeachment of President Fernando Lugo, advocacy of women's rights (such as the legalization of abortion, respect for the women's body, and gender equality), and the struggle against the commodification of life (Martinez 2013).

For ALBA, education constitutes an area of primary importance for the post-hegemonic transformation of the region, as is clearly reflected in the 2009 Declaration of Managua for the Educative Union of ALBA. The declaration considers education to be a crucial means for consciousness-raising and mobilization against neoliberalism. The declaration highlights two major tasks to promote the post-hegemonic production of knowledge. First, the eradication of illiteracy and promotion of post-literacy processes by internationalist brigades. Second, the establishment of a regional structure of undergraduate and graduate education that prioritizes such areas as geopolitics, sciences of education, food sovereignty, and hydrocarbons, based on common curriculum projects and new information technologies. In 2009 alone, close to 14,000 students benefited from ALBA's higher-education programs (Muhr 2010; Gürcan 2010; Gürcan and Bakiner 2015). The Third Meeting of the Council of Ministers of Social Areas, held in the city of Cochabamba on 19 March 2011, approved a new financing of $25 million for the eradication of illiteracy and promotion of post-literacy processes in the region. One should note that projects addressing educational problems were not only developed by the presidents of member countries, but were also shaped through public discussions involving numerous scholars, teachers, and students. An example is the University International Conference that took place in Havana on 12 February 2010: it brought grassroots actors together with 15 ministers, 12 deputy ministers, and 213 university directors. Similarly, the Third Workshop on Education for ALBA, held on 14–15 April 2010 in Caracas, laid emphasis on the need to counter the capitalist-elitist paradigm of higher education that fails to comprehend the real needs of the people (Muhr 2010; Gürcan 2010; Gürcan and Bakiner 2015).

Concrete steps have been taken toward the creation of a common curriculum in the ALBA area. According to Arturo Collado, the Secretary of the *Consejo Nacional de Universidades de Nicaragu*a (National Council of Universities of Nicaragua), the initiative of the *Red de Universidades de los Pueblos del ALBA* (UNIALBA: Network of Universities of the Peoples of ALBA) has led to cooperation in more than 33 areas, including food security, healthcare, scientific development, and environmental protection. In the context of UNIALBA, Cuba designed graduate programs in informatics for Venezuela, Bolivia, Ecuador, and Nicaragua. By 2012, Nicaraguan universities had gained accreditation in both Ecuador and Venezuela (Muhr 2010; Gürcan 2010; Gürcan and Bakiner 2015).

Unlike traditional regionalist institutions, ALBA seems to lay greater emphasis on social justice than on economic and military integrationism. However, ALBA's attempts at regional defense cooperation are also worth mentioning. From the lens of geopolitical economy, the defining feature of ALBA's defense policies lies in their post-hegemonic thrust that challenges US hegemony in Latin America. In 2009, Evo Morales affirmed ALBA's need to develop a closer interest in regional defense and to create a collective defense doctrine. Ultimately, in 2011, the ALBA Defence School opened its doors in the Bolivian city of Santa Cruz with the active support of Iran. The founding of this school cost $1.8 million, and its classroom and dormitory facilities cover an area of 5400 square meters (Manaut and Diamint 2015). At the school's opening ceremony, Morales drew attention to the importance of Latin America's regional defense against the "imperialist threats that seek to divide Latin America". He stated that "peoples of the ALBA-TCP are being besieged, sanctioned and punished by the imperial arrogance just because we are exerting the right of being decent and sovereign … We may not allow that the history of colonization repeats and that our resources are the loot of the empire" (AINS 2011). Morales always had Hugo Chávez's support for regional military cooperation. Chávez was convinced that ALBA needed a NATO-like institution and military school to counter US aggression.

However, in its current form, the ALBA School of Defence does not pursue the NATO model of military cooperation. Instead, the school champions the Chavista doctrine of "civil–military alliance" and the asymmetric warfare concept drawn from the philosophy of Jorge Verstrynge (2014). In this direction, the School also offers semi-official training programs targeting civil elements such as peasant and indigenous communities (Adams and Gunson 2015; Hirst and Sabatini 2015; Manaut and Diamint 2015).

The Unasur experience of post-hegemonic regionalism

ALBA is not the only instance of thriving post-hegemonic regionalism Latin America. The Unasur experience is as important in this regard as ALBA, although Unasur's development has followed a relatively slower, more silent, and protracted time course (Riggirozzi 2012). Overall, Unasur can be seen as an "outgrowth" of the Brazil-led *Comunidad Sudamericana de Naciones* (CSN: Community of South American Nations), which was created in 2004 as an extension of the Andean Community and Mercosur (Bennett 2008; Briceño-Ruiz, 2010). In the language of geopolitical economy, Unasur epitomizes Brazil's hegemonic leadership as a "contender state" that seeks to debilitate US hegemonism in Latin America. However, this leadership initiative differs in form from the ALBA experience in that "ALBA is explicitly critical and, therefore, proposes a new start from a novel background, whereas UNASUR aspires to the convergence of the already existing processes to the new and broader one" (DerGhougassian 2015, 165). In ALBA, the "mortar" that holds its constituents together is a socialistic ideology that attributes an active role to the state in managing the economy, whereas Unasur's common identity is characterized by a broad claim to South American citizenship, human rights and democracy, and a more "balanced" role between the state and the market (DerGhougassian 2015). Moreover, Venezuela and Brazil's earlier perception of Latin America differed in that Chávez's Bolivarianism conceived of Latin America as a single nation, which contradicts Unasur's emphasis on Latin American "nations" (Briceño-Ruiz 2010). This situation may also reflect a conflict of "different hegemonic visions and national interests between Brazil's and Venezuela's leadership aspirations" (DerGhougassian 2015, 178).

Yet in the final analysis, the similarities seem to outweigh the differences. Both ALBA and Unasur are committed to a shared agenda of policy priorities other than free trade and economic integration, including national sovereignty, social development, regional security, health, and infrastructure. Geopolitically speaking, both projects reject US-led governance structures in favour of the multipolarization of global politics, although Unasur seems to prioritize a policy of remedying the liberal governance system while ALBA insists on abandoning liberal governance itself. In the event, ideological differences have not impeded peaceful coexistence and sustained cooperation between Venezuela and Brazil (DerGhougassian 2015).

Unasur's normative framework

Unasur's defining objectives are portrayed as the construction of "a South American identity and citizenship" and the development of "an integrated regional space in the political, economic, social, cultural, environmental, energy and infrastructure dimensions" (Unasur 2008, Preamble, para. 3). Unasur's Constitutive Treaty was signed in 2008: it makes special reference to the importance of multilateralism and international law in the name of a multipolar world order. The Constitutive Treaty enumerates Unasur's founding principles as: respect for national sovereignty and territorial integrity, the right of peoples to self-determination, solidarity, cooperation, peace, democracy, citizen participation and pluralism, universal human rights, mutual dependence, fighting inequalities, and sustainable development (DerGhougassian 2015). From the point of view of geopolitical economy, Unasur's Constitutive Treaty implicitly defies US hegemonism in the global political economy by referring to socioeconomic inequalities and national sovereignty. It essentially targets the neoliberal model of downsizing the state and offering concessions to global capitalism. However, Unasur's constitutive claim to citizen participation still remains controversial in the absence of institutionalized spaces for civil society participation. In fact, CSN, Unasur's predecessor, had established special mechanisms to promote civil society participation and advocacy. CSN's Social Summits were held prior to intergovernmental summits and included forum debates, workshops, and other related events participated in by governments and civil society groups. However, Social Summits were discontinued upon Unasur's creation (Serbin 2012).

Instead, Unasur lays greater emphasis on presidential-level decision-making in view of the potentially constraining effect of bureaucracy on regional cooperation. This being said, one should not ignore Unasur's bureaucratic advances in its institutionalization. The highest authority within Unasur is the Council of Heads of State and Government, under which there exist various councils including the Council of Ministers of External Relationships, Council of Social Development, Health Council, Council of Delegates, Defense Council, and Energy Council. Moreover, Unasur has a general secretariat and several working groups (DerGhougassian 2015).

Unasur's post-hegemonic institutional setting

Unasur's post-hegemonic mechanisms include the Defense Council, the Initiative for the Integration of Regional Infrastructure in South America (IIRSA), and the Health Council. With reference to the geopolitical-economic concern with multipolarization and US hegemonism, the Defense Council is a strong expression of Unasur's post-hegemonic thrust that indirectly challenges US military power in Latin America. Although no anti-US bias has been voiced by Unasur, the Defense Council originates from Brazil's frustrations about US interventionism in the form of the US wars on drugs and terrorism. For example, Brazil explicitly voiced its concerns about Plan Colombia, a US-funded plan to fight drugs and terrorism through military, financial, and diplomatic means; as well as the 2008 reactivation of the US Fourth Fleet that operates in the Caribbean, Central American, and South American regions. The 2009 US–Colombia deal, which involved the deployment of US troops and surveillance systems, created similar concerns on Brazil's part. Brazil believed that Colombia could be used as a base to increase the US military presence in the region. Brazil was also concerned that the US could invade the Amazonia in order to control its vast natural resources (Battaglino 2012).

However, the Defense Council does not draw on the NATO model of military expansionism and aggression. Its primary objectives are rather to prevent foreign intervention and settle territorial disputes. It is also involved in fighting cross-border smuggling and protecting natural resources from foreign threats. In the meantime, the Defense Council seeks to develop a collective security concept that could counter the influence of foreign concepts such as the war on drugs. It also aims to promote region-wide military cooperation by seeking to build endogenous capacities in military industry and weapons technology, and promoting the formation of a regional defense community of political officials and state bureaucracies. Conceived as such, it can be said that the Defense Council undermines the authority of the Inter-American Defense Board of the Organization of American States, which is associated with US leadership in the Americas. In 2011, the Defense Council founded a think tank based in Buenos Aires named the Center for Strategic Defense Studies . The Center publishes annual reports on Unasur's short-term defense strategies. The objectives identified by the 2014 report include the creation of a database on military expenditure trends and resources in South America, examination of the relationship between gender and defense, improvement of cyber-security, opening of the Center's branches in other countries, and organization of conferences and seminars (Briceño-Ruiz and Hoffmann 2015; Manaut and Diamint 2015; Battaglino 2012). Similarly, the Defense Council's plan for 2010–2011 included the following:

> (1) development of a digital network that serves to exchange information on defence policies; (2) organization of a combined peacekeeping regional exercise in 2011 to promote military interoperability, also on the table is the possible creation of an inventory of national defence capabilities to support humanitarian operations; (3) construction of a database containing information on military and civilian defence specialist training centres in order to establish a network of academic centres in member countries; (4) and finally the development of a South American Defence training programme.
>
> (Battaglino 2012, 96–97)

Alongside regional defense, infrastructural development is a priority area in Unasur's agenda. Viewed from the angle of geopolitical economy, this initiative was intended to cause a significant blow to US financial monopoly in international development by laying greater emphasis on long-term development goals that could geo-economically benefit the creation of an internal regional market dominated by regional hegemons such as Brazil. In this context, the IIRSA has been taken over by Unasur. This initiative was originally proposed by Brazil in the 2000 South American Summit: it seeks to connect the region by developing its infrastructure of international transportation. Having initiated several investment projects to build roads, bridges, and border crossings, the IIRSA has so far produced a total of $96 billion in investments and 524 construction projects. Unasur also founded the Bank of the South (BancoSur) in order to fund these investment initiatives and promote other development projects independently of US-led financial structures. In 2007, this bank was expected to have an initial capital of $20 billion. Its expected year of operationalization was 2017 (Ganem 2015; Carciofi 2012; Gürcan 2010; Gürcan and Bakiner 2015).

Another area in which Unasur has progressed is health. Created in 2009, Unasur's Health Council seeks to improve public health services and to liberate pharmaceutical production and distribution from the yoke of multinational companies. It also has the conventional objectives of disease control and training health personnel. The Health Council has been building expert networks in order to facilitate research in critical areas such as HIV and cancer, and to coordinate the exchange of knowledge and training opportunities in the Unasur zone. With the aim of liberating the pharmaceutical industry, the Council has created databases, developed common mechanisms of price negotiation and production, and built a pharmaceutical monopoly against multinational rule. Attempts to institute an autonomous pharmaceutical sector are closely coordinated with the Defense Council (Briceño-Ruiz and Hoffmann 2015; Riggirozzi 2014, 2016).

The Health Council is home to the South American Institute of Government in Health, which is tasked with assisting the Council in fulfilling its objectives. The Institute's 2013 budget was estimated at $2.5 million. The Institute expresses a socialistic vision of public health, which conceives of public health as a universal right that cannot be left to the mercy of free-market mechanisms. It highlights the social determinants of health and acknowledges the intimate relationship between social inequality and well-being (Briceño-Ruiz and Hoffmann 2015; Riggirozzi 2014, 2016).

Finally, Unasur's health activities coincide with disaster relief initiatives and sustainable agriculture. Unasur provided Haiti with substantial assistance following the 2010 Haiti earthquake, including $100 million in assistance for 144 different relief projects as well as medical materials and equipment to fight against cholera. Unasur support was also involved in the provision of training in low-input sustainable agriculture for Haitian farmers within the framework of the Pro Huerta project (Riggirozzi 2016).

Review and discussion

ALBA has done more than just create a strong politico-cultural imaginary of Latin American solidarity: it has also succeeded in translating these ideals into practice. The ALBA experience, founded on a post-hegemonic normative structure centered on social justice, social developmentalism, and anti-imperialism, reveals that regionalism can be turned into a powerful weapon to undo the socioeconomic disasters caused by neoliberalism. Meanwhile, Unasur's experience draws attention to the fact that regionalism is not necessarily confined to free trade and economic cooperation. It also has tremendous potential to create long-term and lasting results in other critical areas such as health, social development, and culture. ALBA and Unasur have added a new dimension to South–South cooperation and post-hegemonic regionalism via the creation of stable channels for social movement participation in regionalism, alternative media outlets, anti-corporate development enterprises and autonomous pharmaceutical industries, development banks, and mechanisms of asymmetric military cooperation. Military cooperation, and the promotion of the concept of asymmetric warfare, could be regarded as important achievements of Latin America's post-hegemonic regionalism at the expense of US hegemony in the region. However, the mere formulation of a collective defense strategy and the creation of a defense school do not seem to suffice for fully deterring US aggression in Latin America. What appears to be missing is any tangible attempt to create stable military arrangements and an integrated command structure to implement the already devised collective defense concept in the region.

Despite tangible advances in Latin America's post-hegemonic regionalism, the sustainability of these regionalist practices is still open to debate. The development of Latin America's post-hegemonic regionalism under presidential initiatives has overshadowed bureaucratic institutionalization. Simple changes of government and the replacement of charismatic left-wing presidents by right-wing alternatives might reverse the hard-won advances of regionalism since the early 2000s. The ALBA experience is closely associated with the names of Hugo Chávez, Evo Morales, Rafael Correa, and Daniel Ortega, and Chávez's passing in 2015 has already slowed down the pace of ALBA cooperation. Similarly, the rightward shift in Argentine and Brazilian politics since 2015 has adversely affected Unasur cooperation. The continental rightward shift has illustrated the fragility of Latin America's post-hegemonic regionalism due to its excessive reliance on charismatic leaders and dependence on extractivism. In particular, extractivism relates to the left's failure to make a definitive break with neoliberalism.

References

Adams, David and Phil Gunson. 2015. "Chávez and ALBA." In *Decline of the U.S. Hegemony?: A Challenge of ALBA and a New Latin American Integration of the 21st Century*, edited by B. M. Bagley and M. Defort, 33–42. Lanham: Lexington Books.

AINS. 2011. ALBA School of Defense and Sovereignty Opens. *Anti-Imperialist-News-Service*, June 14. http://www.anti-imperialist.org/alba-school-of-defense-opens_6-14-11.htm

AMSA. 2012a. *Movilización* [*Mobilization*]. Articulación de Movimientos Sociales hacia el ALBA (Coordination of Social Movements Towards ALBA). http://www.albamovimientos.org/category/movilizacion

AMSA. 2012b. *Periódico del ALBA de los Movimientos Sociales hacia la Cumbre de los Pueblos*. http://www.albamovimientos.org/2012/06/periodico-del-alba-de-los-movimientos-sociales-hacia-la-cumbre-de-los-pueblos/ [no longer available online].

Artaraz, Kepa. 2012. "Cuba's Internationalism Revisited: Exporting Literacy, ALBA, and a New Paradigm for South–South Collaboration." *Bulletin of Latin American Research*, 31(s1): 22–37.

Azzellini, Dario. 2016. "ALBA-TCP: Building Solidarity and Autonomy Among Nations." *NACLA Report on the Americas*, 47(3): 47.

Ballvé, Teo. 2006. "From Resistance to Offensive: NACLA and Latin America." In *Dispatches From Latin America*, edited by V. Prashad and T. Ballvé, 23–34. New Delhi: LeftWord Books.

Bárcena, Alicia, Antonio Prado, Osvaldo Rosales, and Ricardo Pérez. 2015. *Latin America and the Caribbean and China: Towards a New Era in Economic Cooperation*. Santiago: United Nations Economic Commission for Latin America and the Caribbean.

Barker, Robert L. 2003. *The Social Work Dictionary*. Washington, DC: NASW Press.

Barragán, Juan Manuel Gil and Andrés Aguilera Castillo. 2017. "China and Latin America: Strategic partners or competitors?" *Revista Escuela de Administración de Negocios*, 82(1): 73–90.

Barrett, Patrick, Daniel Chávez, and Cesar Rodriguez-Garavito, eds. 2008. *The New Latin American Left: Utopia Reborn*. London: Pluto Press.

Battaglino, Jorge. 2012. "Defence in a Post-Hegemonic Regional Agenda: The Case of the South American Defence Council." In *The Rise of Post-Hegemonic Regionalism: The Case of Latin America*, edited by M. P. Riggirozzi and D. Tussie, 81–100. New York: Springer.

Beasley-Murray, Jon, Maxwell Cameron, and Eric Hershberg. 2010. "Latin America's Left Turns: A Tour d'Horizon." In *Latin America's Left Turns: Politics, Policies, and Trajectories of Change*, edited by M. Cameron and E. Hershberg, 1–22. Boulder and London: Lynne Rienner.

Bennett, Jackson. 2008. "The Union of South American Nations: The Newest Regionalism in Latin America." *Suffolk Transnational Law Review*, 32(1): 103–133.

Borbón, Josette Altmann. 2015. "ALBA: Ideology Overcomes Integration?" In *Decline of the U.S. Hegemony?: A Challenge of ALBA and a New Latin American Integration of the 21st Century*, edited by B. M. Bagley and M. Defort, 67–98. Lanham: Lexington Books.

Briceño-Ruiz, José. 2010. "From the South American Free Trade Area to the Union of South American Nations: The Transformations of a Rising Regional Process." *Latin American Policy*, 1(2): 208–229.

Briceño-Ruiz, José and Andrea Ribeiro Hoffmann. 2015. "Post-Hegemonic Regionalism, UNASUR, and the Reconfiguration of Regional Cooperation in South America." *Canadian Journal of Latin American and Caribbean Studies*, 40(1): 48–62.

Burbach, Roger, Michael Fox, and Federico Fuentes. 2013. *Latin America's Turbulent Transitions*. London: Zed Books.

Cameron, Maxwell A. and Kenneth E. Sharpe. 2010. "Andean Left Turns: Constituent Power and Constitution-Making." In *Latin America's Left Turns: Politics, Policies and Trajectories of Change*, edited by M. A. Cameron and E. Hershberg, 61–80. Boulder: Lynne Rienner.

Carciofi, Ricardo. 2012. "Cooperation for the Provision of Regional Public Goods: The IIRSA Case." In *The Rise of Post-Hegemonic Regionalism: The Case of Latin America*, edited by P. Riggirozzi and D. Tussie, 65–80. New York: Springer.
Castañeda, Jorge. 2006. "Latin America's Left Turn." *Foreign Affairs*, 85(3): 28–43.
Castañeda, Jorge. 2008. "Where Do We Go from Here?" In *Leftovers: Tales of the Latin American Left*, edited by J. Castañeda and M. Morales, 231–243. New York: Routledge.
Castañeda, Jorge and Marco Morales. 2008. "The Current State of the Utopia." In *Leftovers: Tales of the Latin American Left*, edited by J. Castañeda and M. Morales, 3–18. New York: Routledge.
Castorina, Emilia. 2014. "The Reproduction of Democratic Neoliberalism in Argentina." In *Crisis and Contradiction: Marxist Perspectives on Latin America in the Global Political Economy*, edited by Susan J. Spronk and J. R. Webber, 73–97. Leiden: Brill.
Dawson, Alexander. 2010. *Latin America Since Independence: A History with Primary Sources*. New York: Routledge.
DerGhougassian, Khatchik. 2015. "The Post-Washington Consensus Regional Integration in South America: Convergence and Divergence in ALBA and UNASUR: A Comparative Perspective." In *Decline of the U.S. Hegemony?: A Challenge of ALBA and a New Latin American Integration of the 21st Century*, edited by B. M. Bagley and M. Defort, 159–184. Lanham: Lexington Books.
Domínguez, Roberto. 2015. "ALBA and Economic Regionalization in Latin America." In *Decline of the U.S. Hegemony?: A Challenge of ALBA and a New Latin American Integration of the 21st Century*, edited by B. M. Bagley and M. Defort, 237–258. Lanham: Lexington Books.
Ellner, Steve. 2014. "Complexities of the Twenty-first Century Radical Left in Power." In *Latin America's Radical Left: Challenges and Complexities of Political Power in the Twenty-first Century*, edited by S. Ellner, 1–22. Lanham: Rowman & Littlefield.
Flacks, Richard. 1988. *Making History: The American Left and the American Mind*. New York: Columbia University Press.
Ganem, Marcela. 2015. "UNASUR: Constructing the South American Identity." In *Decline of the U.S. Hegemony?: A Challenge of ALBA and a New Latin American Integration of the 21st Century*, edited by B. M. Bagley and M. Defort, 203–222. Lanham: Lexington Books.
Grugel, Jean and Maria Pia Riggirozzi. 2012. "Post-Neoliberalism in Latin America: Rebuilding and Reclaiming the State after Crisis." *Development and Change*, 43(1): 1–21.
Guerra, Antonio Tinoco. 2012. "La Integración Cultural: Una Propuesta para América Latina [Cultural Integration: A Proposal for Latin America]." *Nueva Politica*, 1: 11–25.
Gürcan, Efe Can. 2010. "New Regionalisms and Radical Identity Formation in Latin America." *Journal of Social Research and Policy*, 1(2): 19–33.
Gürcan, Efe Can. 2013. "National-Democratic Struggle and Contradictions of Venezuelan Socialism." *Dialectical Anthropology*, 37(3): 341–356.
Gürcan, Efe Can and Bakiner, Onur. 2015. "Beyond Neoliberal Hegemony in Latin America: Alianza Bolivariana para los Pueblos de Nuestra América ALBA." In *Gramsci and Foucault: A Reassessment*, edited by D. Kreps, 131–153. Farnham: Ashgate.
Hilfer, Tony. 2014. *American Fiction Since 1940*. New York: Routledge.

Hirst, Joel D. and Christopher Sabatini. 2015. "A guide to ALBA: What Is the Bolivarian Alternative to the Americas?" In *Decline of the U.S. Hegemony?: A Challenge of ALBA and a New Latin American Integration of the 21st Century*, edited by B. M. Bagley and M. Defort. Lanham: Lexington Books.

IMF. 2017. Indices of Primary Commodity Prices. Washington, DC: International Monetary Fund. http://www.imf.org/external/np/res/commod/Charts.pdf

Katz, Claudio. 2005. "Real and Imaginary Bourgeoisies." *International Socialism*, 160. http://isj.org.uk/real-and-imaginary-bourgeoisies/

Levitsky, Steven and Kenneth M. Roberts. 2011a. "Democracy, Development, and the Left." In *The Resurgence of the Latin American Left*, edited by S. Levitsky and K. M. Roberts, 399–428. Baltimore: John Hopkins University Press.

Levitsky, Steven and Kenneth M. Roberts. 2011b. "Latin America's 'Left Turn': A Framework for Analysis." In *The Resurgence of the Latin American Left*, edited by S. Levitsky and K. M. Roberts, 3–30. Baltimore: Johns Hopkins University Press.

Lievesley, Geraldine and Steve Ludlam. 2009. "Introduction: A 'Pink Tide'?" In *Reclaiming Latin America: Experiments in Radical Social Democracy*, edited by G. Lievesley and S. Ludlam, 1–20. London and New York: Zed Books.

López, Liza Elena Aceves and Guiseppe Lo Brutto. 2016. "Popular Power and Regional Integration: An Analysis of the ALBA-TCP." In *Popular Sovereignty and Constituent Power in Latin America*, edited by E. Betances and C. F. Ibarra, 183–202. New York: Palgrave Macmillan.

Luna, Juan Pablo and Cristóbal Rovira Kaltwasser. 2014. "The Right in Contemporary Latin America." In *The Resilience of the Latin American Right*, edited by J. P. Luna and C. R. Kaltwasser, 1–24. Baltimore: Johns Hopkins University Press.

Lynch, Nicolás. 2007. "What the 'Left' Means in Latin America Now." *Constellations*, 14(3): 373–383.

Macdonald, Laura and Arne Ruckert. 2009. "Post-Neoliberalism in the Americas: An Introduction." In *Post-Neoliberalism in the Americas*, edited by L. Macdonald and A. Ruckert, 1–20. New York: Palgrave Macmillan.

Macpherson, Sholto. 2006. "Interview with Aram Aharonian, Director General of teleSUR." *New Internationalist*, January 2. https://newint.org/columns/makingwaves/2006/01/01/aram-aharonian

Madrid, Raúl L., Wendy Hunter, and Kurt Weyland. 2010. "The Policies and Performance of the Contestatory and Moderate Left." In *Leftist Governments in Latin America: Successes and Shortcomings*, edited by K. Weyland, R. L. Madrid, and W. Hunter, 140–180. New York: Cambridge University Press.

Manaut, Raúl Benítez and Rut Diamint. 2015. "The South American Defense Council vis-à-vis ALBA: Dilemmas and Contradictions of the New Security Diplomacy." In *Decline of the U.S. Hegemony?: A Challenge of ALBA and a New Latin American Integration of the 21st Century*, edited by B. M. Bagley and M. Defort, 223–236. Lanham: Lexington Books.

Martinez, Jennifer L. 2013. "The ALBA-TCP Council of Social Movements." In *Counter-Globalization and Socialism in the 21st Century: The Bolivarian Alliance for the Peoples of Our America*, edited by T. Muhr. New York: Routledge.

Mhone, Guy. 2004. *Organisational and Institutional Implications of a Developmental State*. Pretoria: Human Research Council.

Moreno-Brid, Juan Carlos and Igor Paunovic. 2010. "Macroeconomic Policies of the New Left: Rhetoric and Reality." In *Latin America's Left Turns: Politics, Policies,*

and Trajectories of Change, edited by M. Cameron and E. Hershberg, 193–208. Boulder and London: Lynne Rienner.
Muhr, Thomas. 2010. "Counter-Hegemonic Regionalism and Higher Education for All: Venezuela and the ALBA." *Globalisation, Societies and Education*, 8(1).
Muhr, Thomas. 2013a. "Counter-Globalization and a Revolutionary Politics of Place, Space and Scale." In *Counter-Globalization and Socialism in the 21st Century: The Bolivarian Alliance for the Peoples of Our America*, edited by T. Muhr, 46–62. New York: Routledge.
Muhr, Thomas. 2013b. "Introduction: The Enigma of Socialism." In *Counter-Globalization and Socialism in the 21st Century: The Bolivarian Alliance for the Peoples of Our America*, edited by T. Muhr. New York: Routledge.
Panizza, Francisco. 2009. *Contemporary Latin America: Development and Democracy beyond the Washington Consensus.* London: Zed Books.
Petras, James. 2011. "Latin America's Twenty-First Century Socialism." In *21st Century Socialism: Reinventing the Project*, edited by H. Veltmeyer, 11–32. Black Point and Winnipeg: Fernwood.
Petras, James and Henri Veltmeyer. 2011. *Social Movements in Latin America: Neoliberalism and Popular Resistance.* New York: Palgrave Macmillan.
Riggirozzi, Pía. 2012. "Reconstructing Regionalism: What Does Development Have to Do with It?" In *The Rise of Post-Hegemonic Regionalism: The Case of Latin America*, edited by P. Riggirozzi and D. Tussie, 17–40. New York: Springer.
Riggirozzi, Pía. 2014. "Regionalism through Social Policy: Collective Action and Health Diplomacy in South America." *Economy and Society*, 43(3): 432–454.
Riggirozzi, Pía. 2016. "Regionalism and Health Policy in South America: Tackling Germs, Brokering Norms and Contesting Power." In *Regional Organizations and Social Policy in Europe and Latin America*, edited by A. C. Bianculli and A. R. Hoffmann, 271–290. New York: Palgrave Macmillan.
Rivera-Quiñones, Miguel A. 2014. "Macroeconomic Governance in Post-Neoliberal Argentina and the Relentless Power of TNCs: The Case of the Soy Complex." In *Argentina Since the 2001 Crisis: Recovering the Past, Reclaiming the Future*, edited by C. Levey, D. Ozarow, and C. Wylde, 67–86. New York: Palgrave.
Robinson, William I. 2008. *Latin America and Global Capitalism: A Critical Globalization Perspective.* Baltimore: Johns Hopkins University Press.
Robinson, William I. 2017. "Passive Revolution: The Transnational Capitalist Class Unravels Latin America's Pink Tide." *Truthout*, June 6.https://truthout.org/articles/passive revolution-the-transnational-capitalist-class-unravels-latin-america-s-pink-tide/
Rodríguez-Garavito, César, Patrick Barrett, and Daniel Chávez. 2008. "Utopia Reborn? Introduction to the Study of the New Latin American Left." In *The New Latin American Left: Utopia Reborn*, edited by P. Barrett, D. Chávez, and C. Rodríguez-Garavito, 1–41. London: Pluto Press.
Rossi, Federico M. 2015. "The Second Wave of Incorporation in Latin America: A Conceptualization of the Quest for Inclusion Applied to Argentina." *Latin American Politics and Society*, 57(1): 1–28.
Saad-Filho, Alfredo. 2005. "The Political Economy of Neoliberalism in Latin America." In *Neoliberalism: A Critical Reader*, edited by A. Saad-Filho and D. Johnston, 222–229. London: Pluto Press.
Sader, Emir. 2009. "Postneoliberalism in Latin America." *Development Dialogue*, 51 (1): 170–179.

Salö, Freja. 2007. "Telesur: 'Tele-Chávez' or the Public Service of Latin America? A Case Study." Thesis, Södertörn University College, Stockholm. http://docplayer.net/45136063-Telesur-tele-chavez-or-the-public-service-of-latin-america-a-case-study.html
Serbin, Andrés. 2012. "New Regionalism and Civil Society: Bridging the Democratic Gap?" In *The Rise of Post-Hegemonic Regionalism: The Case of Latin America*, edited by P. Riggirozzi and D. Tussie, 147–166. New York: Springer.
Singham, Nate. 2015. "The Latin American Left: Challenges for 2016 and Beyond." *teleSUR*, December 27. https://www.telesurenglish.net/analysis/The-Latin-American-Left-Challenges-for-2016-and-Beyond–20151227-0010.html
Stretton, Hugh. 1976. *Capitalism, Socialism and the Environment*. Cambridge: Cambridge University Press.
Unasur. 2008. *Constitutive Treaty of the Union of South American Nations.* Brasilia: Ministry of ForeignAffairs. https://en.wikisource.org/wiki/Constitutive_Treaty_of_the_Union_of_South_American_Nations
Vargas-Llosa, Alvaro. 2007. "The Return of the Idiot." *Foreign Policy*, 160(1): 54–61.
Veltmeyer, Henri and James Petras. 2014. "A New Model or Extractive Capitalism?" In *The New Extractivism: A Post-Neoliberal Development Model or Imperialism of the 21st Century?* edited by H. Veltmeyer and J. Petras, 21–46. London and New York: Zed Books.
Verstrynge, Jorge. 2014. *La Guerra Periférica y el Islam Revolucionario. Orígenes, Reglas y Ética de la Guerra Asimétrica* [*Peripheral War and Revolutionary Islam: Origins, Regulations, and Ethics of Asymmetric War*]. Barcelona: El Viejo Topo.
Villazana, Libia. 2013. "The Politics of the Audiovisual Cultural Revolution in Latin America and the Caribbean." In *Counter-Globalization and Socialism in the 21st Century: The Bolivarian Alliance for the Peoples of Our America*, edited by T. Muhr, 188–202. New York: Routledge.
Vivares, Ernesto, Leonardo Diaz Echenique, and Javier Ozorio. 2009. "Argentina: Reforming Neoliberal Capitalism." In *Reclaiming Latin America: Experiments in Radical Social Democracy*, edited by G. Lievesley and S. Ludlam, 199–216. London: Zed Books.
Webber, Jeffery R. 2010. "Neostructuralism, Neoliberalism, and Latin America's Resurgent Left." *Historical Materialism*, 18(3): 208–229.
Webber, Jeffery R. 2011. *From Rebellion to Reform in Bolivia: Class Struggle, Indigenous Liberation, and the Politics of Evo Morales.* New York: Haymarket Books.
Webber, Jeffery R. 2017a. "Social Theory from the South." *New Left Review*, 103: 151–160.
Webber, Jeffery R. 2017b. "Assessing the Pink Tide." *Jacobin*, November 4. http://www.jacobinmag.com/2017/04/lula-correa-rousseff-left-pink-tide
Webber, Jeffery R. and Barry Carr. 2013. "The Latin American Left in Theory and Practice." In *The New Latin American Left: Cracks in the Empire*, edited by J. R. Webber and B. Carr, 1–30. Lanham: Rowman & Littlefield.
Weyland, Kurt. 2010. "The Performance of Leftist governments in Latin America: Conceptual and Theoretical Issues." In *Leftist Governments in Latin America: Successes and Shortcomings*, edited by K. Weyland, R. L. Madrid, and W. Hunter, 1–27. New York: Cambridge University Press.
Weyland, Kurt. 2011. "The Left: Destroyer or Savior of the Market Model?" In *The Resurgence of the Latin American Left*, edited by S. Levitsky and K. M. Roberts, 71–92. Baltimore: Johns Hopkins University Press.
World Bank. 2016. DataBank. http://databank.worldbank.org

Wylde, Christopher. 2011. "State, Society and Markets in Argentina: The Political Economy of Neodesarrollismo under Néstor Kirchner, 2003–2007." *Bulletin of Latin American Research*, 30(4): 436–452.

Wylde, Christopher. 2016. "Post-neoliberal Developmental Regimes in Latin America: Argentina under Cristina Fernandez de Kirchner." *New Political Economy*, 21(3): 322–341.

Yates, Julian S. and Karen Bakker. 2014. "Debating the 'Post-Neoliberal Turn' in Latin America." *Progress in Human Geography*, 38(1): 62–90.

Yeates, Nicola. 2014. "The Socialization of Regionalism and the Regionalization of Social Policy: Contexts, Imperatives, and Challenges." In *Transformations in Global and Regional Social Policies*, edited by S. A. Kaasch and P. Stubbs, 17–43. New York: Springer.

Zibechi, Raúl. 2003. "Globalization or National Bourgeoisie: An Outdated Debate." *Focus on the Global South*, October 9. http://focusweb.org/node/189

6 The question of Eurasian security and the Shanghai Cooperation Organisation under US interventionism

Introduction

South–South cooperation and the multipolarization of world politics against US hegemony are articulated differently in different geographical and politico-cultural contexts. While Latin American post-hegemonic regionalism hinges on a social justice-centered paradigm, its Eurasian counterpart brings to the fore a security-centered paradigm that confronts US interventionism and global terrorism. This chapter focuses on Eurasia's case and the SCO experience. Led by Eurasia's two most influential states – China and Russia – the SCO is regarded as the strongest manifestation of post-regionalism in Eurasia.

In fact, US interventionism and global terrorism cannot be regarded as separate phenomena in the Eurasian context. Worthy of notice in this connection is that terror incidents have increased significantly since the 2000s, in parallel with rising US interventionism in Eurasia. According to evidence drawn from the Global Terrorism Database, the region represented by the Middle East, North Africa, and Central Asia suffered only 319 terror incidents in 2000, a year before the US invasion of Afghanistan. It is striking to notice that the number of terror incidents in this region soared to 7,000 in 2014 – a 2,000% increase (GTD 2016). Figure 6.1 shows that the number of terror incidents rose continually between 2000 and 2014. This illustrates how terrorism gained momentum following the US interventions in Afghanistan and Iraq, reaching its peak after the Northern interventions in Libya and Syria. Even though the phenomenon of terrorism cannot be reduced to a single factor, these data point to a bitter truth that Northern interventionism is closely associated with the rise of terrorism and currently presents a direct challenge to Eurasian security.

It would be safe to argue that the emergence of the Shanghai Cooperation Organisation (SCO) can be mostly attributed to US interventionism and the collective reaction of Eurasian countries against the security implications of Northern geopolitical containment strategies that have either directly or indirectly encouraged the rise of terrorism in Eurasia. As depicted by Tang Jiaxuan, China's foreign minister from 1998 to 2003, the SCO is the world's

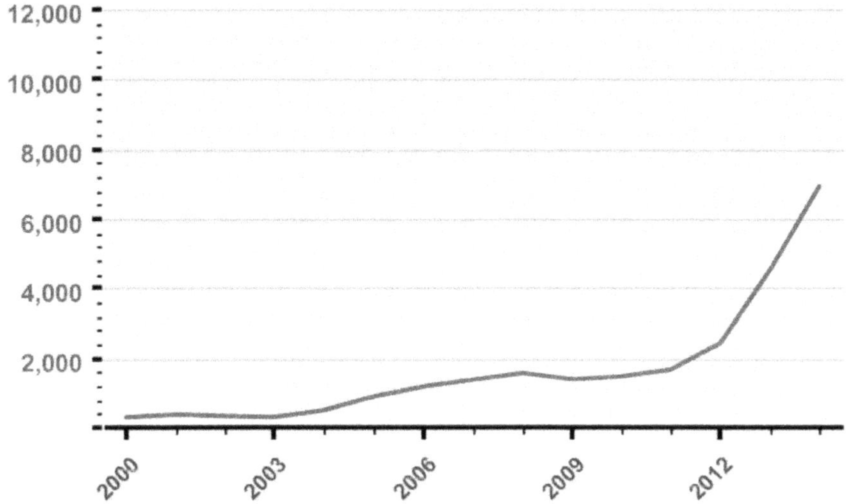

Figure 6.1 Rise in the number of terror incidents in the Middle East, North Africa, and Central Asia between 2000 and 2014
Source: GTD (2016)

first international organization centered on counterterrorism (Peng Chung 2006). In addition, the SCO is the first international initiative to be led by China, which is known for its prioritization of bilateralism in foreign affairs. This suggests that the pressure of Northern interventionism and terrorism in Eurasia has forced China to break with its foreign policy tradition of keeping a low profile in global politics (Song 2016).

The peculiarity of Eurasia's post-hegemonic regionalism is that the SCO has developed a non-conventional approach to the question of regional security by addressing military issues in tandem with the economic, cultural, and technological aspects of security. In view of this peculiarity, the present chapter revolves around the following questions: What are the material and historical conditions that brought the SCO to life and accelerated its pace? What are the region-wide and external factors that keep the SCO experience alive and thriving? In what direction has the SCO evolved, and what have been the major achievements of this experience for Eurasian security? What are the strategic factors that may have impeded the further development of SCO-led regional cooperation?

This chapter opens with an overview of SCO members' strategic interests in joining the organization, which is followed by a section on the SCO's historical and institutional development. The third section addresses China's place within the SCO and its contribution to the organization's normative framework; the fourth elaborates on Russia's place within the SCO. The final section explores the strategic ties that smaller Central Asian member states have developed with one another within the framework of the SCO's regionalism.

Strategic interests of SCO members

Considering the centrality of geopolitical rivalries from the standpoint of geopolitical economy, it is possible to identify a minimum of four factors that have provided the material basis for the SCO's emergence and development: China's desire to disarm its shared border with Russia and settle territorial disputes in Central Asia in the aftermath of the collapse of the Soviet Union; member states' need to address security issues such as smuggling, Islamist terrorism, civil wars, and territorial disputes, which rose to prominence due to the power vacuum created by the collapse of the Soviet Union, the breaking up of Central Asia into weakened states, and US military interventions; concerns shared by China, Russia, and Central Asian states about rising US interventionism in the 2000s; and strategic power relations and competition among SCO members and their desire for a peaceful framework to redress these issues (Aris 2011; Baizakova 2013; Rothacher 2008; Shilong 2012; Yuan 2010).

One could expand upon the above-mentioned arguments as follows.

- The SCO, as a China-led project, has been shaped primarily by China's strategic requirements: securing its borders and stopping Uyghur separatism and Islamist terrorism; diversifying its relationships with Central Asian states in order to maximize market and energy access; keeping US interventionism in check; and constraining Russia's regional control in a peaceful framework. These strategic requirements also lead China to lay greater emphasis on the economic aspects of the SCO (Salter and Yin 2014; Song 2013; Yuan 2010).
- Russia has sought to peacefully counter China's rise in the region and retain its strategic proximity to Central Asian states, therefore it feels obligated to assume a leading position within the SCO. Russia's initially reluctant leadership later turned into a more aspirational attitude following the Northern-supported "color revolutions" in the Balkans and Eastern Europe, which also amplified Russian resentment over NATO's bombing of Yugoslavia and US intervention in Afghanistan and Iraq. In other words, this resentment has led Russia to assume a more active role in the SCO and lay greater emphasis on this institution's security agenda, in contrast to China's emphasis on economic cooperation (Song 2013; Yuan 2010).
- The SCO assumes a vital importance in the eyes of Central Asian countries. These countries consider the SCO to be a peacefully countervailing power against the overwhelming influence of China and Russia; on the other hand, it is also seen as providing an opportunity for Central Asian states to benefit economically from the rise of the two big powers. From this angle, Central Asian states view the SCO's institutional framework as a vehicle for improving their bargaining power in the region. Another factor that encourages Central Asian states to engage in the SCO is that they can maintain their legitimacy in international politics vis-à-vis their

citizens by taking advantage of the SCO's institutional identity. This is important because their international legitimacy has taken a heavy blow from Northern criticism of their so-called "anti-democratic" and "authoritarian" regimes (Aris 2011; Song 2014).

How successful has the SCO been in translating its collective interests into reality? It is hard to ignore the SCO's success in constraining US interventionism, minimizing territorial disputes, largely disarming its borders, and consolidating a unified Eurasian identity at varying levels. For example, the US military presence in Central Asia disappeared when its Manas airbase was emptied in 2014, thanks to the political environment backed by the SCO (Pillalamarri 2014). In addition, the organization has created a relatively strong normative framework that has sustained the rise of Eurasia's post-hegemonic regionalism, which is embodied in China's efforts to advance the notion of "Asian values". Other crucial achievements of the SCO include the strengthening of respect for national sovereignty in the region, and the democratic inclusion of small Central Asian countries in institutional decision-making based on the unanimity principle. Moreover, given the institutional weakness of small Asian states, the SCO's institutionalization has reached unexpectedly impressive levels; especially compared with the relatively poor performance of the Association of Southeast Asian Nations (Yuan 2010).

Despite these crucial achievements, however, the SCO seems to have failed to transcend its status as a loose organization that has prevailed through bilateralism; it has therefore not achieved a sufficiently robust status to be regarded as a collective security organization (Baizakova 2013; Stobdan 2008). There is no scarcity of examples that illustrate the importance of bilateralism for the SCO. For example, at the 2004 SCO Summit, China not only offered $900 million in credit with favourable interest rates for member states, but also signed a $600 million energy agreement with Uzbekistan (Peng Chung 2006; Song 2013). Prior to the 2005 Summit, Hu Jintao, then Chinese President, held private meetings with his Kazakh interlocutor Nursultan Nazarbayev. In these he promised to support Kazakhstan's membership of the World Trade Organization in return for its increased commitment to fighting terrorists from Xinjiang (Peng Chung 2006). At the 2006 Summit, the SCO hosted bilateral agreements worth $2 billion, and Iran signed individual agreements with China and India in order to improve its Yadavaran oil field. China and Kazakhstan also signed agreements to build the Moynak hydropower plant and modernize the Kazakh railway system (Norling and Swanström 2007).

The progress of the SCO is also overshadowed by persisting uncertainties about this organization's institutional identity: that is, whether the SCO is primarily a military alliance or a political union; a defense apparatus or a vehicle for economic cooperation (Baizakova 2013). Besides the different emphases of Russia and China – the former on the SCO's military functions and the latter on its economic functions – it is still uncertain if the SCO is strategically capable of expanding its reach beyond Central Asia, given continuing rivalry between India and Pakistan as well as the SCO's concerns about Iran's nuclear program and confrontational foreign policy stance (Yuan 2010). The challenges that the SCO currently faces take on still greater significance when one considers Russia's continuing efforts to advance its own regionalist vehicles for military and economic cooperation in Eurasia, while maintaining its close involvement with the organization. China also has its own cooperation tools that may potentially undermine the SCO and alienate Russia (Song 2016; Weitz 2011). Finally, the decisions of this organization still lack legally binding force, which has rendered its institutional functioning less efficient than expected in its fight against terrorism. In view of the dialectical interlacement of the SCO's successes and shortcomings, the remainder of this chapter examines the above arguments in the following section devoted to the historical development, institutional structure, and major activities of the SCO; and the subsequent sections that explore the strategic ties that member states have developed with one another within the framework of the organization's regionalism.

The SCO's historical and institutional development

The historical roots of the SCO go back to 1989 and the Sino–Russian rapprochement during the breakup of the Soviet Union. Sino–Russian negotiations to disarm the shared borders resulted in an agreement signed in April 1990. China continued these negotiations with a joint delegation representing Russia, Kazakhstan, Kyrgyzstan, and Tajikistan, which share a 7,000 km border with China. Multilateral negotiations were preferred over bilateralism due to a lack of confidence on the part of the newly emerged and small Central Asian states. The delegations held a total of 22 negotiating sessions, which resulted in a concluding agreement at the 1996 Shanghai Summit (Baizakova 2013; Shilong 2012).

Security concerns also date back to the early 1990s. Islamist extremism had been a major concern since the Tajikistan Civil War that started in 1992, and the Afghani Taliban's rise to power in 1996 generated widespread concerns about rising security problems in Eurasia. China was worried that Islamist unrest in Afghanistan may easily spread to its own Western provinces (Cheng 2011). These concerns played a catalyzing role in the creation of the SCO–Afghanistan Contact Group in 2005 with the aim of establishing a stable channel of exchange between the SCO and Afghanistan. This group is made up of SCO secretariat representatives, officials, and diplomats (Song 2016).

The Eurasian multilateralism of the early 1990s produced beneficial outcomes for China, not only in terms of the disarmament of its borders. Many territorial disputes were decided in favor of China's strategic interests: Kyrgyzstan revoked its claim to a shared mountain range, while Russia relinquished the disputed marshland and islands on the Ussuri River (Rothacher 2008). Central Asian states were no less satisfied by this multilateral experience. In 1998, Kazakh President Nursultan Nazarbayev called for expanding this experience towards other areas of cooperation, namely economic integration and the fight against "Three Evils" (terrorism, separatism, and extremism). The Kazakh media named the first Shanghai Summit in 1998 the "Shanghai Five" (Shilong 2012). Nazarbayev's call resonated well with other Eurasian states; therefore Jiang Zemin, then President of China, proposed at the 2000 Dushanbe Summit to transform the Shanghai Five into a permanent organization. In 2001, the Shanghai Five began calling themselves the SCO (Song 2014).

It is possible to divide the historical development of the SCO into three different periods: the SCO's earlier attempts at institutionalization (2001–2004); the early formulation of the SCO's main agenda (2004–2007); and the implementation of the SCO's agenda (2007 to date) (adapted from Aris 2011). In the first period, the SCO Charter was drafted in the two years following the organization's foundation. By 2004, the SCO had acquired its current institutional structure, with the Council of Heads of State residing at the top of the hierarchy (Aris 2011). The second most powerful SCO organ is the Council of Heads of Government, which annually discusses multilateral cooperation, approves the SCO budget, and addresses organizational priorities. The Heads of Government Summits are organized in coordination with the Council of National Coordinators, which assumes the operational tasks and convenes at least twice a year. Ministerial councils have their own summits in areas such as foreign affairs, national affairs, defense, education, culture, health, finance, and the economy. The operational tasks required to organize and coordinate ministerial summits are assumed by bureaucrats who work in their respective ministries. The SCO also has a Parliamentary Assembly, which is endowed with advisory powers and the authority to bring proposals before ministerial committees. When faced with an agenda of primary importance, SCO decision-making relies on the principle of unanimity, also taking into account the majority vote of the invited representatives from non-member states. Decision-making in regular meetings follows the principle of simple majority (Salter and Yin 2014; Song 2016; Wallace 2014).

The SCO Secretariat is the executive organ of the SCO. It convenes a minimum of three times each year and is responsible for implementing decisions, drafting organizational documents, and coordinating general affairs. Top secretariat executives are appointed by the Council of Heads of Government for three-year terms. Policy recommendations and documents proposed by the Secretariat are subject to approval by presidential and ministerial councils. In the 2005–2006 period, the Secretariat's budget was estimated at \$1.95 million, whereas that of the Regional Anti-Terrorist Structure (RATS) was \$1.25 million (Aris 2009; Peng Chung 2006; Salter and Yin 2014). Aside from the budgetary structure of individual SCO organs, the member states' respective contributions to the general budget are 24% for Russia, 24% for China, 21% for Kazakhstan, 15% for Uzbekistan, 10% for Kyrgyzstan, and 6% for Tajikistan (Salter and Yin 2014; Wallace 2014).

While the Secretariat is located in Beijing, RATS is headquartered in Tashkent. RATS employs a staff of 30, who have diplomatic immunity and border crossing authority. RATS' functioning is sustained via two organs. The RATS Council is formed by a representative from each member state selected from their country's intelligence or defense institutions; these representatives convene a minimum of twice a year. The Executive Committee assumes RATS' operational tasks (Wallace 2014). It is estimated that in 2005 alone, RATS prevented at least 250 terror incidents and compiled a list of 400 wanted terrorists. According to the most recent data available, in 2009, 99 terror incidents were prevented; and while the number of prevented incidents in 2011 was only 10, 400 terrorists were arrested and over 1,000 light arms were confiscated. RATS has taken part in the provision of security at major events such as the 2008 Beijing Olympics, and in 2012 alone its services were used 16 times (Aris 2009; Wallace 2014). In March 2006, Uzbekistan hosted the first RATS' anti-terror drill, which was participated in by regular, special, and police forces. Similar drills continue to be held up to the present day (Salter and Yin 2014). Despite the lack of reliable data, the decreasing frequency of terrorist acts in places such as Chechnya and Xinjiang may be closely associated with the SCO's presence and RATS' activities (Aris 2009). Besides terrorism, RATS is also interested in international crime. Its major activities in this area include the provision of training for 141 security personnel by China and the capture of 17 suspected drug smugglers in the period 2009–2011. Additional functions of RATS are the provision of training via conferences, workshops, and classes, and the creation of a network among Eurasian security communities (Wallace 2014).

The track record of RATS demonstrates that it is much more than a shell institution. However, one should also mention its serious shortcomings, which constrain the further development of regionalization in Eurasia. RATS staff report their progress to their own government rather than the SCO Secretariat, whilst Chinese officials encourage bilateral intelligence sharing. Central Asian states seem reluctant to share delicate intelligence with the Chinese, however; this also applies to Sino–Russian intelligence mechanisms (Aris 2012; Salter and Yin 2014). RATS' performance is also constrained by an inadequate budget, estimated at no more than $2 million. Equally important is the fact that RATS is still not interested in intelligence collection, counter-intelligence, or integrated command creation (Wallace 2014). Even worse, RATS officials have no real jurisdictional power in the SCO area. In anonymous interviews, SCO staff portray the SCO's role as that of a Eurasian Interpol rather than a militarized anti-terrorist unit. In this regard, it is also known that Chinese RATS personnel mostly have policing and national affairs backgrounds, and that they tend not to be fully familiar with military and diplomatic affairs. Therefore, it is often asserted that RATS' real practical value consists of deporting terror suspects and regime challengers (Aris 2009, 2011; Wallace 2014).

The period 2004–2007 was marked by the early formulation of the SCO's main agenda, which was later extended to non-conventional areas of security such as organized crime and drugs. Meanwhile, the member states increased the frequency of joint military drills against conventional threats (Aris 2011). The early security agenda of the SCO mostly stemmed from the Tajikistan Civil War (1992–1997) and the Taliban's rise to power in 1996. In the period 2004–2007, the SCO's security agenda was greatly shaped by Northern-supported color revolutions. In the language of geopolitical economy, the color revolutions thus intensified Eurasian contender states' will to push for multipolarity. Pro-Northern regime changes in countries such as Ukraine (2004) and Georgia (2003), and the Tulip Revolution in Kyrgyzstan (2005), led SCO members to increase their vigilance against Northern strategic attempts to contain the rise of Eurasian powers. Similarly, the Andijan Uprising of 2005 in Uzbekistan and the resurfacing of ethnic conflicts in Kyrgyzstan (2010) served as warnings for Eurasian countries that regime instability and change could create a domino effect across the entire region. The period 2004–2007 also saw the SCO take on increased operational involvement in the question of Afghanistan (Roy 2010; Song 2013).

The acceleration of the SCO's military agenda can be attributed to Russia's increasing involvement in the organization following the outbreak of the color revolutions targeting its power in Eurasia. Prior to this conjuncture, not only did Central Asian states support the US intervention in Afghanistan, but Russia's reaction to this intervention was also much more neutral than expected. The SCO's first anti-terror drill took place in 2003 with the participation of 1,000 troops. Due to increasing strategic tensions with the North and the growing threat of terrorism following the Northern interventions, the SCO's 2005 Peace Mission drill involved 10,000 troops and advanced weapon systems under a stronger Sino–Russian initiative. This was followed by the 2006 anti-terror drill led by China and Tajikistan. The SCO's military agenda in 2007 was busy, hence the 2007 Tianshan-1 drill led by the China–Tajikistan partnership and the Peace Mission 2007 led by Russia. The SCO's military agenda in 2008 was marked by an agenda of antiterrorism. The International 2008 Volgograd exercise had a script that involved terrorists capturing an oil tanker. In fact, this exercise was part of a chain of SCO exercises against unconventional threats. Similar war games took place in 2006 featuring terrorists attacking a nuclear facility in Uzbekistan, and in 2009 featuring terrorists attacking a chemical factory in Tajikistan. The Peace Mission in 2009 was marked by the participation of 3,000 troops under Sino–Russian leadership; the Mission of 2010 involved all member states except for Uzbekistan and included 5,000 personnel mobilizing for a full 17 days. Peace Mission drills continued in 2011 between the Sino–Russian partnership and in 2012 with the involvement of almost 2,000 personnel from all member states. The 2013 Mission led by the Sino–Russian partnership was followed by another in 2014 involving all member states except Uzbekistan: this involved 7,000 troops. In the final analysis, it is safe to assume that the SCO's drills constitute a reaction to US interventionism and the North's containment efforts in Eurasia. It is also believed that these drills have provided Russia and China with opportunities to market their own arsenals for sale in Central Asia and around the world (Song 2013; Yuan 2010).

The SCO's current phase of regionalization, which started in 2007, is important in terms of the implementation of its agenda of non-conventional security engagement, which was still in the planning phase by the end of 2006 (Aris 2011). Historic landmarks in this new phase include the creation of the Energy Club, Business Council, and RATS in 2006; activation of the Interbank Consortium in 2006; establishment of the Youth Council in 2009; and effectuation of the University Network in 2011. The Energy Club is generally perceived as a Russian initiative to counter China's bilateralism and increasing influence in Central Asian energy markets (Song 2014). These strategic concerns seem to have resulted in a neglect of the need to resolve ongoing tensions between Central Asian countries over natural resources, especially water resources, which stand as major impediments to Eurasian cooperation. However, the possibility of energy cooperation within the SCO – as represented by the Energy Club – is a potentially useful idea that could empower Eurasianism at the ideational plan.

The Business Council is driven by three strategic objectives: development and coordination of regional investment initiatives; maximizing exchange among regional business and financial circles; and encouraging governments to take the lead in improving the economic situation in Eurasia. The supreme body of the Business Council convenes at least once a year, makes decisions by unanimity, and is made up of council presidents from each member state. Supreme body meetings evaluate the annual report prepared by the Secretariat of the Business Council, discuss next year's business and finance projects, and appoint the Secretariat's management. The Board of the Business Council comprises three council representatives from each member state, and serves as a platform for open dialogue, exchange, and proposal. In the absence of a formal voting system, it works by the principle of consensus. In turn, the Secretariat's role consists of examining all the proposals and decisions agreed by the Business Council; preparing the draft agenda and annual draft reports; and coordinating council events such as summits, conferences, workshops, and exhibitions (Aris 2011; SCO Business Council 2016; Song 2016).

In its present form, the Interbank Consortium provides a network for coordinating mostly infrastructural investments among banks organized under the umbrella of the Business Council. The members of the Consortium are the State Development Bank of China, Development Bank of Kazakhstan, Bank for Development and Foreign Economic Affairs of the Russian Federation (Vnesheconombank), National Bank for Foreign Economic Activity of the Republic of Uzbekistan, Settlement & Savings Company of the Kyrgyzstan Republic (RSB Bank), and State Savings Bank of the Republic of Tajikistan (Amonatbonk). Furthermore, the Forum of Industrialists and Entrepreneurs functions in parallel to the Business Council and Interbank Consortium as a network of business and economic experts, scholars, and think-tank institutions (Aris 2011; SCO Business Council 2016; Song 2016).

Based on the geopolitical-economy framework, one could point to the geo-economic importance of these business networks, created within Eurasia rather than transnationalized and integrated into Northern-dominated structures.

The question of youth occupies an important part of the SCO's post-hegemonic agenda. The Youth Council is composed of leading youth organizations from member states such as the youth branches of governing parties, civil society organizations, and young business circles. The founding members include the Youth Congress of Kazakhstan, youth wing Jas Otan, National Democratic Party Nur Otan, All-China Federation of Youth, Kyrgyz Youth Community Council, Russian Union of Youth, Youth Public Chamber of Russia, and Union of Youth of Tajikistan. The Youth Council organizes international youth forums to which organizations from non-member states are also invited (Aris 2011; SCO Youth Council 2016; Song 2016). The creation of such youth networks within Eurasia could build a barrier against Northern non-governmental organizations who seek to influence organized youth in the direction of color revolution.

Meanwhile, the SCO seems to have developed a vibrant cultural agenda of its own. Using its influence in the SCO area, China has opened Confucius Institute branches in Kazakhstan and Uzbekistan, offered Chinese-language courses for SCO officials, and accelerated its effort to organize exhibitions and other cultural events in SCO countries. Moreover, the SCO is endowed with permanent multilateral channels to improve cultural integration. Emblematic in this regard is the organization of a total of 12 meetings of ministers of cultural affairs and five meetings of ministers of education by 2015. Fine arts exhibitions and film festivals are regular occurrences during SCO summits and meetings. It is also known that in 2009, Putin proposed to organize a Eurovision-style music competition under the umbrella of the SCO (Dadabaev 2014; Song 2016; Wallace 2014).

Perhaps the strongest area articulated in the SCO's cultural agenda is educational cooperation. Initiated in 2006, ministerial summits on education take place every other year, and are accompanied by meetings of education experts. Other important channels that facilitate educational cooperation are education weeks organized in individual member states, and the Forum of University Rectors. Similarly, the SCO (Academic) Forum brings together several research institutions, including the China Institute of International Studies, the International Institute of Modern Policy (Republic of Kazakhstan), the Institute for Strategic Analysis and Assessment (Kyrgyzstan), the Center for East Asian and SCO Studies at the Moscow State University of International Relations, the Center for Strategic Studies under the President of the Republic of Tajikistan, and the Institute for Strategic and Regional Studies (Uzbekistan). The forum chair rotates on an annual basis among the representatives of the member states (Song 2016).

The SCO University network gathers over 60 universities with the aim of advancing cultural, scientific, and economic cooperation in the SCO area. When Putin first proposed to establish such a network in 2007, he intended the creation of an SCO university; this later evolved into a loose network structure of existing universities. This network prioritizes the creation of joint academic programs in strategic subjects such as area studies, environment, energy, information technology, and nanotechnology. Degree equivalence and the formulation of common academic standards are further priorities of the University network (Dadabaev 2014; Song 2016).

The SCO's advances in the area of education cannot be denied. However, the strategic interests of individual member states also play a key role in advancing the SCO's educational agenda. Certain Russian experts in education claim that Russia benefits from the SCO's educational cooperation mechanisms by maintaining and extending the influence of the Russian language and Russian culture in the former Soviet Republics. In a similar vein, it can be observed that China makes a tremendous effort to maintain its regional initiatives in educational cooperation. China's involvement in the SCO's educational mechanisms is extensive: the Joint Institute of SCO Studies (a think tank created in 2009 with the cooperation of East China Normal University and the China Development Bank), the China National Institute for SCO International Exchange and Judicial Cooperation (created by Shanghai University in 2014), the SCO Public Diplomacy Institute (created by Shanghai University in 2011 and supported by the Chinese Ministry of Foreign Affairs), and Xi Jinping's 2013 commitment to offer 30,000 scholarships to students from SCO member states in the following 10 years (Dadabaev 2014; Song 2016).

The SCO's normative framework and China

The SCO has come a long way on the road to building a sophisticated institutional structure that creates momentum for post-hegemonic regionalism in Eurasia. However, it is still too soon to regard it as a genuinely collective organization that is inextricably embedded in the political matrix of shared activity. Likewise, it would be naïve to suggest that these institutional achievements are a result of pure internationalist and solidarity-minded intentions driven by philanthropic motives of a "Eurasianist dream". Instead, the continuity of this regionalist initiative rests on a delicate balance of individual strategic interests and conjunctural developments. For example, it is thanks to its geoeconomic and geopolitical interests that China has taken the lead as the driving force of Eurasian regionalism by shaping the SCO's intellectual agenda and actively contributing to its institutionalization (Song 2016).

The SCO's normative agenda draws its strength from China's lead. China's efforts to amplify the global influence of its economic power through strong historical and cultural references find their echo in the SCO cooperation process. China seems to have succeeded in maintaining and advancing its leadership position within the SCO by ably using its soft power, understood as the "ability to get preferred outcomes through the co-optative means of agenda-setting, persuasion and attraction" (Nye 2011, 16). China's normative foreign policy framework hinges on Deng Xiaoping's foreign policy conception of "28 Characters" and former President Hu Jintao's strategy of *Sige Buju* (Four Outlines). As stated in Hu Jintao's report at the 18th Congress of the Communist Party of China in 2012, the success of China's foreign policy depends on regarding "major powers as the key; neighbourhood as the priority; developing countries as the basis; and multilateralism as an important platform" (Song 2016, 11). As the first outline suggests, China should avoid engaging in major conflicts in Eurasia with the US as a global power and Russia as a regional power. Ensuring mutual respect and trust in its relationships with these powers should be essential to Chinese foreign policy. China's reservation about Iran's potential SCO membership resonates with this first outline, given Iran's antagonizing foreign policy style. The second outline, concerning the prioritization of good neighborhood relations, is embodied in the SCO process, which is nonetheless undermined by US efforts to antagonize China by building an anti-Chinese coalition with countries such as Japan, Vietnam, the Philippines, and India. The third outline concerns building relationships of solidarity with countries of the Global South, mostly targeting energy-rich countries; this, however, differs from China's Marxist internationalism in the Mao era (Song 2016). Finally, in conformity with the fourth outline, China still maintains a high profile in multilateral institutions such as the United Nations, BRICS, G20, Association of Southeast Asian Nations, International Monetary Fund, World Bank, World Trade Organization, and World Health Organization.

Within the policy of the 28 Characters, the two most influential principles that have until recently given shape to China's entire foreign policy are *Tao Guang Yang Hui* (keeping a low profile) and *Jue Bu Dang Tou* (never become the leader) (Song 2013). In the 1990s, these principles were supplemented by the strategy of *You Suo Zuo Wei* (make some contributions), which was used to justify China's increasing presence in world politics without giving up its claim to modesty. In light of this connection, it is relevant to highlight the shift in China's official language from "peaceful rise" to "peaceful development". This shift was motivated by the potential perception of the meaning of "peaceful rise" as threatening to other countries (Song 2013, 2016).

China champions the notion of "Asian Values", rejecting the universalist claims of the North's values of democracy, human rights, and supranationalism. Asian Values rather center on economic development and national sovereignty. Freedom is conceived in relative terms, taking into account the cultural peculiarities of each Asian nation. Moreover, shared values are given greater weight than the Northern emphasis on institutionalization (Ambrosio 2008; Aris 2011). As such, from the point of view of geopolitical economy, one may anticipate that the creation of endogenous normative frameworks that reclaim regional norms and values could contribute to the multipolarization of world politics by diversifying cooperation strategies that were formerly monopolized by the US-led international system.

Asian Values were also incorporated into China's "New Security Concept", presented at the Association of Southeast Asian Nations in 1997 and officially adopted by the Communist Party in 2002. This being said, both Asian Values and the guiding principles of China's new security approach (equality, dialogue, trust, and cooperation) constitute important parts of the SCO's normative structure. The so-called Shanghai spirit is thus an extension of similar China-patented values: mutual trust, mutual benefit, equality, consultation, respect for cultural diversity, and the pursuit of common development. Similarly, the SCO's claim to the term "harmonious world" seems to be an extension of the notion of "harmonious society" championed by the Communist Party of China (Song 2013). Furthermore, Hu Jintao's references at the 2012 and 2013 SCO Summits to the need for building a "community of common destiny" is also indicative of China's leading initiative in the SCO's normative structure (Song 2016).

Why is China so invested in the SCO? From the perspective of geopolitical economy, China's active involvement in the organization could be said to stem from a myriad of factors, including its desires to peacefully counter Russia's influence in Central Asia while expanding its own hegemony within the region, to strengthen its partnerships with Russia and Central Asia by keeping them away from US influence, to geopolitically secure and diversify its energy supply beyond the Middle East, to expand its export markets, to contain the spread of Islamist extremism and separatism into its own territory, and to limit the US military presence in Eurasia.

The Uyghur question occupies a strategic place in China's attempts to keep the US out of Central Asia. In this regard, it is particularly important to emphasize that China's fight against separatism and religious extremism is conflated with strong geopolitical concerns. The Xinjiang Uyghur Autonomous Region is China's main gateway to the West: this region borders on Kazakhstan, Kyrgyzstan, and Tajikistan, which potentially enables cross-border terrorist activity. Moreover, Xinjiang accounts for as much as 15% of China's territory and serves as a major area for agriculture, grazing, and nuclear testing (Salter and Yin 2014). It possesses 38% of China's coal reserves and 25% of its oil and natural gas reserves. It is the second-largest contributor to Chinese wind and solar power production, and ranks fourth in hydropower reserves. Xinjiang has a total of 122 minerals; for several of these, it has the largest reserves in China (China, 2017; Duan et al. 2016). Besides its own energy resources, Xinjiang connects China to other energy-rich countries in Central Asia (Salter and Yin 2014). Moreover, China's geopolitical concerns about the Uyghur question are also related to US interventionism in Eurasia. The Eurasianist camp claims that the USA supports the World Uyghur Congress and Uyghur Islamist terrorists with the aim of disintegrating China. The US financial support for the World Uyghur Congress is not kept secret: the National Endowment for Democracy gives over a quarter of a million dollars annually (Cartalucci 2015).

Regarding the importance of energy politics, China is the world's second-largest energy consumer, which explains its close interest in Central Asia as a major energy-exporting region. Driven by the intention of establishing closer ties with Central Asian countries in the name of greater energy security, China has become the most important builder of infrastructure in Central Asia (Rahman 2011). China attaches a great deal of importance to the 1,200 km Kazakhstan–Xinjiang oil pipeline, which was completed in 2009 and has reached an annual capacity of over 20 million tons. This pipeline is expected to generate a fourfold increase in Chinese imports of oil from Kazakhstan. Between 2009 and 2012, 12% of China's oil imports came through this pipeline. China is also connected to Kazakhstan via the 1,400 km Beyneu–Bozoi–Shymkent natural gas pipeline, which was completed in 2015. Of similar importance to China's energy security is the 1,833 km natural gas pipeline that runs from Turkmenistan to China via Uzbekistan and Kazakhstan; this has an annual capacity of 40 billion cubic meters. No less important is the 970 km Sino–Russian crude oil pipeline, which was completed in 2011 and has reached an annual capacity of 15 million tons (Movkebaevaa 2013).

Central Asia possesses 4% of the world's energy resource reserves, and its remaining oil and natural gas reserves correspond to 1.9% and 10.6%, respectively, of the world's total remaining recoverable reserves (Hu 2014). By 2010, Central Asia's political and technological dependency on Russia was indisputable, with nearly 99% of Central Asian gas and 76.5% of crude oil exported through Russia (Martín 2010). In 2013 alone, however, the share of Central Asian resources in China's total oil and natural gas imports was recorded at 7% to 9% and 70%, respectively (Hu 2014). China's infrastructural investments, combined with its proximity to the region (Wang 2017), liberate energy-rich Central Asian countries from the political and technological monopoly of Russia.

In this environment, there is little doubt that the increase in China's investments in Central Asian infrastructure is driven mostly by its energy interests. While these investments benefit Central Asia's long-term development, China itself hopes to ensure its energy supply and increase its trade volume (Song 2013). Accordingly, in 2016 China created the Asian Infrastructure Investment Bank to serve countries such as Pakistan, Tajikistan, Uzbekistan, and Kazakhstan. This bank was developed outside of the context of the SCO and the Russian initiative (Panda 2016). However, China has also exhibited a strong interest in developing bilateral ties in Central Asia through the use of the SCO's multilateral platform (Song 2016). At the 2005 SCO Summit, China offered a credit line of $900 million to Central Asian countries; this rose to $10 billion per country at the 2009 SCO Summit (Roy 2010). The year 2015 was marked by China's "One Belt One Road" initiative, which seeks to make substantial investments in infrastructure projects (highways, railways, airports, and pipelines) with an intended budget of $40 billion in 2014. It was announced that China was planning to build a 4,000 km railway system and a 10,000 km highway network in the region (BRICS Post 2015).

When considering China's drive to expand its markets and hegemonic power, the increasing volume of trade within the SCO area could be seen as an indicator of the ways in which the SCO initiative helps China to strengthen its ties with Central Asia. Figure 6.2 reveals that in 2010, China replaced

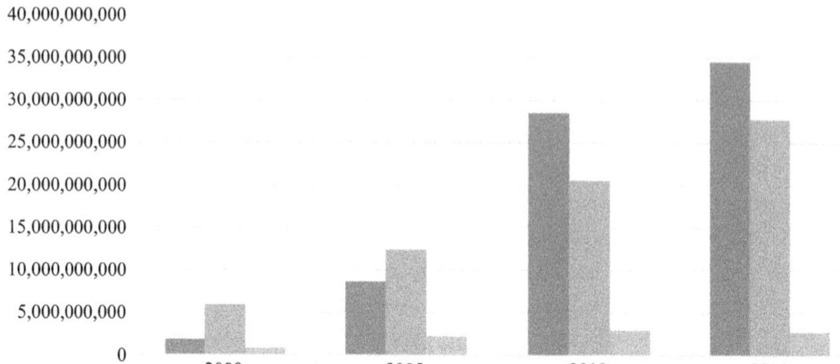

	2000	2005	2010	2014
Çin	1803204296	8616804438	28542928564	34541834764
Rusya	5869963966	12380835159	20571624476	27754852634
ABD	804290890	2187767548	2977178651	2798761730

Figure 6.2 Trade volume of selected countries with SCO members excluding Russia and China (in current US dollars)
Source: United Nations 2017, April 14

Russia as Central Asia's top trading partner. In fact, its trade volume with SCO members excluding Russia soared by 1,816% in the period 2000–2014, compared with Russia's increase of over 370%. Meanwhile, the SCO years have also benefited Sino–Russian trade, which has risen by over 1000% (Figure 6.3). Even more striking from a geopolitical-economy perspective was the 6% decline in US trade volume with SCO members excluding China and Russia in the period 2010–2015 (United Nations 2017). Similarly, US development aid to the SCO region declined by over 65% between 2002 and 2015 (Figure 6.4).

The US has not remained indifferent to its decline and China's rise in Eurasia. The Obama administration launched the "Pivot to Asia" initiative, which consisted of strengthening US military ties with its traditional partners such as Japan, South Korea, and Australia against China. US interest in pitting India and Vietnam against China can also be explained in the same way. These initiatives were closely tied to the US-led Trans-Pacific Partnership in the sphere of international political economy, which sought to isolate China by initiating a new economic cooperation process with Asian countries (Song 2016).

The New Silk Road initiative (One Belt One Road) was therefore China's answer to US military and economic aggression in Eurasia: it was intended to connect Europe and Central Asia through stronger economic partnerships. Its self-proclaimed "novelty" alludes to China's intention to transcend trade-centered forms of economic cooperation based on a strategy of expansion in infrastructure, technology, and the financial sector. The reference to the Silk

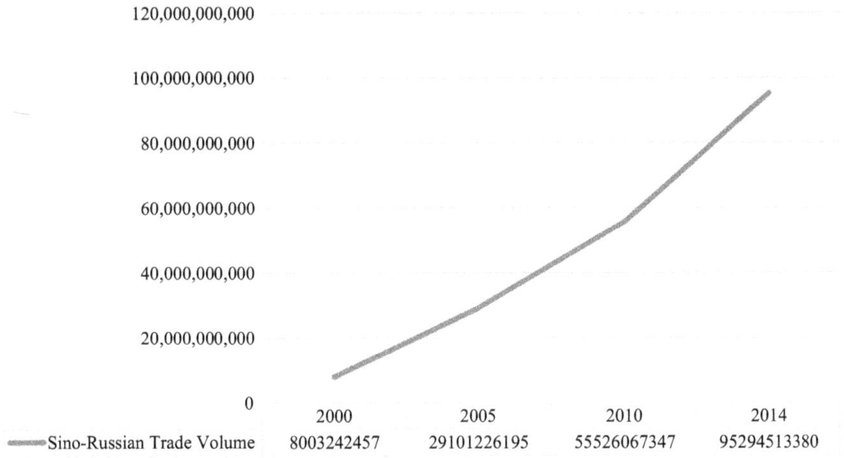

Figure 6.3 Sino–Russian trade volume (2000–2014, in current US dollars)
Source: United Nations 2017, April 14

Road is a symbolic allusion to China's glorious past. Although the Silk Road initiative springs mostly from China's individual efforts, the SCO is closely involved in advancing this agenda, showing that China is keen not to alienate Russia (Song 2016).

However strong China's normative motivation for advancing the agenda of cooperation in Eurasia, it is not interested in an unrestrained enlargement of the SCO at the expense of blurring its geopolitical focus on Central Asia (Song 2014). China's reservations are perhaps best illustrated in its reluctance to allow the inclusion of India and Iran in the SCO prior to 2017. The ongoing rivalry between India and Pakistan has been a defining feature of Eurasian politics, and the inclusion of these countries in the SCO could be a giant step towards Eurasian cooperation (Blank 2013). Although India is an important trade partner of China, the growing Indian influence in the region – especially in energy-rich Central Asia – could potentially undermine Chinese authority. In a similar vein, Russia's active support for Iran's inclusion in the SCO does not seem to be matched by similar enthusiasm among other SCO members. China and the Central Asian countries are not interested in openly antagonizing the Northern world by endorsing Iran's strong anti-American tone and nuclear program (Akbarzadeh 2015).

Russia and the SCO

Russia is another locomotive of the SCO cooperation. However, the reasons for Russia's engagement in the organization are much more complicated than

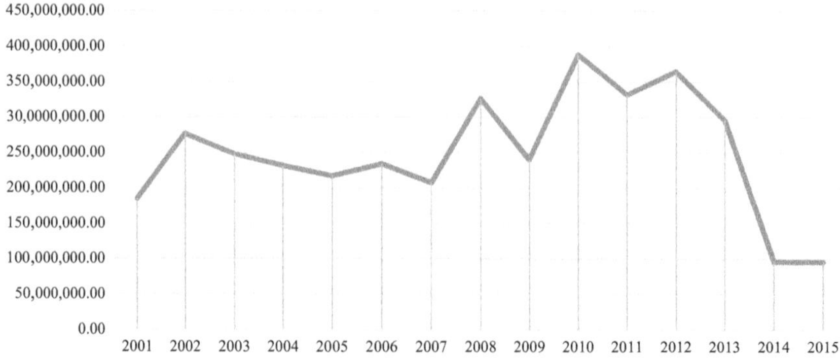

Figure 6.4 US Aid to SCO members Excluding Russia and China (2001-2015, in current US dollars)
Source: USAID 2017, April 14

those behind China's active commitment. The complex nature of Russia's commitment to the SCO stems mainly from its continued efforts to advance Eurasian cooperation through its individual initiative outside the SCO framework. The Russia-led Collective Security Treaty Organization (CSTO) was created in 2002, right after the creation of the SCO in 2001. Another Russia-led Eurasian organization is the Eurasian Economic Union, which is the successor of the Eurasian Economic Community founded in 2001. The Eurasian Economic Union emerged in 2015 as a regional organization that aspires to supranational integration in a similar manner to the European Union. This organization, with its population of 183 million and GDP of over $4 trillion, seems to express an even more ambitious aim for economic cooperation than the SCO. The Eurasian Economic Union has its own supranational court, and aims to achieve free movement of commodities and services as well as common policies in the energy, agriculture, and transportation sectors (Aris 2011; Song 2016). Russia's peaceful hegemonic competition in Eurasia has not been left unanswered by China, as shown by the creation of the Asian Infrastructure Investment Bank in 2016 and the launching of the Belt and Road initiative in 2013. China's proposal to merge the SCO and the Eurasian Economic Union at the 15th Summit in Russia in 2015 could similarly be regarded as a Chinese attempt to advance the New Silk Road project and block Russian efforts to consolidate its control. On the one hand, Russia cannot easily oppose China's blocking efforts, given its current economic difficulties and military encirclement by the North. On the other hand, China's leading status within the SCO does not necessarily create a zero-sum situation for Russia. On the contrary, the overall outcome of the 15th Summit, for example, might even help to further convince Russia of the SCO's potential to advance its post-hegemonic agenda. The 15th Summit is considered to have been a landmark in the SCO's history. It was organized jointly with the 7th BRICS Summit, and produced a concrete and comprehensive roadmap for the SCO's future, which was mapped out in a document entitled *Development Strategy of the SCO until 2025* (SCO 2015). The admission by the SCO of Belarus to observer status and Armenia to the position of a dialogue partner may strengthen Russia's hand within this institution, since these two countries are Russian allies and members of the Eurasian Economic Union (Song 2016).

The CSTO is also worth looking at as a major Russian initiative in Eurasia. There are significant overlaps between the areas of activity of the CSTO and the SCO, but Russians seem to be more inclined to rely on the CSTO when addressing security-related issues in Eurasia (Weitz 2011). It is known that certain Chinese analysts regard the CSTO as a Russian initiative to counter China's rise in Central Asia (Song 2013). It is also safe to assume that Russia's fear of China has not disappeared completely, despite significant improvements in Eurasian cooperation. For example, Russians are still concerned about the expansion of Chinese settlements in Russia's Far East and Siberia (Stobdan 2008). Therefore, Russia's insistence on setting up the CSTO separately from the SCO may be partially attributable to the Chinese factor. Interestingly, however, at the 13th SCO Summit, Tajikistan's representative Khudoberdy Kholiknazarov proposed a merger between the SCO and the CSTO in favor of Chinese interests (Salimov 2014).

Compared with the SCO, the CSTO seems to assume a more concrete character in its institutional existence and functioning. Its stated purpose is "to address new threats and challenges through a joint military command located in Moscow, a rapid reaction force for Central Asia, a common air defence system and 'coordinated action' in foreign, security and defence policy" (quoted in Aris 2011, 149). To achieve this, in 2009 the CSTO created the Collective Rapid Reaction Force against foreign attacks, terrorism, crime, and natural disasters (Aris 2011). This development is of significant importance considering the SCO's lack of permanent military arrangements.

Like the SCO, the CSTO holds annual military drills. One of the largest was held in 2011 with the participation of 10,000 troops and over 70 fighter jets. The 2014 drill involved 3,000 troops, during which the CSTO also tested its psychological and cyber warfare capabilities. As many as 95,000 troops participated in the drill of 2015, using over 7,000 pieces of military equipment (Miller 2011; Silk Road Reporters 2014; Sputnik 2015). On an anecdotal note, the question of cyber warfare has also been taken quite seriously by Russia. It is known to already have installed its own Internet and telecommunications monitoring system (the System for Operative Investigative Activities) in SCO member states' telecommunications infrastructure (Wallace 2014).

Overall, from the perspective of geopolitical economy, both the CSTO and the SCO could be said to contribute to the consolidation of Russia's military presence in Central Asia, while also consolidating the multipolarization of global politics to the detriment of US military supremacy. The presence of

Russian troops at military bases will continue until 2042 in Tajikistan and 2032 in Kyrgyzstan. Russia has also modernized its fighter jets at the Kyrgyz Kant Air Base, and its troop presence in Tajikistan will be increased from 5,900 to 9,000 by 2020. Russia's military base in Tajikistan is its largest foreign base (Abdurasulov 2015). Thanks to the CSTO it has strengthened its military influence in Central Asia, which is not confined to troop deployment and military modernization. In fact, Russia's initiative in the CSTO has imposed significant restrictions on members of the organization in terms of participation in foreign alliances and the construction of foreign military bases: Russia retains a veto power in these matters. Moreover, any attack on a CSTO member state is regarded as an attack on the organization itself (Radyuhin 2011).

Despite significant military advances by the CSTO and SCO, however, the military credibility of these organizations has been undermined by a handful of critical incidents. For example, Kyrgyzstan's former President, Kurmanbek Bakiyev, had to seek asylum in Belarus after widespread looting and his replacement, Roza Otunbayeva, called for Russian intervention in order to stop ethnic conflict between the Kyrgyz and Uzbek populations. However, Russia and the SCO declined Otunbayeva's request due to the absence of evidence pointing to intervention by foreign powers: the SCO forbids military action unless foreign intervention is suspected (Aris 2012). Another crisis that undermined the military credibility of Russia took place when Belarus declined to recognize South Ossetia and Abkhazia during the Russia–Georgia war of 2008, and Russia imposed sanctions on Belarus despite its status as a CSTO member. As such, the CSTO is still believed to be far from justifying its claim to supranationalism. In the military sphere, it functions more as a mechanism to facilitate coordination and technology transfer between national armed forces (Aris 2011).

Central Asian countries within the SCO: Mutual dependence and problems

A closer look at the underlying strategic reasons for Central Asian states' involvement in the SCO reveals that Central Asian regionalism is more than a pure love affair. The key factor is reinforcing new strategic power-balancing mechanisms so as to counter the influence of Eurasia's biggest powers, maximize trade benefits, and restrain US hegemony (Aris 2011; Song 2014). In this section, therefore, I will take a closer look at the case of each Central Asian member state, starting with Central Asia's most influential SCO members (Kazakhstan and Uzbekistan) and ending with its most vulnerable SCO members (Kyrgyzstan and Tajikistan).

Kazakhstan

Kazakhstan is known for its self-proclaimed leadership role in Central Asia, which is facilitated by its vast natural resources, its strategic geographic position linking Central Asia to Europe, and its status as Russia's closest regional ally (Aris 2011). Energy abundance is key to Kazakhstan's regional power: it has 30 billion barrels of proven oil reserves and 2.4 trillion cubic meters of proven natural gas reserves. Kazakhstan is globally ranked 12th for its oil reserves and 5th for its natural gas reserves. It is the world's largest uranium producer, holding 20% of the global reserves. Its energy abundance boosts its bargaining power within the SCO (Rahman 2011; Salter and Yin 2014; Song 2016).

Kazakhstan's strategic proximity to Russia has not prevented it from establishing a closer relationship with China and supporting Pakistan's membership of the SCO (Aris 2011). Given Kazakhstan's lack of direct access to the sea and thus global markets, the country attaches strategic importance to a closer relationship with China. Relatedly, Kazakhstan has emerged as a key energy provider for China, which has developed a strong economic presence in the smaller nation, particularly in the areas of energy and trade. Leading Kazakh corporations such as Eurasian Group and Kazakhmys are known to be actively lobbying for the expansion of China's market share in the country's economy (Cheng 2011; Movkebaevaa 2013). Nonetheless, despite China's increasing influence in Kazakhstan, there remain strategic frictions between the two nations. For example, Chinese troops were denied to use Kazakhstan's territory as a conduit point during an SCO military drill in 2007 (Salter and Yin 2014). Interestingly, increasing Chinese influence seems to have generated certain tensions on the part of the Kazakh population. In 2006, some parliamentarians joined protests aiming to impose a threshold of 40% on China's energy investments in Kazakhstan, and a large proportion of the Kazakh population are not favourable towards Chinese migrants (Dadabaev 2014).

Other SCO members in Central Asia benefit from the SCO's protective shield to constrain Kazakhstan's assertive foreign policy, which serves as another factor that consolidates the SCO's role in the region (Aris 2011). As for Kazakhstan's close relationship with Russia, Kazakhstan has developed its relationships with South Ossetia and Abkhazia in line with Russian strategic interests. However, it has also expressed an interest in joining the Baku–Ceyhan pipeline project, which passes through Georgia and excludes Russia. Moreover, Russia's 2008 intervention in Georgia was strongly resented by Kazakhstan, due to its concerns over a possible Russian intervention in its own northern territory under a similar pretext (Katz 2008; Song 2016). Kazakhstan is also concerned about the separatist tendencies of its Russian population within its borders. By the most conservative estimations, Russian ethnic groups make up 20% of Kazakhstan's population. It is important to note that Russia's intervention in Georgia was also resented by China as its timing coincided with the Beijing Olympics (Katz 2008; Song 2016).

Uzbekistan

As one of the world's leading natural gas exporters, Uzbekistan has 1.8 trillion cubic meters of natural gas reserves; it is Kazakhstan's most important rival in Central Asia (Rahman 2011). It possesses significant reserves of gold, copper, lead, zinc, tungsten, and uranium. Uzbekistan failed to participate in the SCO's 2003 military drill, and denied entry to the Kazakh military during the SCO's Peace Mission drill in 2012. The rivalry between these countries is expressed not only in the personal conflict between Islam Karimov (former Uzbek President) and Nursultan Nazarbayev (Kazakh President), but also in border disputes, roadblocks, bridge explosions, and mining disputes (Rothacher 2008; Song 2013; Wallace 2014). Uzbekistan also faces a separatist challenge in its Karakalpak and Tajik regions (Katz 2008). The size of the Tajik minority in Uzbekistan is disputed: official figures put it at 5% of the population, but other estimates make it over 20%. Interestingly enough, Uzbekistan assumed a catalyzing role in SCO cooperation when the 2005 Andijan Rebellion – led by the Islamic Uzbekistan Movement and Hizb ut-Tahrir – resulted in 1,500 casualties. The suppression of this rebellion by the state met with Northern condemnation; as a result, Uzbekistan found refuge in the SCO and ended the US military presence on its soil (Aris 2011; Blank 2013).

Kyrgyzstan

A major security-related factor that draws Kyrgyzstan closer to the SCO is ethnopolitical tensions that have been threatening Kyrgyz stability since 2005. In Kyrgyzstan, it is estimated that over 14% of the population are ethnic Uzbeks, which is a major source of contention in Kyrgyz politics (Aris 2012). As mentioned earlier, this country is crucial to Russia's military presence in Central Asia. However, Kyrgyzstan underwent a so-called "Tulip Revolution" in 2005. This incident overthrew the regime of former President Askar Akayev, who ruled the country with his family and allied clans (Aris 2012). Kurmanbek Bakiyev, former Kyrgyz President and Akayev's successor, failed to maintain order when he broke his promise to impose limits on presidential powers. This resulted in political unrest; he resigned and was replaced by Roza Otunbayeva as the Interim President. Unfortunately, the turmoil continued to grow with the killing of hundreds of Uzbek Kyrgyzs; during the fighting that took place in June 2010, thousands of victims of the conflict fled to Uzbekistan.

The ethnopolitical unrest in Osh resurfaced in June 2011 with pro-Bakiyev ethnic groups leading the way. Russia and the SCO's refusal to intervene generated certain doubts on the part of Kyrgyzstan about the security-related benefits of Eurasian regionalism (Aris 2012). However, the SCO's inaction was justified by the absence of foreign (i.e. Northern) intervention as the catalyst for social unrest. The organization's institutional philosophy prioritizes the principles of non-interventionism and national sovereignty in security matters, and a driving concern is that unjustified intervention may cause a domino effect, encouraging other interventions in the region. In fact, the fear of interventionism is so intense that most SCO countries were concerned about Russia's 2008 war with Georgia, although then President Mikheil

Saakashvili was a representative of Northern interests in the region (Aris 2012; Weitz 2011).

Finally, the rapid pace of Eurasian regionalization has not fully reversed Sinophobia in Kyrgyzstan. Similar to the situation in Kazakhstan, Sinophobic anti-migrant protests are no rarity in Kyrgyz politics. A major issue of contention is that certain Chinese entrepreneurs regard Kyrgyzstan as merely a resource provider for China and prefer to import their workers from China instead of relying on Kyrgyz labor (Dadabaev 2014).

Tajikistan

The security question in Tajikistan is perhaps the most delicate of all Central Asian SCO members: the country suffered from a large-scale civil war that cost approximately 100,000 lives during the period 1992–1997. The threat of Islamist terrorism has also not lost its crucial relevance in contemporary Tajikistan; this helps to consolidate its ties to the SCO. Ethnic Uzbeks make up 15% of Tajikistan's population, and separatism is another major security concern in this country. Moreover, Tajikistan was hit by a severe energy crisis in the period 2007–2009, which effectively paralyzed its economy (Aris 2011; Katz 2008; Rahman 2011).

Tajikistan experiences constant disputes with Kyrgyzstan and Uzbekistan over the control of water resources, and these disputes prevent the first two countries from reaching their potential in hydropower generation. Tajikistan and Kyrgyzstan are among Central Asia's poorest countries, but they also have the region's largest water resources, namely the Syr Darya River which has its source in Tajikistan, and the Amu Darya River which flows out of Kyrgyzstan. Hydroelectric power is of strategic importance for relieving these countries' excessive dependence on Uzbek natural gas. Furthermore, they expect to export their excess energy production to countries such as China, Afghanistan, and Pakistan. Tajikistan and Kyrgyzstan's ambitions to realize their potential in hydroelectric power production constitute a major source of contention with neighboring countries; particularly Uzbekistan and Kazakhstan, whose agriculture could be negatively impacted by the loss of water resources. For example, Uzbekistan is among the world's top ten cotton exporters, so access to water is critical for the Uzbek economy. It is possible that the Russian military presence in Tajikistan and Kyrgyzstan deters Uzbekistan from resorting to military action to secure its water resources. In addition, access to water is also a subject of contention among Kyrgyz and Tajik farmers as the construction of dams disrupts the cross-border river flow (Stratfor 2012; Water Politics 2014).

Perhaps most worryingly, it is estimated that nearly half of Tajikistan's population depend on narco-trafficking for survival. Tajikistan is globally ranked third for the amount of confiscated narcotics: it is estimated that 80% of all narcotics confiscated in Central Asia are passing through Tajikistan territory. The combination of these security, economic, and criminal challenges renders Tajikistan reliant on the SCO's support to maintain order and public safety (Aris 2011; Song 2016).

Finally, Russia is the largest economic and security provider for Tajikistan. Meanwhile, under the influence of SCO cooperation, Sino–Tajik relationships are rapidly strengthening, as evidenced by the opening up of the border from both sides. At the 2005 SCO Summit, China provided Tajikistan with a $900 million loan for use in infrastructural investments such as hydroelectric production and highway tunnel construction (Aris 2011).

Review and discussion

Eurasia's experience of post-hegemonic regionalism constitutes a highly comprehensive and sophisticated cooperation process. Eurasian cooperation, led by institutions such as the SCO, the CSTO, and the Eurasian Economic Union, is an expression of a concrete agenda of post-hegemonic development centered on the fight against Northern interventionism, terrorism, separatism, and religious extremism. Aside from combating the threat of Eurasia's military encirclement by the US, the SCO's case demonstrates that competition between regional powers such as China and Russia has been successfully mediated within a peaceful framework, which also renders peaceful cooperation prevalent over strategic conflict. All of this is sustained by a strong normative and institutional structure that regulates Eurasian diplomacy based on the principles of national sovereignty, non-interference, non-interventionism, and mutual trust.

The prioritization of infrastructural development not only has enabled the rise of big Eurasian powers such as China and Russia at the expense of US aggression; it also provides less powerful Eurasian countries with long-term and lasting opportunities for all-round development. The SCO's experience with the Business Council and Interbank Consortium indicates that Eurasian regionalism is not merely a state-led project, and that the integration of business elites is part of this post-hegemonic struggle. Military cooperation is one of the SCO's highest priorities, not only serving a symbolic role in deterring US interventionism, but also facilitating the integration of military circles, coordination among national armies, and transfer of technology.

Eurasian regionalism exhibits a less impressive performance in civil society engagement than its Latin American counterpart, which is characterized by the experience of ALBA's Council of Social Movements and the creation of alternative media outlets. However, one should not downplay the SCO's strong potential for cultural cooperation and soft power. The SCO's Youth Council fills an important void in politicizing the youth in favour of post-hegemonic regionalism. In a similar vein, the creation of an alternative network of universities and research centers points to another strength of the SCO's cultural potential.

A major weakness of post-hegemonic regionalism in Eurasia is the persisting emphasis of key Eurasian powers (China and Russia) on bilateralism, which potentially undermines the institutional power of regionalist organizations. Similarly, China and Russia's individual pursuit of creating their own regionalist institutions with overlapping boundaries may undermine the advance of post-hegemonic regionalism in the long run, despite recent attempts to merge these initiatives. Finally, Eurasian regionalism is also marked by ambivalence about how to reconcile its emphasis on national sovereignty with supranational institution-building. Cases in point are the SCO's failure to subject RATS to a centralized and fully operational command structure, and the lack of supranational jurisdiction on the part of SCO officials. On the other hand, the CSTO's advances in creating a court of justice and permanent military arrangements constitute grounds for some level of optimism.

References

Abdurasulov, Abdujalil. 2015. "CIS Summit: Russia to Bolster Central Asia Military." *BBC News*, October 16. http://www.bbc.com/news/world-europe-34538051

Akbarzadeh, Shahram. 2015. "Iran and the Shanghai Cooperation Organization: Ideology and Realpolitik in Iranian Foreign Policy." *Australian Journal of International Affairs*, 69(1): 88–103.

Ambrosio, Thomas. 2008. "Catching the 'Shanghai spirit': how the Shanghai Cooperation Organization Promotes Authoritarian Norms in Central Asia." *Europe–Asia Studies*, 60(8): 1321–1344.

Aris, Stephen. 2009. "The Shanghai Cooperation Organisation: 'Tackling the Three Evils'. A Regional Response to Non-traditional Security Challenges or an Anti-Western Bloc?" *Europe-Asia Studies*, 61(3): 457–482.

Aris, Stephen. 2011. *Eurasian Regionalism – The Shanghai Cooperation*. New York: Palgrave Macmillan.

Aris, Stephen. 2012. "The Response of the Shanghai Cooperation Organisation to the Crisis in Kyrgyzstan." *Civil Wars*, 14(3): 451–476.

Baizakova, Kuralai I. 2013. "The Shanghai Cooperation Organization's Role in Countering Threats and Challenges to Central Asian Regional Security." *Russian Politics and Law*, 51(1): 59–79.

Blank, Stephen. 2013. "Making Sense of the Shanghai Cooperation Organization." *Georgetown Journal of International Affairs*, 14(2): 39–49.

BRICS Post. 2015. "China's Silk Road wins big at SCO Summit." *The BRICS Post*, July 11. http://thebricspost.com/chinas-silk-road-wins-big-at-sco-summit/#.W4aHLOhKj1U

Cartalucci, Tony. 2015. "Turkish-Uyghur Terror Inc. – America's Other Al Qaeda." *New Eastern Outlook*, September 23. http://journal-neo.org/2015/09/23/turkish-uyghur-terror-inc-americas-other-al-qaeda

Cheng, Joseph Y. S. 2011. "The Shanghai Co-operation Organisation: China's Initiative in Regional Institutional Building." *Journal of Contemporary Asia*, 41(4): 632–656.

Dadabaev, Timur. 2014. "Shanghai Cooperation Organization SCO Regional Identity Formation from the Perspective of the Central Asia States." *Journal of Contemporary China*, 23(85): 102–118.

Duan, Jinhui, Shuying Wei, Ming Zeng, and Yanfeng Ju. 2016. "The Energy Industry in Xinjiang, China: Potential, Problems, and Solutions." *Power*, January 1. http://www.powermag.com/energy-industry-xinjiang-china-potential-problems-solutions-web

GTD. 2016. Terror Incidents by Region. *Global Terrorism Database*. https://www.start.umd.edu/gtd/

Hu, Bin. 2014. "Oil and gas cooperation between China and Central Asia in an environment of political and resource competition." *Petroleum Science*, 11(4): 596–605.

Katz, Mark N. 2008. "Russia and the Shanghai Cooperation Organization: Moscow's lonely road from Bishkek to Dushanbe." *Asian Perspective*, 32(3): 183–187.

Martín, Miguel Á. Pérez. 2010. "Geo-Economics in Central Asia and the 'Great Game' of Natural Resources: Water, Oil, Gas, Uranium and Transportation Corridors (WP)." *Real Instituto Elcano*, 59: 1–27.

Miller, J. Berkshire. 2011. "Russia Launches War Games." *The Diplomat*, September 23. http://thediplomat.com/2011/09/russia-launches-war-games/

Movkebaevaa, Galiia A. 2013. "Energy Cooperation Among Kazakhstan, Russia, and China within the Shanghai Cooperation Organization." *Russian Politics and Law*, 51(1): 80–87.

Norling, Nicklas and Niklas Swanström. 2007. "The Shanghai Cooperation Organization, Trade, and the Roles of Iran, India and Pakistan." *Central Asian Survey*, 26 (3): 429–444.

Nye, Joseph. 2011. "American and Chinese Power after the Financial Crisis." *The Washington Quarterly*, 33(4): 143–153.

Panda, Ankit. 2016. "Revealed: The Asian Infrastructure Investment Bank's First Projects." *The Diplomat*, April 20. http://thediplomat.com/2016/04/revealed-the-asian-infrastructure-investment-banks-first-projects/

Peng Chung, Chien. 2006. "China and the Institutionalization of the Shanghai Cooperation Organization." *Problems of Post-Communism*, 53(5): 3–14.

Pillalamarri, Akhilesh. 2014. "The United States Just Closed its Last Base in Central Asia." *The Diplomat*, June 10. http://thediplomat.com/2014/06/the-united-states-just-closed-its-last-base-in-central-asia/

Radyuhin, Vladimir. 2011. "CSTO Tightens Foreign Base Norms." *The Hindu*, December 22. http://www.thehindu.com/todays-paper/tp-international/article2736607.ece

Rahman, Khalid. 2011. "Central Asia, Energy Security and Shanghai Cooperation Organization." *Policy Perspectives*, 8(1): 65–76.

Rothacher, Albrecht. 2008. "Allying with an Evil Axis? The Ambivalent Role of the Shanghai Cooperation Organisation in Central Asia." *RUSI Journal*, 153(1): 68–73.

Roy, Meena Singh. 2010. "Role of the Shanghai Cooperation Organisation in Afghanistan: Scope and Limitations." *Strategic Analysis*, 34(4): 545–561.

Salimov, Oleg. 2014. "SCO-CSTO Merger Raised at Dushanbe Conference." *Central Asia-Caucasus Analyst*, June 4. http://www.cacianalyst.org/publications/field-reports/item/12983-sco-csto-merger-raised-at-dushanbe-conference.html

Salter, Michael and Yinan Yin. 2014. "Analysing Regionalism within International Law and Relations: The Shanghai Cooperation Organisation as a Grossraum?" *Chinese Journal of International Law*, 13(4): 819–877.

SCO. 2015. *Development Strategy of the Shanghai Cooperation Organization until 2025*. Beijing: Shanghai Cooperation Organization. http://eng.sectsco.org/load/200162

SCO Business Council. 2016. *Official Website*http://bc-sco.org/?level=2andlng=en [no longer available online].

SCO Youth Council. 2016. Official Website. http://www.forumsco.com/?lng=en [no longer available online].

Shilong, Yang. 2012. "China's Outlook on the Shanghai Cooperation Organization." *Chinascope*, 58: 23–27.

Silk Road Reporters. 2014. "Armenia to Participate in Kazakhstan CSTO Drills." December 8. http://www.silkroadreporters.com/2014/08/12/armenia-participate-kazakhstan-csto-drills [no longer available online].

Song, Weiqing. 2013. "Feeling Safe, Being Strong: China's Strategy of Soft Balancing through the Shanghai Cooperation Organization." *International Politics*, 50(5): 664–685.

Song, Weiqing. 2014. "Interests, Power and China's Difficult Game in the Shanghai Cooperation Organization SCO." *Journal of Contemporary China*, 23(85): 85–101.

Song, Weiqing. 2016. *China's Approach to Central Asia: The Shanghai Co-operation Organisation*. New York: Routledge.

Sputnik. 2015. "95,000 Russian Troops Join Massive CSTO Military Exercise." Sputnik, September 14. http://sputniknews.com/russia/20150914/1026966249.html

Stobdan, P. 2008. "Shanghai Cooperation Organization: Challenges to China's Leadership." *Strategic Analysis*, 32(4): 527–547.

Stratfor. 2012. *Central Asia's Looming Conflict Over Water, Part 1: The Upriver Countries. Assessments*, November 12. http://www.stratfor.com/analysis/central-asias-looming-conflict-over-water-part-1-upriver-countries

United Nations. 2017. International Trade Statistics Database. http://comtrade.un.org

USAID. 2017. Foreign Aid Explorer. https://explorer.usaid.gov

Wallace, Thomas. 2014. "China and the Regional Counter-Terrorism Structure: An Organizational Analysis." *Asian Security*, 10(3): 199–220.

Wang, Henry K. H. 2017. *Energy Markets in Emerging Economies: Strategies for Growth*. New York: Routledge.

Water Politics. 2014. "Conflicts in Kyrgyzstan: Foreshadowing Water Wars to Come?" *Water Politics*, June 17. http://www.waterpolitics.com/2014/06/17/conflicts-in-kyrgyzstan-foreshadowing-water-wars-to-come/

Weitz, Richard. 2011. "Shanghai Cooperation Organization: A New Force in Asian Security?" *Korean Journal of Defense Analysis*, 23(1): 133–148.

Yuan, Jing Dong. 2010. "China's Role in Establishing and Building the Shanghai Cooperation Organization SCO." *Journal of Contemporary China*, 19(67): 855–869.

Conclusion

In this book, I have provided a geopolitical-economic analysis of how, in the 2000s, global politics took a sharp turn toward multipolarity at the expense of US global hegemony. In particular, two different but complementary developments have been discerned in the multipolarization of global politics: the bankruptcy of hegemonic global governance under the crisis of Northern capitalism; and the intensification of South–South cooperation in a post-hegemonic direction. I have thus shed light on the historical, political-economic and geopolitical contexts in which these developments have taken shape, based on the cases of Europe, Latin America, Eurasia, and Africa.

Relative decline of US global hegemony

As discussed in Chapter 3, the erosion of US global hegemony is discernible in several key areas. First, the loss of US supremacy in the global political economy is shown by the way that the Global South is fast becoming the center of gravity of global production and exports. This is also true of US financial superiority amid the deep-seated economic crisis since 2008, which has resulted in the BRICS countries (Brazil, Russia, India, China, and South Africa) increasing the share of foreign investment and development credit going to the Global South. However, the economic superiority of the US is far from having vanished completely, given its status as the top performer in GDP per capita and the fragility of China's development. Second, US military power is fast being stripped of its deterrent effect, regardless of the continuing status of the US as the world's strongest military power. This is shown most obviously by events in the South China Sea as well as Russia's advances in Syria and Ukraine. Russia has already outpaced the US in military expenditure as a percentage of GDP and is a global leader in the arms trade. Third and fourth, the major states contending against US global hegemony are distinguished not only by their territorial strength and substantial energy access, but also by their demographic superiority and expanding reserves of skilled labor. Institutional capacity and global cultural influence constitute the fifth and sixth areas in which US global hegemony is being tested. The global influence of US culture is still unrivaled, but it exhibits a lack of commitment to global governance, is undergoing a substantial loss of legitimacy within global governance institutions, and faces the challenge of alternative institutions in the Global South.

The crisis of capitalism and the bankruptcy of hegemonic global governance

In Chapters 1 and 2, I explored the crisis of Northern capitalism and the bankruptcy of hegemonic global governance based on the cases of open regionalism in Latin America and Europe. Once presented as the most advanced model of integration into global capitalism, the case of the North American Free Trade Agreement (NAFTA) is emblematic of the bankruptcy of hegemonic global governance: it has now been depicted as a "trading disaster" by the US President (Frisk 2017). However, by the time the disaster caused by the NAFTA regime reached a point of critical mass, it had already been of great use in advancing the US geopolitical agenda. Not only did it serve to resolve trade disputes in favor of the US and facilitate free trade in line with US geo-economic interests, it also heavily exploited economic asymmetries with other NAFTA members in order to subordinate Mexican and Canadian foreign policy to US geopolitical interests. Prior to the implementation of the accord, Mexico's accession to the organization was celebrated as proof of the rise of this country from the ranks of the Third World to the First World. However, Mexico proved to be unable to compete with the US and Canadian economies in a free-trade environment, and is now the country that has suffered the greatest human and economic losses due to NAFTA's impositions. The bankruptcy of agriculture, constrained employment opportunities, and mass migration have led Mexico to become a failed state wracked by narcotrafficking, human trafficking, and arms trafficking, all under the NAFTA regime. Sadly, global crime has been the sole sector that has benefited from the liberalization of trade.

In Latin America, US hegemonic decline and the subsequent rise of South–South cooperation in a post-hegemonic direction have been built on the success of the continental movement against the Free Trade Area of the Americas. This was followed by the fall from grace of the *Mercado Común del Sur* (Mercosur: Southern Common Market) and the Organization of American States, as well as the founding of alternative (i.e. post-hegemonic) regional institutions in the 2000s. However, the movement against the Free Trade Area of the Americas and the leftward shift in Latin America were not the only instances in which the acuteness of the crisis of hegemonic global governance reached a zenith. The diffusion of the US economic crisis to Europe has exposed the bankruptcy of the neoliberal model of open regionalism and the narrow strategic interests of German neo-mercantilism. As with the NAFTA experience, neoliberalism and free trade have led to the widening of economic asymmetries between Europe's neo-mercantilist elite and the peripheral majority. This Southern peripheral majority has been scapegoated for its alleged financial irresponsibility and laziness. Europe's crisis is actually a direct outcome of neoliberal policies centered on excessive deindustrialization, financialization, and indebtedness under the comforting shade of imports and credit from Europe's neo-mercantilist core. Indeed, the bankruptcy of hegemonic global governance also finds its expression in the deepening of Europe's strategic crisis. Amplifying the far-reaching effects of the crisis of capitalism since 2008, the Northern intervention in Syria and Europe's Russophobic stance over Ukraine have fueled racism, xenophobia, and Euroscepticism accompanied by massive migratory flows from Syria and the consolidation of Europe-wide far-right movements that feed on the Ukrainian conflict.

Multipolarization and South–South cooperation

The crisis of Northern capitalism and bankruptcy of hegemonic global governance have created a facilitative environment for post-hegemonic initiatives. As elaborated in Chapter 3, the BRICS countries have taken advantage of this environment to wage a bifrontal struggle that links together the aspiration of transforming hegemonic global governance from within and the aim of building alternative institutions to rival US hegemony. The strategy of transformation from within has been implemented in the BRICS' attempt to reform the United Nations by democratizing the structure of the Security Council and extending its membership to Brazil and South Africa, as well as its intention to democratize decision-making at the International Monetary Fund. In turn, the aim of post-hegemonic institution building has been translated into practice with the creation of a new development bank, credit rating agency, and contingency reserve arrangement. The BRICS' proposal to replace the US dollar with an alternative currency for world reserve and global trade could be seen as another post-hegemonic attempt to constrain US hegemony.

It is possible to identify a number of challenges that are slowing down the pace of the erosion of US global hegemony and the multipolarization of global politics. Most importantly, South–South cooperation suffers from a relatively low level of political synchronization in globally important matters. India's oscillation between membership of the Shanghai Cooperation Organisation (SCO) and allying with the US raises well-founded concerns about the future of South–South cooperation. India's ongoing tensions with China and Pakistan, and China's military assertiveness in the South China Sea, constitute potential impediments to multipolarization and South–South cooperation. In the early BRICS era, a major source of contention was the rift between BRICS countries regarding the liberalization of international trade during the Doha Rounds. The same goes for BRICS countries' significant disagreements on climate change and the Kyoto Protocol. In addition, BRICS' support and abstention from the UN Security Council vote on foreign intervention in Libya has had irreparable ramifications for the entire Eurasian continent, with the spread of a chaotic environment and jihadist terrorism. A similar situation occurred when China abstained from voting on a UN resolution on the alleged chemical attack in Syria, despite Russia casting a veto (Fedschun 2017).

Extending the previous chapter's discussion on BRICS, Chapter 4 showed how Africa has become a strategic base for rising multipolarization and South–South cooperation. From a geopolitical-economic point of view, Africa testifies to the decline of US global hegemony amid the increasing involvement of BRICS countries. The post-hegemonic transformation of the African political economy finds its expression in the rise to prominence of a horizontalist approach to "development cooperation", which undermines the Global North's verticalist understanding of "conditional development assistance". African countries seem to benefit from the BRICS' increasing involvement in the continent, which allows them to multiply their foreign policy options and prospects for development. On the other hand, BRICS' resource-driven engagement ends up exacerbating Africa's dependency on extractivism and arms trade.

Aside from BRICS cooperation, post-hegemonic regionalism is perhaps the political arena where South–South cooperation is practiced most intensely, as explored in Chapters 5 and 6. A geopolitical-economic assessment of Latin America and Eurasia reveals that post-hegemonic regionalism constitutes a multi-front struggle centered on four main areas that underpin the multipolarization of global politics: culture, economy, financial cooperation, and regional defense. Regarding the cultural aspects of regionalism, both the Latin American and Eurasian forms of post-hegemonic regionalism hinge on strong normative frameworks and firm commitments to the regionalization of an endogenous culture and an educational system free from US hegemonism. In the case of the SCO, Eurasian regionalism brings forth the so-called "Asian values", which prioritize economic development and national sovereignty over the Northern hegemonic conceptions of liberal democracy, human rights, and supranationalism. In the case of the *Alianza Bolivariana para los Pueblos de Nuestra América* (ALBA: Bolivarian Alliance for the Peoples of Our America), Latin American post-hegemonic regionalism draws on Bolivarianism, a form of anti-imperialism that looks to past continental struggles against Spanish colonialism and US imperialism. Other post-hegemonic political values encouraged by Latin American regionalism are inclusion and participation; these find their application in ALBA's creation of a Council of Social Movements and other networks of anti-imperialist and anti-neoliberal progressive movements such as the *Articulación de Movimientos Sociales hacia el ALBA* (AMSA: Coordination of Social Movements towards ALBA). Although Latin America's left-wing politics is substantially different from Eurasian political culture, the SCO's Youth Council is important in terms of the region-wide politicization of the organized youth, its participation in the post-hegemonic project, and distanciation from Northern hegemonism.

In the field of cultural regionalization, worthy of special mention is the SCO's creation of a network of universities, strategically targeted research programs, education experts, and think tanks in a forum setting. The same is true of ALBA's attempts to organize educational workshops and create a regional university of its own. Indeed, ALBA's cultural activities go beyond the sphere of education and extend to regionalization in the media and cultural industries. Examples include the creation of teleSUR as an alternative to hegemonic US media outlets, and the mobilization of cultural *grannacionales* and not-for-profit agencies to facilitate anti-imperialist and endogenous art creation and distribution, including short films and documentaries. These cultural initiatives take on a greater relevance when considering the fact that culture – "soft power" – is one of the areas in which US global hegemony is strongest, to the detriment of post-hegemonic initiatives.

Not every country has the resources to become a global hegemon. However, it is possible for any country to erode US global domination and contribute to the multipolarization of world politics by simply taking part in a post-hegemonic initiative of international cooperation. When it comes to economic strength, the unmatched competitiveness of US power is beyond doubt. Nonetheless, Latin American and Eurasian forms of post-hegemonic regionalism have taken their own paths in using economic cooperation as a tool to foster endogenous development and challenge US global hegemony. A common feature of Latin America and Eurasia's experiences is that they both see economic regionalization as an issue that concerns more than free trade. Instead, they attach primary importance to social and infrastructural development. In this regard, it is relevant to mention the focus on de-commodifying health and liberating the pharmaceutical sector by the *Unión de Naciones Suramericanas* (Unasur: Union of South American Nations) through its Council of Social Development and Health. Of similar importance is Unasur's prioritization of infrastructural development through the Initiative for the Integration of Regional Infrastructure in South America (IIRSA) and energy security. In ALBA's case, an important feature to notice is this organization's use of *grannacionales* and social missions as strategic tools to advance the agenda of social justice, fair trade, and bottom-up development through the active participation of local communities. As for Eurasian regionalism, the SCO is closely involved in infrastructural development and energy security (via the SCO Energy Club). It also has its Business Council, which allows Eurasian states to promote local development and their own regional business "champions".

Post-hegemonic regionalism, as one of the strongest manifestations of rising South–South cooperation, also shares a common agenda of financial cooperation, which is equally critical for eroding US global hegemony and fostering multipolarization. The SCO's Interbank Consortium is of strategic importance for this post-hegemonic agenda of financial development in terms of funding domestic projects of infrastructural development and entrepreneurship. Similar support for infrastructural projects is intended to be offered by Unasur's Bank of the South. As for ALBA, its development bank and *Sistema Unitario de Compensación Regional* (SUCRE: Unified System for

Regional Compensation) constitute the backbone of its financial infrastructure, which is used as the main source of funding for social development programs.

A final area that reflects the shared agenda of post-hegemonic regionalism is regional defense. From a geopolitical-economy perspective, defense and military cooperation is the *sine qua non* of multipolarization and the resistance to US interventionism. The US is known for its habit of resorting to so-called "pre-emptive" strikes based on falsified or non-existent threats, as happened in the 2003 invasion of Iraq and over the 2017 Shayrat missile strike in Syria (Carden 2017; Left et al. 2004). Faced with the threat of US interventionism, the greatest progress toward military regionalization has been observed in Eurasia. Post-hegemonic organizations such as the SCO and the Collective Security Treaty Organization hold regular drills that draw massive participation, the scale of which suggests that they are about far more than counterterrorism. Rather, they aim at deterring potential military interventions from Northern countries, especially the US. As such, Eurasian drills also incorporate psychological and cyber warfare into their practices. The SCO's setting up of the Regional Anti-Terrorist Structure (RATS) indicates that Eurasian regionalism pays attention to the issues of counter-terrorism and international crime, hence the organization of targeted training sessions, smaller-scale drills, and security operations. Furthermore, these regionalist arrangements also allow for the transfer of military technology, and provide national security and intelligence communities with the opportunity to forge region-wide networks.

The social justice-oriented focus of Latin American regionalism does not prevent its post-hegemonic agenda from addressing the question of regional defense. The ALBA School of Defense, Unasur's Defense Council, and the Research Center of Strategic Defense attest to the importance of military cooperation for Latin America's post-hegemonic regionalism. This being said, a peculiarity of the Latin American experience lies in ALBA's emphasis on the concept of asymmetric warfare and a civil–military alliance, besides the Unasur Defense Council's concern with creating an endogenous pharmaceutical industry. Familiarity with asymmetric warfare and the creation of stable channels for a civil–military alliance are of strategic importance for the Global South, because most Southern countries are unable to compete with the technological superiority of the US military. As for the pharmaceutical industry, this area is monopolized by a handful of Northern multinational companies, "which hold the patents for key medications and vaccines used in infectious-disease campaigns" (Waitzkin and Jasso-Aguilar 2015, 118). This impedes local research and the production of low-cost medicines. The Unasur Defense Council's involvement in de-commodifying health as a regional security problem is thus a valuable contribution to the post-hegemonic struggle of the Global South.

In sum, Latin American and Eurasian regionalism have succeeded in contributing to the perceived, if not actual, decline of US global hegemony. They have demonstrated that there is an alternative to US hegemonism, and have laid the normative and institutional foundations of multipolarity by waging a multifrontal struggle. However, merely focusing on the advances of these experiences would result in an incomplete understanding of post-hegemony and the multipolarization of global politics. With reference to my earlier portrayal of post-hegemony as a reversible and contradictory process, one should also acknowledge the limitations and contradictions of the Latin American and Eurasian experiences from the point of view of geopolitical economy.

In Latin America, a severe problem that contradicts the regionalist claim of anti-imperialism and refutation of neoliberalism is the inability of ALBA and Unasur to transcend the extractivist model of development, which is traditionally associated with the imperialist pillage of natural resources and neoliberal globalization in terms of commodification and excessive dependence on global trade. Despite ALBA's claim to fair trade, Latin America's regionalism seems to have failed to formulate a coherent alternative model of development. This failure is even more pronounced in the case of Eurasia, where a security-centered focus neglects the importance of formulating an alternative model of economic development to US-patented neoliberalism. In Eurasia, the problem of democratic participation and popular legitimacy has not been thoroughly addressed; rather, it is overshadowed by the authority of strong leaders and top-down processes. Due to the political character of Eurasian regimes, the participation of labor and other progressive sectors in the building of a multipolar world is almost nonexistent. In turn, this situation constitutes a potential impediment to the cultural integration of the Eurasian continent, since the working masses who do not directly associate themselves with regionalist projects can develop no substantial interest in maximizing cultural interactions.

Moreover, post-hegemonic governance currently faces an unresolved tension between national sovereignty and supranationalism, which is particularly evident in the regionalization of military cooperation. Even Eurasian regionalism, which has attached greater importance to military cooperation than its Latin American counterpart – especially in the case of the SCO – suffers from the absence of a centralized military command and cross-border jurisdiction. In Latin America, both ALBA and Unasur have refrained from extending military cooperation to an operational level; they also lack coordinated intelligence mechanisms to resist US attempts to destabilize left-wing governments.

Finally, despite significant achievements in the institutionalization of post-hegemonic regionalism, both the Latin American and Eurasian experiences have been mostly led by strong personalities – Vladimir Putin in Russia, Evo Morales in Bolivia, and formerly Hugo Chávez in Venezuela and the Kirchners in Argentina. The way that post-hegemonic regionalism rests excessively on the shoulders of individual leaders is a likely source of future instabilities and interruptions in South–South cooperation. Indeed, the slowing down of post-hegemonic regionalism in Latin America attests to serious leadership vulnerabilities following the weakening of the Bolivarian government in Venezuela, as well as the defeat of the left in Argentina and Brazil.

References

Carden, James. 2017. "The Chemical-Weapons Attack in Syria: Is There a Place for Skepticism?" *The Nation*, April 19. https://www.thenation.com/article/the-chemical-weapons-attack-in-syria-is-there-a-place-for-skepticism/

Fedschun, Travis. 2017. "UN Draft Resolution on Syria Attack: Vote Fails with Russia Veto, China Abstains." *Fox News*, April 12. http://www.foxnews.com/world/2017/04/12/un-draft-resolution-on-syria-attack-vote-fails-with-russia-veto-china-abstains.html

Frisk, Adam. 2017. "Donald Trump Again Attacks Canada's Dairy Industry, Calls NAFTA a 'Trading Disaster'." *Global News*, April 20. http://globalnews.ca/news/3392010/donald-trump-canada-dairy-industry-nafta-disaster/

Left, Sarah et al. 2004. "Iraq War 'Waged on False Intelligence'." *The Guardian*, July 9. http://www.theguardian.com/world/2004/jul/09/usa.iraq2

Waitzkin, Howard and Rebeca Jasso-Aguilar. 2015. "Imperialism's Health Component." *Monthly Review*, 67(3): 114–129.

Index

For Product Safety Concerns and Information please contact our EU representative GPSR@taylorandfrancis.com
Taylor & Francis Verlag GmbH, Kaufingerstraße 24, 80331 München, Germany

www.ingramcontent.com/pod-product-compliance
Ingram Content Group UK Ltd.
Pitfield, Milton Keynes, MK11 3LW, UK
UKHW022123190926
475702UK00013B/1611
9781032338408